The *Strong Winds* series

The Salt-Stained Book, A Ravelled Flag and *Ghosting Home*: The series begins when Donny, aged 12, arrives in East Anglia with his profoundly deaf mother, Skye. They are separated and Donny is taken into care at Erewhon Parva vicarage. There he meets Anna, Luke, Liam and Vicky. Anna's mother, Lottie, seems to have abandoned them and the younger children's father, Bill, is in prison.

Donny and Skye's family has been badly affected by Second World War tragedies. Now the arrival of Donny's previously unknown great-aunt Ellen in her Chinese junk *Strong Winds* brings new and far-reaching complications. His friendship with Anna and their alliance with Xanthe and Maggi Ribiero helps Donny survive the tumultuous events of the first three books.

The Lion of Sole Bay: Two years later it is Luke who finds himself alone. He has chosen to spend half term with his father on the dilapidated fishing boat, *Lowestoft Lass*, but Bill is hospitalised after an accident involving hyperactive redhead 'Angel' Vandervelde. It's Hallowe'en, a dark time of year, and there are dark deeds planned.

Black Waters: During the following summer it seems that Xanthe Ribiero's dream of sailing for her country is at an end. She takes refuge in a remote village on the Essex marshes where she helps investigate a long-running local feud and avert a future outrage.

Pebble: Donny, Anna and their Allies are sixth-formers, looking ahead to their future lives. Luke has blotted out his frightening adventure in *The Lion of Sole Bay* but for Liam, now almost ten years old, forgetting the past is not so easy.

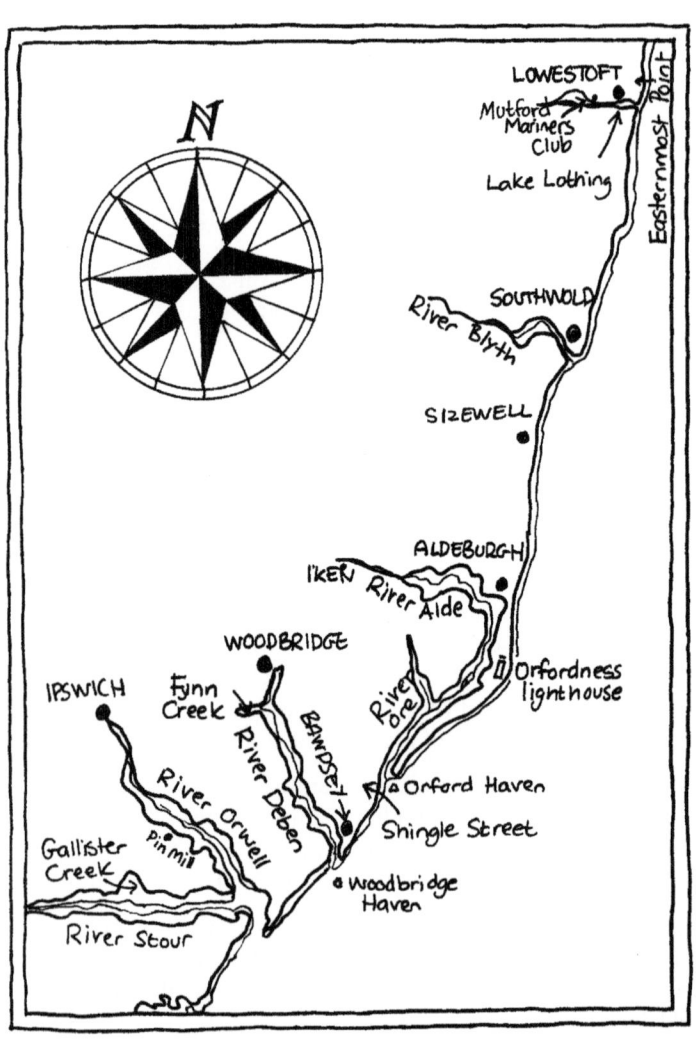

Pebble

Julia Jones

VOLUME SIX
OF THE *Strong Winds* SERIES

Illustrated by Claudia Myatt

*This book is dedicated to all the people from many countries who work
conscientiously and kindly in care and nursing homes, especially those in
The Moat House, Essex, who looked after my mother, June.
Your round-the-clock care was invaluable. Thank you also for your friendship.*

First published in 2018 by Golden Duck (UK) Ltd.,
Sokens,
Green Street,
Pleshey, near Chelmsford,
Essex.
CM3 1HT
www.golden-duck.co.uk

All rights reserved
© Julia Jones, 2018

ISBN 978-1-899262-39-7

All illustrations © Claudia Myatt 2018
www.claudiamyatt.co.uk

Title font (Old Rubber Stamp) by Rebecca Simpson
rebeccasimpsondesign@gmail.com

Design by Megan Trudell

e-book conversion by Matti Gardner
matti@grammaticus.co.uk

Printed and bound in the UK
by Biddles, King's Lynn

Contents

1.	A lost carnelian	9
2.	A lighthouse left astern	20
3.	A shanty, shared	37
4.	A murdered apple tree	47
5.	An expedition north	70
6.	A snorkel and a face mask	85
7.	A bowl of chicken soup	99
8.	An unfriendly seal	113
9.	An item of early evening news	126
10.	A human mollusc	138
11.	A hard place	149
12.	An unidentified object	164
13.	A newly-varnished oar	175
14.	A private ambulance	187
15.	A well-filled sketchbook	198
	Pages from Heike's sketchbook	210
16.	A forgotten crew list	212
17.	A shelduck family	225
18.	A choice of guitars	238
19.	A travelling thumb	249
20.	A place to anchor	263
21.	A white arm from the sky	274
22.	A lump of amber	292
	Fact checker	304

Some characters you may have met already…

Luke and Liam Whiting	sons of Bill Whiting and Eva (who has died), aged almost ten and about 13 in this story.
Vicky Whiting	daughter of Bill Whiting and Lottie Livesey, soon to be six years old.
Anna Livesey	daughter of Lottie Livesey, aged 16. Her father died flying out to a North Sea oil rig.
Lottie Livesey	singer, Anna and Vicky's mother, Luke and Liam's stepmother. Her own mother (Theodora) was a successful novelist and her uncle (Callum) a research scientist but bitter quarrels in the past mean that their money and possessions have passed to Anna (and Vicky).
Bill Whiting	former fisherman, dock-worker, shanty singer; father of Luke Liam and Vicky, disabled in boatyard accident, struggling to restore old fishing vessel, *Lowestoft Lass*.
Donny Walker	son of Skye Walker and unknown father (Hermann), aged 16. Lives on board Chinese junk *Strong Winds* which was left to him by his great-aunt Ellen (otherwise known as Gold Dragon).
Skye Walker	Donny's mother. Brain-damaged before birth. Brought up by her great-aunt Edith (otherwise known as Old Nokomis). Father was Native American. Has a half-brother named Defoe.
Wendy & Gerald:	An overworked vicar and her husband, former foster parents to most of the children. Now with their own small daughter, Ellen, aged about three.

The Ribiero family	Joshua and June, Xanthe (18) and Maggi (16). Successful professional family. (Absent from this story as involved in the 2012 Olympics.)
Old Mrs Everson	very old lady with delightful habit of popping up just when she's needed.
Miss Grace Everson	former farmer and owner of the Fynn Creek moorings.
Edward	Anna's (and Vicky's) Trustee. Former friend of Anna's great-uncle and admirer of Donny's great-aunt. Does his best to act as a Mr Fixit when his legal responsibilities allow.
Ben, the dog	black terrier, rescued from ill-treatment in *A Ravelled Flag*. Comforts Luke in *The Lion of Sole Bay*.

Full fathom five thy father lies;
Of his bones are coral made.
Those are pebbles that were his eyes.
Nothing of him that doth fade,
But doth suffer a sea change
Into something rich and strange.
Sea nymphs hourly ring his knell,
Ding dong!
Hark now I hear them,
Ding dong bell.

(There's a word change here.
Thanks, William Shakespeare, for the rest.)

CHAPTER ONE

A lost carnelian

Liam had already lost his lucky stone before he missed the penalty. It was an orangey-red stone that you could nearly see through. It had extra circles of colour hidden inside and he'd found it on the day they'd heard that his brother Luke was safe.

Liam and his younger sister Vicky collected pebbles and shells, crab casings, driftwood and sea glass. They didn't take them far, only up the cliff to a hiding place in the garden of their house, which they were using as their treasury. Vicky said they were gifts for her magic sea people: Liam mainly just liked the pebbles. It was something to do with the way they felt and that you could never find the same one twice. And they were so old. If you were scrunching on a pebble, it could have been scrunched on by a dinosaur.

The lucky stone had been something different. It had been waiting for him on the beach when he ran out to look where Luke and the witch-women had passed them in the night. It was like a message, glinting in the winter sun as the water sucked away. Its wild swirls of orange-red reminded him of a lion's mane, a real lion, not a carved wooden pub sign. Or the crazy red hair of Luke's new friend, Angel, who had been in danger with him.

That was more than a year ago and you'd think people had forgotten about it. But Liam hadn't. Anna had had the stone polished for his Christmas present and he'd kept it in his pocket ever since – left hand because that was his special side. He'd have given it to Luke, if Luke had ever needed it. Or to Angel.

But now he couldn't give it to anyone because he'd lost it – and he'd lost his touch as well.

The ball was on the penalty mark; the goalie from the other side waiting, looking tense; his team mates watching, ready to cheer. Liam took a deep breath, ran a few strides, kicked…and missed. Not missed obviously but missed the ball's sweet spot. His boot connected okay and sent it in the right direction but it didn't lift and curve and fly for that corner at the top of the net which was where he'd had in mind.

"Bad luck, Liam."

"Close one, mate."

"Come on lads, don't give up now."

The game went on. Liam was always there or thereabouts, running hard as ever. He was a trier, everyone knew that and they didn't lose by much, only that single goal.

"Better luck next time, lads. See you Monday after school."

Liam excused himself. He had a school music trip on Monday and he couldn't make the match next Saturday either.

The coach looked as if he couldn't quite believe what he was hearing. "Last match of the season, mate! I did get told about the music trip but what's stopping you on Saturday? Did I ought to have a word with someone?"

He looked around the edge of the pitch where kids were collecting their gear, finding their parents. He had to check they all left safely.

"Your mum not here?"

"Step-mum. No sir."

"Step-mum then. My mistake. How're you getting home?"

The lad seemed a bit low. Hadn't been playing well for the last few games. Coach hadn't said anything. He was a good lad. Bad patches like that could get people down. He'd been sorry when he noticed Liam'd had taken his name off the list for the half term activity camp. Wondered about calling the parents. Wasn't quite certain who he should ask for…

"Walking, sir. It isn't far."

Liam pointed to where you could see one of the Bawdsey Manor pinnacles poking upwards to the sky, beyond the belt of dark green pines.

"Posh place."

Liam sort of shrugged. It used to make him feel awkward when people said that but he'd got over it. Living in the Manor was better than being looked after at the rectory and very likely better than the Lowestoft caravan park where they'd lived after he'd been born. He didn't remember that far back.

"Your step-mum's Lottie Livesey. I bought her first album. Must be doing well to have a place like that."

"It's not her place, it's my sister's. We live in the flat at the top. The rest of it's a school."

"School?"

"Not a normal sort of school. It's kids from abroad learning English. We don't see them much."

"Oh. Right. Your step-mum's headlining at Luminal. You all going to be there?"

"Not sure. Sometimes she thinks we're too young to be at festivals. Anna goes to most things. She's the oldest. She's sixteen."

Liam needed to get away. It would have been different if he'd been playing well. He'd have chatted all evening then. Nothing felt okay since he'd lost his lucky stone.

There was a bodyguard keeping lookout on the beach. That meant Aleksandr was somewhere around – 'Zander', as he'd told them to call him. It was 99 percent certain Zander would be being private with Anna in one of the caves or some hidden corner of the garden. Luke didn't like it and kept trying to tell Anna that she shouldn't be seeing the young Russian. Anna, predictably, flared up and said it wasn't any of Luke's business. Luke and Anna rowed a lot these days.

The presence of the bodyguard meant that the gate in the chain link fence would have been unlocked. He could get straight in from the beach. But Liam had other plans. He was going further along the shoreline, then up the cliff near where the defence station used to be. He'd got his phone and a note book. The phone had been bought for him after the attempted kidnap – even though phones didn't seem to have been much help in any of his friends' problems. They usually got dropped overboard. There must be hundreds of them out there. He wondered what Vicky's sea-people made of these unknown rectangular objects spiralling slowly down...

Liam didn't plan on taking his phone out to sea. Anna had downloaded him an app called ShipTrack. It worked because of satellites and also something called AIS – Automatic Identification System. AIS was so ships didn't run into each other but you could also use it to track them from the land. The app showed ships all over the world but Liam used it to check on the ships he could actually see or that might be heading in their direction. In case they were bringing trouble. It was better up the cliff because he could see further. Though that hadn't been working so well recently.

He started along the beach. Millions and millions and millions of pebbles; all of them different when you looked close up and all blurring together into a long sweep of golden brown. The tide was low so he could have walked on the harder surface where the stones were mixed with some sand, but that would have meant jumping or climbing over the ends of the breakwaters. He'd misjudged the heights a couple of times and it could have been then that he'd lost his lucky stone.

Except it was more likely he'd lost it on the day he hadn't noticed that all the shingle had been swept off the metal launching track which led from the hut under the cliff to the water. That had totally taken him by surprise. He couldn't think what the track might be going to be used for: the hut wasn't big enough for any sort of boat. He tried the door but it was locked and the padlock looked new. When fishermen had used the track, their boats had lain out on the beach. There weren't any fishermen or any boats anymore. But someone was using that track for something.

Liam trudged through the dry, deep shingle above the high water mark. He skirted the fleshy clumps of sea cabbage, picked up a few random bits of plastic for his litter bag and climbed to the top of the sandy cliff.

The horizon was blurry again today but the app wasn't bothered. It used satellites so it didn't mind what you could actually see. Liam turned the screen brightness up to max and zoomed in to each separate vessel to try and read their info and add it to his book. He had a headache now and he was glad when it was done. He'd almost lost his brother off this coast. You didn't get over that sort of thing. Next time there were enemies approaching he'd be looking out for them.

It wasn't a high cliff. It was mainly sand, coarse and reddish, held together by plants whose names Liam didn't know. At the top there was grass, dry and rabbit-nibbled, and clumps of brambles which were hard to get around but could give cover if you needed it. People didn't come this way much. And no one could get inland from here because of the high chain mesh fencing topped with barbed wire surrounding the jumble of abandoned buildings and the bare grassy space that used to be the defence station.

Donny had once said casually that all fences had a gap in them if you looked hard enough but Liam and Luke had searched every centimetre of this one, all the way round, getting badly scratched and dirty in the process, and they hadn't found as much as a loose link. When they told Donny, he said he was sorry, he'd mainly meant school fences or building sites, not former RAF defence stations. And this place hadn't just been for defence, it had missiles.

Liam didn't much want to go inside anyway. As well as the half-hidden buildings there were random metal structures and covered mounds. They gave him bad feelings. He kept his back to it and watched the sea.

It was a bright May afternoon with a breeze blowing straight inland. That meant it was coming from the East. Liam wondered what it might be bringing with it. A few people were sailing. They looked as if they were having fun. Donny had said he might come round with *Strong Winds* when it was half term and that was straight after next week.

His eyes felt gritty. He must have got some sand in them climbing up. He blinked a lot and used some spit but he wasn't sure they felt much better. His left hand reached into his pocket but the lucky stone still wasn't there. He could climb back down to the beach and search for another, he supposed. There wasn't much to go home for: Lottie and Vicky were out, Anna was somewhere with Zander and Luke was at Angel's. After that he was staying with their dad at Fynn Creek. Liam wished he was staying there as well.

Dmitri, the bodyguard from Kaliningrad, wished he was at home. He'd got this job because he was okay with kids. He had a top service record from his time with the Baltic Fleet and he needed money. Most people in Russia needed money and protecting billionaires' children was very well paid. Then the pressure had been put on. Unofficial jobs. Reconnaissance. Extra hours. Extra cash. Nothing to be talked about but an uneasy feeling that this wasn't something that could be refused. Then last night a delivery. Received and hidden. No questions asked. It had been heavy and today he felt tired. Bone-tired.

Dimitri checked up and down the beach, watched out to sea, kept his radio link with the gatehouse at the main entrance. Held on to the key to the beach gate in case the young master chose to take a stroll. Guessed that he wouldn't – Aleksandr Arkadyevich Ivanov wasn't what you'd call the outdoor type.

Dimitri missed his own kids. The weather would be warming up now that it was May, though colder there than here. Vassily and Tatiana were energetic and adventurous. They might be on the beach; biking, dune-sliding or looking for amber. Keeping out of trouble, he hoped. He sighed as he thought of the pale light on the blue-grey sea, the miles of sand and the miles of forest. He wanted to know what his children were doing and who they were with. He'd never get back the time he was losing from their lives.

He'd watched the little lad from the top floor flat picking his way along the beach and climbing the low cliff. He was the boy with the crippled father. Dmitri had made it his business to investigate the family as soon as Zander began showing such an interest in the oldest girl. He couldn't see they were any sort of threat. Though if he'd been that boy's dad he'd have made it his business to be round more often.

Dmitri tried to convince himself that this separation from his family wasn't any different from when he'd been with the fleet. They had often been away for months at a time, could be years. Living conditions were much harder on a sub, pay was poor and there was a lot there you couldn't talk about. Everything, really.

But this job was so lonely. No chance to get drunk and grouse about the officers. And again, too much he couldn't talk about, even when he rang his wife back home. He didn't like the extras he was being asked to do.

Dmitri comforted himself with the rate he was earning. Not too much longer and he'd be helping his own son get through college, though it wouldn't be a place like this. He'd want Vassily to get some proper learning. Zander wasn't enjoying it much. Kept saying that he'd rather be in London. Dimitri saw his point but it wasn't his place to say so. This had been the Boss's choice for his only child and there was no doubt that surveillance was easier here.

Dmitri'd been issued with a top-of-the-range GPS tracking device linked into his phone so he could always check Zander's whereabouts – as long as the young master consented to wear the corresponding wristband, expensively incorporated into his designer watch – or carry his modified phone. Dimitri was savvy enough to know that both usually got left in the language school when the lad was with his girlfriend.

"I'd have him micro-chipped if he were mine," Dmitri grumbled to himself. But that reminded him again that his own children were a thousand miles away.

He could be home in less than twenty four hours if the Boss loaned him one of his fleet of fast cars. But his work was here, guarding Zander – and doing those other jobs – until the school term was over and the Ivanovs decided where they were heading for the summer. Dmitri dreamed of weeks in a dacha, berry-picking and mushroom-hunting, family time.

Bodyguards weren't paid to dream. And billionaires were much more likely to spend their summer cruising on a super-yacht than deep in the forest telling tales round the samovar.

Dmitri began to wonder whether he was going down with something. He'd been sick when he'd got in last night, felt a bit feverish when he'd gone to bed and his breakfast had gone straight though him this morning. Hadn't felt like eating since.

He looked out to sea again and along the beach. Then he got a message on his phone –'Pretty Girl. Alone?' and a picture of Tatiana walking home from her music lesson.

Dmitri felt hot, cold and sick to his gut. The palms of his hands were slippery with sweat. He had no idea who'd sent the photo but he knew only too well what it could mean. His worst nightmare – every parent's worst nightmare – looked as if it was about to come true. There was someone he didn't know watching his daughter.

He checked Zander's location. The GPS tracker showed he was in the school study area where Dmitri knew he wasn't. He didn't have time to search. He wanted to pull the jet ski out of the hut on the beach where he'd been told to hide it, run it down the metal track across the shingle and head straight across the water, east and north. He knew that was stupid.

Dmitri texted his wife: 'Keep children close. On my way. Love you.' Then he switched his mobile off, took out a pad and scribbled a note. Set off along the beach to climb the low cliff, shivering as he ran.

"I need your help," he said to Liam. They hadn't ever done more than nod and smile before now. Dimitri was panting, sweating, holding out a piece of paper. "This is for Zander – Aleksandr Ivanov. You know who he is? It's important that he gets it but nobody else. He's with your sister. Can you give it to him for me?"

Liam couldn't read any of the writing.

"It's in Russian. Zander will understand. They'll be in the garden, probably in one of those caves. If you can't find him in one hour, give it to the principal. But you will."

Liam nodded. The man's thank-you was left floating on the air as he plunged down the cliff again and lurched back along the beach. Liam took the private route along the top even though there were places where he had to crawl. He reckoned he knew where Zander and Anna would be. He didn't want to meet anybody else.

The app on Liam's phone couldn't register a wooden dinghy with no AIS and Dimitri's powerful binoculars couldn't see twelve miles to the northeast, round a point and through a lighthouse. So neither of them had spotted the little boat that was struggling south against the ebb. And both of them had left their lookout points before it was engulfed in sea fog.

CHAPTER TWO
A lighthouse left astern

The edge of the Manor gardens spilled over into the top of the cliff. It had been strengthened and engineered so there were pathways and rock plants, sudden turnings and narrow openings, places to sit and read, talk or flirt. Anna and Zander were in one of the artificial caves with seats that the rich people had made. They'd moved a small table in there so they could play chess and share books. He was teaching her his language in return for English conversation practice.

Luke had had another go at Anna about it only yesterday. "You didn't ought to have anything to do with that Russian. His dad's filthy rich. He'll be one of those oligraphs selling off their country. They probably all used to be in the secret police."

"You mean the KGB – *Komitet gosudarstvennoy bezopasnosti*," Anna had answered confidently. "That's been gone since before Zander was born. And why are you being so prejudiced just because his father's rich? People can't help that, you know. And, by the way, it's oligarch, not oligraph."

"I think he's a spy."

"Spying on what?" Anna had been totally contemptuous. "He's at a language school, FGS! The Cold War's over. This place hasn't been a missile station for years. Catch up, Luke. History's about the past. Zander's like us. He's living his life now."

Liam hated arguments so he hadn't stayed to listen any more. Luke got very fired up about history these days and he wasn't scared of Anna – in fact they were really good friends – but she was incredibly clever and stubborn and neither of them would be backing down any time soon. Life in the Manor was more peaceful when Luke stayed over on *Lowestoft Lass*. Except that Liam missed him.

Zander and Anna weren't what most people would have called flirting. They had a pile of books with them and a chess set.

"*Pree-vyét*," said Anna, looking up at Liam with a smile. She'd recently had her short mouse-coloured hair dyed black. It still gave him a shock.

"I've got a note. It's for Aleksandr from his bodyguard."

Zander took the note and read it. He stood up, leaving the chess game and gathering his books.

"I apologise," he said to Anna. "I have a difficulty and must speak with the principal."

He didn't give her any time to answer or ask questions.

"Is the gate in the fence still open?" he asked Liam. "Could you make sure it's closed again, please?"

He turned back to Anna. "I believe you have a key. Perhaps you would be good enough to ensure the gate remains locked."

He gave them a stiff little bow and was gone.

"Did you read the note?" Anna asked Liam.

"I couldn't. It was funny writing."

"Cyrillic," she said automatically. "It scared Zander."

"The man who gave it me was scared too."

They went down to check the gate but it was already closed

and locked. Dmitri had done what he could to leave the Manor secure.

"So how did you get in?" Anna asked. "I thought you said there weren't any gaps in the fence? You didn't go all the way round to the main entrance?"

"There's a tree."

"You'd better show me. We may need to have it taken down."

"Why? No I won't." Anna thought she could do anything just because she owned the flat and had a posh boyfriend. "That's killing things and it isn't even in the grounds. It's a wild tree and you can't."

"Li, I'd do anything to protect my friends." He knew this was true. Anna was ruthless. "Zander is at kidnap risk every day of his life. Think about it."

Liam thought about it but he wasn't changing his mind. "Kidnappers would have to get him out. My tree's only for getting in. If there's any other ways I don't know them."

Fog had come blowing in from the sea and clung where the long strip of bare shingle narrowed and turned westwards. It had come out of nowhere on a sunny afternoon.

Heike had left Lowestoft in the dinghy soon after it was light. She'd worked late in the bar the previous evening because George had needed extra help. That meant she'd only had a couple of hours sleep but it had totally been worth it as he'd asked one of the club members, setting off across the North Sea, to give her a tow down Lake Lothing and cast her off once they were outside the harbour entrance.

George didn't know she hadn't any oars. He was just doing

her a favour, like he always did when he could. She wouldn't have got away at all otherwise. Both the wind and tide were against her and without oars she was powerless. She should have had oars. She'd made a pair in the first term of her course – it was one of their first tasks, a requirement. Then she'd needed money so badly that she'd sold them. Didn't realise how much they'd matter – and that they weren't exactly hers to sell. She should have made another pair.

The yacht had turned northeast and she'd headed south, with the wind nicely on her port side. She'd made good progress for the first few hours and had felt utter happiness in the way her dinghy skipped and chuckled in the playful waves. She allowed herself to relax and be proud of her achievement. She'd learned so much since she'd arrived at the Shipwrights' College but it was working with wood that she loved and this dinghy had been her personal project. Months and months of repair and rebuilding, then sanding and varnishing, layer upon layer until the different woods gleamed like caramel or liquid amber.

She hadn't met the dinghy's owner – Ms Anna Livesey hadn't visited the college or asked to see any progress photos. Money for materials had come from a trust fund and all Heike's work was provided as part of the diploma. Ms Livesey had been informed that the dinghy was finished and would be delivered this weekend but she probably assumed it would arrive on a road trailer.

If she thought about it at all. All the discussion about changing the rig from traditional cat-rigged to a light lugsail had been managed by Ms Livesey's lawyer. Even the dinghy's name – *Theodora* – had been communicated to the college via the lawyer. The owner wasn't bothered.

♀ PEBBLE ♀

This was Heike's first weekend away from Lowestoft since she'd arrived in England. If she'd had more time to get familiar with the Suffolk coast maybe she'd have realised that forty miles in a twelve-foot sailing dinghy with no oars or outboard was only going to work in optimal conditions. But she'd had no time. She'd snatched a few sailing sessions on Lake Lothing and Oulton Broad to check all was well with *Theodora*'s rig and gear. Such a pretty boat. Handling so beautifully. Heike didn't believe that Ms Anna Livesey, who could afford all the money, deserved her.

Maybe that was unfair. Maybe she just felt jealous of anybody who didn't have to lie about their age and do agency work in care homes at least three nights a week and every weekend simply to pay their tuition fees. The course itself was often physically demanding and there were plenty of days she needed to take painkillers because her muscles hurt so much: plenty of nights she was living off caffeine and sugar to keep her energy going. Heike never sat down when she was working; she was too afraid she'd fall asleep and then she'd lose her job.

For the first part of the day the wind and tide hurried her along and there was plenty to see. She stayed close to the coast, passing caravan parks and beach huts, a seaside town with a harbour and a pier, then the giant puffball of the nuclear power station. She watched an Environment Agency boat laying a yellow buoy between the two sets of markers that showed where the seawater went in and out. The people on board waved and she waved back. She'd read something in the local free sheet about the extra environmental monitoring that was happening before the music festival which was going to be there. Luminal.

It sounded good. Heike had thought she might try to get time off and go. But then she'd seen the ticket prices…

Only halfway and more than half the day already over. The tide had turned against her and she was passing the coast so slowly she felt she could have counted every stone. There was no rest from steering and trimming the sheet. She shifted around trying to get more comfortable. *Theodora*'s wooden thwarts were hard, however beautiful they looked. She needed to stand and stretch but couldn't: the waves were choppy and she had to keep her weight low. She trailed a hand over the side when she could and splashed water on her face to stay awake. It was startlingly cold.

More beach huts and another picture-postcard town. She wished she could stop and go ashore. Buy an ice cream – or watch other people eating theirs. Lie down in the sun. Rest.

But she couldn't. She had a dinghy to deliver and she was beginning to wonder whether she wouldn't be quicker walking it to Bawdsey.

After the town the coastline was bleak. She noticed the massive aerials of a radio-transmitting station and a huge block building without any windows. A slab of a place. Like something the Soviets would have built. Totally creepy.

This was a deserted shore. Heike wondered whether she should go further out to sea. She had a very old chart that she'd borrowed from one of the derelict yachts at the college. It showed there was a point ahead with squiggly lines that meant rough water. They were called overfalls and someone at the club had said they would be worse on the ebb. There was a lighthouse on the point. She could already see waves splashing up against the shore.

Heike turned *Theodora* away and began tacking at right angles from the coast. They were going sideways faster than they were going ahead. She felt the air growing damp and the colour fading from the day. There was a bank of thick fog rolling in from the sea. She was pointing straight into it. Heike shivered.

Within minutes she and her dinghy were alone in a wet grey world. It was crazy to continue. She hadn't got a compass and there were sandbanks ahead as well as the overfalls. She turned back towards the land, hoping desperately that she could remember the direction she'd been heading. The breeze didn't seem quite so strong now it was carrying the fog with it. If she hit the land she hoped she wouldn't hit it too hard. Visibility was maybe ten metres; it was hard to be sure.

Heike strained to look ahead. Most lighthouses made some noise in fog. This one didn't. Would she spot any gleam from its light?

Her eyes ached from peering at nothing. The fog was in her hair, on her cheeks and up her nose. If she opened her mouth she could almost taste it.

The shape of the waves changed. There was a darker grey mass in the greyness ahead. Some of the wave tops peaked and spurted into small transparent water fingers. Heike realised just in time that they were telling her she had reached the shore. She swung the dinghy sideways, pulled up the centreboard and rudder and let her sail come down with a rush.

She was too tired to care exactly where they were. She pulled the dinghy up the steeply sloping beach and tied its painter round her ankle. Then she spread a jacket on the shingle, lay down with her head on her rucksack and fell blissfully asleep.

A LIGHTHOUSE LEFT ASTERN

Theodora woke her with a good sharp tug. She was floating and eager to continue their voyage. The fog had cleared and the flood tide was racing past the shoreline. No more spurting peaks and pointing fingers: the waves were more like a team of galloping horses now, surging along in the direction she should go. She was very near the red-and-white striped lighthouse but there was no time to explore. The daylight wouldn't last much longer. Could she make it to the River Deben entrance in time?

She scrambled back into *Theodora*, ignoring hunger pangs. Once she was round the point at the end of this long shingle spit – the Ness, it was called – she'd be able to see her way across the bay until she closed the coast again. Then they would reach the Deben. But would there be any light left and how should she get in? She'd felt so insecure earlier, when she'd tried beating out to sea, away from the shore, and it would be dark by then. Her chart seemed to show that there could be a side entrance immediately underneath the Bawdsey cliff. There weren't any marker buoys shown on the chart – not for the side channel – and it was obviously shallow. You wouldn't go there in a yacht but the dinghy ought to be okay. It felt safer to stay close to the land.

Theodora pulled eagerly away in the freshening breeze. This would be their last sail before the handover. There would be other boats in Heike's life but she was going to hold this moment in her heart for ever.

Two – maybe three? – hours later. The daylight had gone and so had the inshore channel. If it had existed at all. The friendly lighthouse with its regular five second flash was far behind them and forgotten. The clanging bell at the previous river mouth had left no echo in her memory. Black water and white spray was all that she could see, swirling on every side as *Theodora* drove helplessly towards the beach. The dinghy couldn't answer when she'd tried to tack away; the forces were too strong. They were going to smash.

Heike scrambled forward and released the main halyard. The sail bellied and stuck. She reached up and grabbed at the wooden spar, tugging it until she almost tipped over the bows when it came. The dinghy slowed but didn't stop.

She pulled up the centreboard too. Realised – too late – that she should have incorporated some adjustment into the rudder. There was surf all around her now; the water rushing madly on.

The chart had shown a channel but all she could see were mounds and plateaus of shingle, like bergs and icefloes. The chart had lied.

Theodora slammed to a stop, caught by her rudder as if it was a stern anchor. The brass pintles were strong. They were holding her. They couldn't last.

The shingle growled beneath the planking. The wood felt thin. Heike's instincts told her she must lighten the load. She stepped out into the dark, cold, racing water.

Theodora lifted at once. Her rudder freed. She was eager to float on. The pebbles were firm beneath Heike's feet. Maybe she could walk them through, onwards in this inky dark.

The dinghy twisted round. Heike grabbed the stern. Braced her legs and back, clung on and used all her weight to hold the dinghy stationary as the tide rushed past. The rudder was wildly askew. She needed to get it out but she couldn't risk losing her grip. The wood was slippery. Her fingers were cold.

Very carefully, she leaned forward into the dinghy so the rudder dug hard down into the shingle. She reached inside for a loop of mainsheet then, still using her weight to keep *Theodora* grounded, she wrapped the rope around the stern thwart and wrapped it round herself with a quick release knot. Even if she got dragged, she didn't care. The dinghy could not break free.

She tried again to lift the rudder out from its pintles. It was impossible. Something must have bent. Then she stood up slowly, allowing the dinghy to float a short rope's length away, and walked behind, legs stiff, muscles tensed, following wherever the water forced them to go.

A frothing white fringe showed a shingle mound ahead. She grabbed *Theodora*'s side, pulling her around the danger. And another. Then the depth plummeted. Heike almost lost her footing, hung on desperately and heaved herself back on board, bruised and gasping.

They were through the banks and into the river. If only she'd had oars.

In with the tiller, down with the centreboard, up with the sail. She headed for the right-hand shore where the big house lay hidden. She spotted a small quay and a jetty, marked with a few dim lights and steered the dinghy towards them. Then she dropped the sail for the last time and tied up. There were signs forbidding this but Heike took no notice. *Theodora* needed to be left safe while she set off to meet Ms Livesey. This was the scariest moment of the voyage.

Bawdsey Manor. It had an entry barrier and a gatehouse. There was no way Heike could look like anything other than a skinny teenager who'd sailed all day and got soaked. She knocked on the toughened glass window.

"Yes?" The man inside answered though a voice com. He didn't sound pleased.

"I've come to meet Ms Anna Livesey."

The man ran his finger down a list but without even looking at it. "She's not a student here," he said.

Heike had imagined Ms Livesey as a retired lady, indulging a whim to sponsor a boat, then losing interest. If this was a school maybe Ms Livesey was a teacher?

"All I have is this address. I'm delivering her dinghy from North Suffolk Shipwrights."

A second man came out of the lodge.

"What's your vehicle?"

There were headlights bright behind her. A motorcycle driving towards them and a car following it. Powerful lights. Dazzling.

"I haven't…" Heike started to say. The motorcycle rider was alongside them. He pushed his visor up.

"Mr and Mrs Ivanov. Barrier up."

The gate staff weren't going to be hurried. The guard who had been talking to Heike turned away, walked across to the big car and greeted the occupants, doing a brief check at the same time. A driver in front; Mr and Mrs Ivanov (she assumed) in the back. Russians! Heike caught a glimpse of a man with short grey hair and wire-rimmed glasses and a woman wearing furs. Furs in May!

The barrier lifted and Heike stepped backwards out of the light as the Russians were waved through. She watched as the vehicles drove briskly along the road to the main house. Felt the familiar prickle of hatred.

She needed to remember that she wasn't here for herself. Ms Livesey's sponsorship had been to the college and she was their representative. She returned to the window, politely.

"I need your help to contact Ms Anna Livesey. She's expecting her dinghy to be delivered."

"You want to phone 'em in the top floor flat," the man told his colleague. "Just give us a minute, miss." He didn't ask her to come inside.

Heike could see lights shining out as the doors of the main house were opened and the Russians welcomed in.

"Sorry, miss," said the man who'd made the call. "Her mother says it's not a good moment. Could you leave it somewhere safe and they'll take a look in the morning? She says to thank you for taking the trouble. They're all very excited and she's sure it'll be lovely. There's a dinghy park by the quay," he added helpfully. "It's kept locked but I've a key here you can use."

Heike didn't believe in Anna Livesey's family's 'excitement'. She wished she could stomp off into the dark and sail her dinghy away. Ms Anna Livesey probably wouldn't even notice. But that would be worse stealing than when she had sold those oars. Which hadn't felt like stealing at the time but was obviously bad when she thought about it now.

She had money for her train fare back to Lowestoft but she hadn't worked out how she was getting to the station.

"When do your last buses go?" she asked. She had to make sure *Theodora* was okay first.

"Saturdays? Half four ain't it, Bob?"

"Cross to Felixstowe, walk up the town and you'd ketch one

a bit later. Not now though, foot ferry stopped at six. What's your problem, miss?"

She was about to say she didn't have a problem but the two men had looked at each other and made a decision.

"There's a bit of trouble going on there. Security-related. They don't tell us much more than keep an extra lookout for anyone who don't seem quite right. Not saying that's you," he added hastily. "But if there's people about who aren't quite right, then we wouldn't want you getting mixed up with them. How old are you anyway?"

"Eighteen." It was her usual lie.

"They're all eighteen," said the man with the list of students on his desk. "Except when they're not."

"You're expecting to meet Ms Anna Livesey. And your name is…?"

"Heike Kaleva. She doesn't know me. I'm from the North Suffolk Shipwrights' College and I'm delivering her Columbia dinghy. I sailed here. The dinghy's tied up on the jetty."

"But you haven't got no further transport and there's no one either with you or expected to collect you."

"Yes."

"Then you come in here with us and we'll make another call to the house."

Her legs were shaky now. She found a chair and sat without being asked.

"Lottie Livesey says she's coming herself," one man said to the other and there was a look passed between them that Heike didn't understand. Like they'd swallowed the cream.

"This is so very kind of you," Lottie said to the security men, coming to the door of the lodge. "And thank you, too, for bringing my daughter's dinghy safely all this distance." She gestured towards Heike, including her in the charmed circle she was drawing round them all.

Lottie Livesey was beautiful in a bony sort of way. Her face was all angles and her forearms stuck out from her sleeves as if her wrists were extra-long, leading to her large, expressive hands. She wasn't smartly dressed, just a thin blouse tucked into jeans. Heike began to think she might have seen her somewhere.

There were two children with her. A little girl with red-gold hair and a boy of about nine or ten. She might have meant them to stay in the car but they hadn't.

"My younger daughter, Vicky," she introduced them, "And Liam. You'll know them both already," she said to the security men. She had a lovely voice or was it the personality? Lovely but vulnerable. Made you want to respond. Reach back to her as she was reaching out to you.

"Now, what do you need from me?" she asked Heike. "How can I help you? But first, do please tell me your name."

When you looked closely, Lottie Livesey's cheeks were hollow and her eyes were tired. Heike knew what that felt like. Like a care home at three in the morning. Residents shouting, moaning, walking round, wanting another plate of biscuits, another pad change and you had to smile and speak politely while you worked. Even when they called you names or tried to kick you.

If they stayed up all night, they could sleep all day, tucked round with rugs in an armchair, while you were lying on the yard floor underneath a keelboat with a peening hammer and a mouthful of copper fastenings. Heike disliked Anna Livesey even more for sending her already-exhausted mother to see about her dinghy. She wasn't an eccentric teacher; she was a spoiled brat.

"I need to hand over Ms Anna Livesey's dinghy. It's a delivery from North Suffolk Shipwrights' College. I have moored the dinghy to the jetty right now, but if you can tell me where there is a trolley I'll pull her into the dinghy park."

"Have you sailed here?" asked the boy. "From Lowestoft? Because I was looking out and I didn't see you."

"Looking out for me?"

"Just looking out."

"Yes, I have sailed here but during this afternoon I took a break. There was a fog. I think you call them 'haars'. So I landed near the lighthouse and I slept longer than I meant. That's why I'm late. I didn't find the right entrance to the river either."

She needed to be honest. "It's possible the lower rudder pintle's bent. I'm sorry. I ought to take a look when she's out of the water. Perhaps, if we get her on a trolley now, one of you might have a torch? If there's a repair needed I'll come back and do it, of course." That meant bus fares and train fares, all that time spent travelling, but they were problems for later. She needed to see if there was damage first. Maybe the rudder had stuck because she was panicky and pulling it wrong.

"What a day!" said Lottie, "You must be utterly wiped out! Couldn't we leave looking at the dinghy till tomorrow and you could come back then?"

"The dinghy is tied to the jetty. I don't know if it's acceptable for her to be there."

"Can't leave her there," said one of the security men. "Ferryman'll need access in the morning. Oughta put her in the park if we can. I don't mind giving you a hand. What yer think, Bob? I'll have me radio on. If there's callers I'll come straight back."

"Don't see why not. There's been a flap but it's almost ten. Harry'll be on his way. He's night shift. The Ivanovs have brought their own security. We've done our bit."

Heike was watching Lottie. She saw her tense.

"You know that's terribly sweet of you. But as things are tonight I don't think we should do anything to take you from your post. If this kind girl can just show me where she's left the dinghy now, then I'll make absolutely certain we're up early and we'll move it before the ferryman arrives. I'm sure my daughter has a key and a trolley already organised. She'll be so disappointed not to meet you," she added, turning to Heike. "There's been an unexpected situation connected with the language school and she's involved."

Heike noticed the boy about to say something. But then not.

"So, all we need to do," continued Lottie, "Is be a little bit lazy and pop into the car. We'll check that the dinghy's alright and then I'll run you to the station. If we're quick you should catch the last train."

Heike said nothing. It wasn't her place. Owners (or owners' mothers) knew best.

"She could have had Luke's bed for the night," Liam said to Lottie as they watched the rear lights of the train leave for Lowestoft. "Luke wouldn't have minded. It was like when Donny first came. She'd nearly fallen asleep in the car. At least Rev Wendy gave him some pyjamas."

Lottie turned to stare at him.

"I'm sorry, sweetheart, I'm not sure what you mean. They have a security crisis in the language school. That dear girl was delivering a dinghy. We have to keep it in proportion."

"She was cold and hungry and she'd been shipwrecked. The language school isn't anything to do with us."

"Except that it was you who delivered the message and it's Anna's friend who has been left dangerously unprotected."

"I was on lookout but I didn't see her. She could have drowned and I wouldn't never have noticed."

Lottie put her arm round him. "You can't watch all of the coast all of the time. Someone would have raised the alarm if she'd been in serious difficulty. But I think it's wonderful the way you're taking such a caring attitude. I should have taken more notice myself. I'm sorry. When this next album's out and Luminal's over, I promise I'm going to be there for you again. I absolutely will. And we could have a lovely trip up to Lowestoft and take her some flowers or something."

CHAPTER THREE
A shanty, shared

Liam bashed his finger with the hammer and the nail dropped onto the deck, skittered away under the bulwarks and fell into the mud of the creek. His eyes misted as he struggled with the pain. That was the third time he'd hit that finger in the about ten minutes he'd been trying to do this job.

"Thought you were the practical one," Luke said, not really noticing. "We won't have no nails left if you keep chucking them over the side. Ducks'll grow iron teeth."

Liam had thought he was the practical one, too, but that was before he found he couldn't knock a nail through a sheet of ply. It was Sunday afternoon and they were up Fynn Creek trying to help their dad. Bill had an old fishing boat there, *Lowestoft Lass*. He'd bought her a couple of years ago with some salvage money and she was his project that had gone wrong. And now the moorings and the Fynn Creek boatyard had a new owner and people like Bill were under pressure to get out.

Lowestoft Lass needed serious work if she was ever going anywhere. She looked strong enough from a distance but some of her planks were rotten and the nails that held her together were rusted. (Those ones weren't called nails, they were called fastenings, Liam wasn't quite clear about the difference but he knew it was a bad problem.) His dad, Bill, was a fisherman and a dockworker but he'd taken a job in a boatyard in the town to learn the proper ways of ship-building. Then he'd had an accident and now he couldn't walk any more.

And he hadn't learned how to be a ship-builder either.

Everything was difficult for Bill though they'd rebuilt the gangplank so he could get the wheelchair on board and he'd made all sorts of handholds where he needed them. There was an amazing sort of ramp with a rope pulley that he could use to get down from the wheelhouse to the cabin. The old boat's leaks were terrible but Luke and Liam knew he was happier living here than he was at the Manor even though that had an electric lift and a specially adapted shower and the right sort of mattress.

It was quite hard to see how their dad and Lottie had got together in the first place, except they'd both been pub singers and both widowed. Then they'd had Vicky. After that, there'd been trouble. Bill had gone to prison and Lottie had gone underground. But that was history and Lottie was on her way to being a mega-star and Bill seemed to have given up even going to his shanty group.

Liam picked up another nail and tried again. Couldn't just be a cry baby whinger. Needed to man up.

"Hang on, mate," Bill stopped him, "I reckon we could have a go using epoxy here, never mind them nails. There ain't nothing much to fix on to, anyway. Even if we're going get pushed out we'll want a dry cabin over our heads. I got us a bit of stuff we could mix up. Then we'll stick that ply on top and paint it."

"Couldn't you live down our end of the river, Dad?"

Liam had given up pretending that his bashed finger didn't hurt and was sucking it, trying to keep the swelling down. It was the index finger of his left hand. He'd be useless with his guitar if he couldn't bend it.

"Could do – if they'd have me. But we'd drag the keel out if we tried ter shift her now. Needs proper work done by someone who knows what they're about. Not a useless cripple and a couple of lads."

The new owner wanted the top end of Fynn Creek made into a marina, with waterfront housing and leisure facilities. It got funding as a reclamation scheme. So Fynn Brook, which came down for miles through the meadows, was going to be held all the way between banks. There were going to be dykes and a pumping station and a water-powered generator to drain the reed beds and make land for shops and more houses. Then there would be a big dam further down that would make the whole creek into a basin with a lock entrance and deep water at all times. Looked like another world on paper.

But first, the ramshackle collection of mooring-holders – 'creekies' as they called themselves – with their decaying liveaboards and meandering home-built walkways would have to pay up, smarten up or move out.

Some of them had already gone. There'd been a fire at the moorings. It had probably been started by criminals but it could have been an accident with fireworks so most people's insurances were still arguing. Miss Grace, the lady who had owned the moorings then, had been really understanding about financial problems. But she'd got lung damage from something toxic in the smoke and couldn't do nothing more. The moorings had been sold and her farm lay empty with the lawyers arguing.

The last time Luke had seen Miss Grace they were rescuing the mad old man who lived in the woods. Maybe he was trying to get to his ruined yacht. They'd both been worried about the old man and got him an ambulance but it had been Miss Grace who had collapsed.

By that time Luke had been out at sea, kidnapped by some crazy Dutch women. Bill had been in rehab after his accident. So none of them had been back to Fynn Creek for a while. That winter was when *Lowestoft Lass* had really gone downhill.

Luke didn't usually talk about that time he'd been staying there on his own, but today, when they were sitting in the wheelhouse reading instructions for how to mix epoxy, he suddenly started up. It had been All Souls and someone had told him about lighting candles for people who had died. He'd tried lighting one for their mum (who was dead) and walking round with it but it hadn't really worked. No reason why it should.

Then, later in the night, he'd remembered her holding him. She was showing him the moon and telling him that Liam was on the way and making it feel something magic, like a story.

Bill's eyes went a bit misty. "She were a one for stories, your mum. Reckon that's where you got yer imagination. Didn't come from me, no how."

"What about me?" Liam wanted to ask. "What did I get? I don't even remember our mum."

But he didn't say anything and when epoxy was ready you had to get on and spread it before it went hard.

"Are you paying your bills alright Dad? They can't chuck you out because of that, can they?" Luke asked before they left.

"Don't you worry, lad, I'm getting by. Anything I've got spare I'm spending on paint. Brightening the old girl up. Flash git manager called her a hulk t'other day."

"I'll come after school tomorrow. I could paint the wheelhouse.

Do it bright white like she's a cruise liner. Okay if I stay over? I'll bring clothes and that."

Liam wished he could come and stay over too but he was still in primary school and that was the other end of the river. Luke was in secondary and he could pretty well do as he liked. Same as Anna.

"The Russians' big house in London got burgled last night," Liam told them. "Anna thinks that man giving me the note and running off might have been some kind of diversion to get Zander's parents out of the way. Making them come down here so the burglars could get in there. I dunno. I thought the man was really upset. He didn't seem like he was faking."

"Did they? Steal stuff, I mean?"

"Maybe a car."

Luke and Bill weren't much interested in cars. Liam might have been but he couldn't really on his own.

"And Anna's got that dinghy, now, what her great uncle left her. It's in the dinghy park. Show you when we get back."

"That'd be cool. Play me that shanty of yours as well if you like."

"Maybe." Liam's finger throbbed and here was Lottie to collect them, in a hurry as usual but trying not to show it.

They eased the old man into a chair by the door so he could join in the concert. Liam's school was playing in the local care home. Liam was on the end of the row nearest the old man because he needed space for his guitar.

When the music group started singing the old man looked up as if he was trying to hear but they were too far away or the songs were too modern. After a bit his head dropped down and he started mumbling. Their head teacher had given them a talk about dementia that morning so most of the kids understood that he had an illness; he wasn't being rude or mad.

Liam was doing a solo, near the finish of the concert. It was a shanty he'd learned from his dad. About men who'd been whaling in the frozen north and were rolling home to old Maui with a shipload of packed blubber and oil which they were going to sell and then they were going to get drunk and spend all their money so they'd have to go back to the north again. Hunt more whales.

The guitar part was difficult and his finger was still sore. Liam blanked the women talking to each other in the kitchen space as they got the urn boiling. He blanked the phone ringing in the care home office and he blanked the fact that he didn't need to blank the old man's muttering. He didn't notice that the old man was disentangling himself and sitting up and looking round towards the music. Leaning forward and his face sort of clearing.

Like a flower growing towards the light, someone poetical said afterwards.

Liam was playing as best he could for those old sailors who were coming down from the northern sea with their ship in tatters and ice in the rigging and the wind blowing a gale behind them. Then he heard the old man joining in, his old voice getting stronger all the time, like he too was looking out for them palm trees and the white sand beaches and island girls bringing rum.

They asked Liam to play it straightaway again when he'd finished. He played it twice and the activity leader videoed the old man on her phone.

The music teacher reminded her that she'd have to get

permission for Liam to be in the video because he was a child.

"And what about his permission?" She pointed at the old man. Then she remembered her manners and asked him directly. "I'm sorry, sir, I don't know your name. Thank you for joining our song."

The old man didn't seem to have heard so the activity leader answered for him.

"We call him John – like John Doe? We're not sure we know his real name. There was nothing at all when he was discharged from hospital last year. We didn't even think he spoke English. Maybe someone will recognise him off a video if I put it on social media. It could be his best interests. Do you know any other songs like that?" she asked Liam.

Liam did a couple more easy shanties and the old man sang them as well. Other people joined in too.

It was a truly wonderful feeling but the concert was way past its finish time and they needed to be getting back to school. The other old people were being given tea and biscuits. They were smiling at the children, slopping their drinks as they tried to wave. The old man didn't want his tea. He was staring at Liam and making sounds that didn't come out as words you could understand.

Liam felt responsible. "I could come again," he said.

The old man looked at Liam as if he was seeing him in the same way he'd been hearing him. Like they were connected.

"I could bring my guitar after school. Lottie won't mind. She's always saying I don't practise enough."

"She's Lottie Livesey, the singer," the teacher told the activity leader. "I'm sure she'd give permission. Liam plays a lot of football, though. I'm not sure how often he'd come."

He didn't tell her he wasn't doing football any more. It felt too painful.

It didn't matter because the activity leader was rushing on, filled with enthusiasm.

"We'd love to see him anytime. Children and pets. They do our residents so much good. I'll check with safeguarding but as long as he's always with one of us…" She was beaming like a heat source. "Perhaps you could let me know when you've asked his mum," she said to the teacher.

"Step-mum." Liam made the correction on auto-pilot.

The old man's face was freezing over as the children left. There was a ribbon of clear snot hanging from his nose like an icicle. Liam hoped he hadn't actually killed whales. Though you could think whaling was basically the same as fishing, only bigger. Liam's own family used to be fishermen.

"I'll come after school," he told him. "I'll come tomorrow. I'll get Lottie to ring. Or I could ask Anna."

The TV was on in the big room when Liam turned up the next day. It was a quiz show and it didn't look as if anyone was watching: there were a few old people asleep in their chairs, an old lady rocking a pram and another staring intently at a table. There was an old man tidying boxes and another old lady in a wheelchair who kept getting stuck round the edges of things and shouted at anyone who tried to help her. It seemed to be her full-time occupation: wheeling and getting stuck and jiggling to and fro until she got herself free again, then zooming away and getting stuck and rocking and shoving and being angry and on the move again.

Liam felt uncertain now.

⚓ A SHANTY, SHARED ⚓

"You've got a visitor, John," said the carer who'd brought Liam in. "He's never any trouble," she told Liam. "Except when he's having his hair cut or being shaved. That takes three of us! You're his first visitor I've ever heard of. You're not family, are you?"

"No," said Liam. "I came with my school."

"I heard about it. You did a concert and John started singing."

"It was a shanty. My dad used to sing shanties."

"I'll let you get on with it then. Would you like a glass of squash or anything?"

"Water would be okay."

"I'll bring a beaker for John as well. Prompt him if you can. It's hard to get him to drink or eat."

Liam played 'Old Maui' but he wasn't getting any response.

The carer came back with water. "I don't think he knows you're there. Move so you're in front of him."

"John," she said loudly. "Look! Visitor!"

"Vanya?" said the old man, suddenly, clearly, raising his head. Liam couldn't quite see but he could feel the blaze of hope in the old man's face.

"I'm Liam. I've come to play sea shanties."

The old man started to droop again. Liam got playing as quickly as he could. His singing was better than his playing and he'd picked up plenty of words from his dad. 'Farewell and adieu to you Spanish ladies', 'What shall we do with the drunken sailor?' 'Leave her, Johnny, leave her.'

The old man began to cry. It was completely horrible. Old men shouldn't cry like that. It hurt to hear him.

The carer had gone off somewhere. Liam put his guitar

down and looked round for a tissue. He couldn't see one. So he did the bravest thing he could and put his hand on the old man's shoulder.

The old man stopped as suddenly as he'd started. "Vanya?" he tried again but he didn't seem too upset when Liam said no.

Liam gave him some of the water, which he gulped. Then he coughed and the end of the snot got stuck on the side of the glass. This had all been a very bad mistake.

But the old man had gone back to 'Old Maui'. Now he was singing it to Liam. Not with many of the words but it was him singing it.

Liam didn't bother with his guitar. He just joined in. The old man's voice wasn't so mumbly once he got going; it sounded much younger than the rest of him. They did all the verses of 'Old Maui' that they could. Several times. And some of the other songs too. It was better than doing it with that lady and her phone. He should get his dad to come here. And Luke too. Be like they were a mini shanty group.

The activity leader was watching from behind the coffee bar. Children and dogs, she'd always said, they did her residents so much good.

CHAPTER FOUR

A murdered apple tree

Liam went to the care home every day for the rest of that week. It was the only thing that was going well in his life. Him and his football boots seemed to have lost touch with each other and school work wasn't good either. He couldn't seem to understand what the teacher was showing them. She thought he wasn't trying but he was.

The old man got a bit brighter and the carers said it cheered them all up, Liam being there. It would have been good if his dad could have come with him but Lottie pointed out that someone needed to look after Vicky if he wasn't going to be there after school. Normally they walked home together, when he didn't have football, and messed around till Luke or Anna came back. Went on the beach. Picked up pebbles. Made plans for their treasury that would make it one of the wonders of the world.

"I absolutely love it that you're going to this place and playing to the dear people. Perhaps we might do them a concert together one day. The problem just now is that I've so much work for Luminal. I'm going to have to ask Bill to step in. I'll get him a taxi or there's community transport if he doesn't want to accept. It's too late by the time the older ones get home and it isn't fair to Vicky to keep her indoors in this lovely weather. Of course they can't get onto the beach with his chair but I don't think she'll mind. And then we've got London at half term, though Wendy may have invited Vicky to spend the week with Ellen at the Rectory."

"*London…?*"

"Had you forgotten? We're all going. Except Vicky might not be and Luke's spending the week with Bill, working on that boat of his and Anna says that Zander's family have asked her if she'd like to visit them while we're up. But I'll love having you with me," she added hastily. "There'll be quite a lot of PR interviews but you liked the recording studio that time we were in Italy, didn't you? This time there'll be sessions with the band!"

Italy. That was when they'd gone away before and Luke had stayed in Fynn Creek and they'd nearly lost him. They should have been sticking together, looking out for each other. Liam didn't want to go to London with Lottie but it seemed like nobody else wanted to have him. Not even his brother and his dad.

"We should have talked about it properly," Lottie said, putting her arm round him. "It's my fault. I'd assumed you'd be going to the football camp but your coach says you crossed your name off. He sounded upset…?"

"The camp's only an activity thing. They've finished all the matches."

"I'm sure we'll manage to have some fun. The language school doesn't have an official half term so Zander will only be in London for a few days. I couldn't say no when they invited Anna to their house. She says you and she can go to the Science Museum when she's not with them."

Lottie seemed to think there wasn't any more to be said. Or

maybe she didn't have time to say anymore. She gave him a special hug anyway

Luke was angry that Liam could've even thought he wasn't wanted at Fynn Creek.

"It was that football thing. How was we to guess you weren't going on the residential? It's what you always do. Obviously you can come on *Lassie* though there's only two bunks and only one of 'em's dry. But we're fixing it if we can get the epoxy on them decks. Ought to get it done if the weather holds. Or I could go stay at Angel's."

Liam felt like he was everybody's pity pick. "Don't see why I can't stay here in the flat. Language school kids don't have half term."

"But you ain't a language school kid and they ain't going to let any of us be on our own anymore. Especially not after last weekend."

The brothers were silent. Both of them resenting the Russians.

"Have you seen Zander's new bodyguard?" Liam asked Luke. "He's called Iakov. He's well grumpy. I was going up the cliff and he yelled at me about the defence site. As if I were going to go in there anyway."

"Yuck-off! I saw the other one in there once. Right in the site."

"The one who left?"

"Think so."

"That's quite weird. We didn't find any way in, did we?"

"Not through the fence. But there must have been ways before this was a school… Angel's dad was telling us about the Cold War. There was a lot of it round here."

Luke was obsessed about history. Liam wasn't. And he didn't like war stories.

"You coming down the beach? Give you a skimmer challenge."

Luke sounded awkward. "Thing is I've got Pokémon Amber for tonight. Show you if you want."

Liam didn't want. Nintendo screens were too small. He was even struggling with his ship identifier app. Even when it was zoomed right in.

He headed for the beach but stopped at the dinghy park first. That had a fence that you could get through easily enough. He found Anna's new dinghy and ran his hand down the stern. It felt beautiful except the metal bit at the bottom was right out of shape. You could see the rudder wouldn't work. There were bad scratches there too. He wished the delivery girl would come back and mend it because after she had he was going to ask Anna if he could use the dinghy sometimes. It was no good hoping for an outboard but he could row about. Cross over to Felixstowe without using the ferry or take himself to that bit of sand that only showed up at low water. He wondered whether she'd let Vicky come with him.

Except there weren't no oars. But Donny'd promised he'd teach him to sail someday. Then he'd be able to get all the way up the river to *Lowestoft Lass*. If he was allowed.

It was evening now and the sea was slopping about, pearly grey and thick like mercury. He didn't have homework and Lottie'd said supper was a help yourself as she was doing some gig in Norwich or somewhere. She'd made a pasta bake that would feed all of them and Skye was coming to put Vicky to bed and stay over.

Liam liked Skye. They all did, even if they couldn't much talk to her or understand what she said. Anna and the older ones had learned BSL which was a special language where you talked to people with your fingers. They should all have learned it really. Skye had loads of problems connected with being deaf and dyslexic but she was understanding and she totally got it about making patterns with stones and things. He was tempted to go back and join with her and Vicky but it was about three days since he'd done a proper lookout from up the cliff. It had given him a bad feeling finding Yuck-off there.

That was a good name Luke had thought of. He didn't ought to let Zander's bodyguard keep him off of his cliff. Anyway language school were on a trip today so Yuck-off would have to have gone as well.

The gate in the chain link was shut and locked and there were notices making certain no one from outside thought they could go into the Manor. They'd put all new security cameras on the main entrance and there was going to be lights that would come on in the grounds. It was obvious they weren't so sure that it was about some burglary in London.

The man who'd given him that note... He'd been scared. It had poured off him like sweat. Liam didn't think he'd been setting up a burglary. Not of his own choice.

The water was a bit blurry today, when he got close to it. Tried a couple of skimming stones but he couldn't quite get the knack. Nothing like that had properly worked since he lost his lucky one.

Liam sat down on a warm slope of pebbles and began to feel his way carefully through them. They were mainly mudstones and flints but there were so many differences in the roughness of the outsides and then the mix of ultra-smooth and vicious-sharp. He got a good flint today but his best find was two small pieces of green sea-glass. You could hardly see that they'd been green, so frosted from tumbling about all those years in the other pebbles and the salt until they weren't jagged any more but quite flat and their edges rounded. They must have come from some long ago broken bottle and these two bits had managed to stay pushed around together while the others could be miles away. Skye would love them.

Liam chose a whitish, veined sandstone for Vicky. It had lumps and lines where it had been squashed together all them millions of years ago. Found her a bit of sea-sponge too, to wash her fairies' faces. Then he put all his finds deep into his pocket before he headed for the cliff. His lucky stone was still gone. Anna and him had looked it up. It had been a banded carnelian but he didn't know much more. Maybe he oughter ask her if she'd take him to that museum that had rocks and things. She was a good sister. Probably they'd have to get used to her having boyfriends.

"I don't never want to go anywhere with you ever! I think you're cruel and wicked and you can have your phone back and your app and its screen is rubbish anyway. And I wish I didn't have to live in this house. I'm going to ask my dad if I can go to Fynn Creek and never come back. I don't care if I get rained on every day. I hate you."

She'd had his tree cut down. All that was left was a stump, creamy white and jagged like a raw wound. And flecks of sawdust and a jumble of branches, chopped into smaller pieces then dragged away and dumped. Someone with a chainsaw had killed it. Probably hadn't taken more than a few minutes but that tree had been living there for years. It was a little wild apple tree. It had felt like a friend.

It wasn't only because it was his way in – instead of going all the way back round through the main gates he and Luke could climb up and along the branch and over the fence into bushes – it was because it was a nice tree. It had saucers of pink and white blossom in the spring. It wouldn't ever have them again. And the buds that were left now the blossom had gone wouldn't never turn into neat little green apples that nobody came to get because they didn't know it was there.

Most of Liam's hatred was for himself because he'd told his sister about the tree. She wasn't his proper sister anyway. And she never would be. She was a wicked witch rich bitch.

No one had ever heard Liam talking like that. He was screaming. Screaming straight at Anna with his face red and scratched and his clothes all crumpled and tears pouring down and making a tideline of greyish dirt. They stared at him as he threw the phone at her then blundered away into his own room and slammed the door. They could hear him sobbing on his bed.

Hundreds of miles away a man who'd crashed his stolen car racing north up the *autobahn*s died without regaining consciousness. His daughter, who he loved so much, wouldn't see him again and he wouldn't be there, full of pride, when his clever son went to college. But in his wife's heart he would live for ever as her memories brought his spirit home to the pale light on the blue-grey sea, the miles of sand and the miles of forest. She would do her best to help their children remember him there.

His body had been kept for an autopsy. The authorities didn't know yet what they would find.

"What was that about?" Luke asked Anna.

She was white and blotchy red.

"I have N.O. idea," she answered, breathing as if she'd been punched. Then her brain began clicking back into action. "Is there some place where you and Li go on lookouts?" She'd picked up the phone and was staring as if it might explain.

"Up the cliff by the end near the defence site. He does, but I don't so much. Not recently. It's since that business with the crazy Dutch women when you didn't know that Angel and I and her dad were being abducted right past you."

"I just thought he was ship-collecting: seeing how many tankers or container ships or whatever he could spot – like in those 'I Spy' books. It's why I gave him the app." She thought a bit more. "There'll be a tree you use to get back over the fence without coming round to the gate. He got really upset when I said it might have to come down. I didn't even think about it again. But what did Li mean about this screen being rubbish? I can't see anything wrong with it."

"Reckon he was saying anything what came into his head. He's well moody at the moment. It's weird him not going to football anymore."

Skye, who had watched without hearing, took Vicky into the

kitchen and made a drink for Liam. She put some cookies on a plate and they carried them into his room and put them by the bed. Vicky kissed him but he didn't look round.

Heike, up in Lowestoft, had worked extra night shifts all week to cover for a colleague whose child was sick. So she took her courage in her hands and asked the manager for an advance on her pay.

It was only by a week but they wouldn't do it. Asked her why she wanted it. She couldn't explain that she needed the money to buy wood because she'd sold that first set of oars and didn't want to meet Anna Livesey until she'd at least started making the replacements. They maybe thought she was about to take unscheduled time out to visit Estonia or something. They did offer an advance if she'd let them keep her passport but she wasn't going to do that. Other foreign workers had warned her that that was something you should never do. A copy maybe, but not the real thing.

Afterwards she wished she hadn't asked. Maybe when she'd finished her diploma the miracle would happen and she'd get a job in ship-building that would pay her enough to live on and maybe even be able to send some money home. But at the moment there was nothing. No chance.

She'd told her tutor about the accident on the Deben Bar and the damage to *Theodora*'s rudder pintle. He'd got her straight onto welding a replacement and showed her the technique of scarfing in a piece of wood if she thought the transom had been weakened. She explained her idea about re-modelling the rudder so the blade could pivot up while still keeping some steering capability and he was so helpful that she nearly explained about needing wood to make another pair of oars.

But she was too ashamed. How could she have thought it was okay to sell that first pair?

She'd get the repair done, then buy the wood when she had the extra shift money in her pocket. She'd have to make two trips back to Bawdsey. It was going to be hard to budget in the fares but she was looking forward to going back to that river in daylight. There'd be no need to go near the big house or those Russians.

Anna didn't need Liam to apologise when they finally had to meet up the next day. She knew what it felt like when you totally lost it. She managed to convince him that the tree hadn't been destroyed because of her. Iakov had been authorised to carry out a total security audit and he'd seen it as a risk and got onto it.

She went with Liam along the beach and up the cliff when he got back after the care home. They looked at the stump and she agreed that it was a really sad thing and maybe they could have moved the fence instead. Privately, she was glad she hadn't had the job of trying to put that suggestion to Iakov. He wasn't like the other man – Dimitri – and she saw that Zander was scared of him.

"You've got to understand their situation," she tried telling Liam. "They've had such big changes. Zander's father used to be in the intelligence service (I haven't exactly told Luke that) but he's totally forward-thinking and he tries to use his money and his newspaper to help people know the truth about things and get connected up to the rest of the world. But that makes enemies and there was some big row that meant they had to leave Russia about ten years ago. Zander was about six then. He doesn't know what it was about."

When she had a bit more time, after exams, she would do a search and find out. She didn't really understand why Zander hadn't done that for himself.

"If my father wishes me to know, then he will tell me," was all he'd said. Anna couldn't have coped with that. Her father had died in a North Sea accident and she'd read the enquiry reports as soon as she'd worked out how to use the internet. Her mother hadn't told her anything.

"I think Zander's dad is just trying to protect him," she said aloud to Liam. "The way things work out there his wife and Zander are his two weak points."

"What's the matter with Mrs Ivanov? Why can't she look after herself?"

Or look after Zander, he thought. He didn't get it why those people's problems meant that someone like Yuck-off could just come round cutting his tree down. There was a clearance zone being made all along the fence. Sound of chainsaws and smoke from fires.

"She's ill. It's a hereditary disease that she gets because of her race. She's an Ashkenazy. Genetically, they're really interesting." The scientist in Anna popped out for a moment but was quickly squashed by her new emotions. "Mrs Ivanov is a lovely person and very brave. She used to be a cellist. They have a charity that researches the condition and she uses herself as a volunteer to try new drugs."

"Is Zander going to get the illness too?"

"Probably not."

Then they got quite involved in calculations about what the odds were if you had half your parents from one genetic group but they had mixed races of grandparents from other groups and then you might not know what race at least one of your great-grandparents was from so that put a random factor in. Liam loved mental maths and somehow he and Anna found they were friends again.

Though he still didn't want his phone back and the idea of going to London for half term made him feel dead.

He and Anna took a detour to the dinghy park on their long walk back from the lookout cliff to the main gate. The girl from Lowestoft was working there. She'd found some wood to chock the dinghy up and was repairing the place where the rudder fitted on to the transom. The new pintle was ready to attach but she'd decided to fit an extra knee inside for strengthening. Then she was going to sandpaper out the scratches and make everything as new. It had taken longer than she'd originally expected. Good jobs usually did.

"Do you have some varnish?" she asked. They'd introduced themselves and Anna had managed to say something about how nice the dinghy looked and what a lot of work it must have been.

"You definitely got the name right?" she asked. "It wasn't something to do with swallows?" She'd been left this dinghy in her great-uncle's will. He'd been a famous scientist and inventor who'd worked on radar and direction-finding systems during the war. It was because of him that they lived in their top flat in the Manor. Anna had always thought she would be a physicist or a computer scientist as well but recently she hadn't felt so sure.

She needed to decide soon. She had to fill out her UCAS form.

Anna's great-uncle could be quite childish. He and his friends (some of them were Donny's relatives) liked to make out they were the Swallows and Amazons children from those famous stories. Anna had assumed she'd been left this dinghy so she could do the same. And because she wasn't particularly interested in children's stories – or in pretending – she hadn't bothered to go and look at it.

"Shouldn't it have been called *Swallow* or *Scarab*…or something?" she asked, as if this boatyard girl would know.

She was going to have to face the fact that her great-uncle hadn't named the boat from a story book. Theodora had been his sister, Lottie's mother. Anna had never met her because Lottie had quarrelled with her so badly in the days before she'd discovered how to use charm. They'd never made up and it was too late now because Theodora was also dead.

"This dinghy should have been left to Vicky as well… Why do I have to keep dealing with all this family stuff?" She wasn't talking to the girl or Liam, she was talking to herself.

"Vicky won't mind," said Liam. "She'll think she's the Lady Galadriel anyway. It's a really cool boat. Donny and Skye have got one with a mast right forward like that. But theirs is bigger and it's plastic. This one sort of gleams." Like a wet beach in sunshine, he thought but didn't say.

"That's the varnish," said the girl. "We gave her sixteen coats. Technically she's about a hundred years old but there's almost nothing of the original left. You probably gathered that from the costs of your sponsorship. You should think of *Theodora* as new."

"All the paying was done by the lawyer," said Anna. "It's

a Trust. I don't usually see what's going on until they send accounts at the end of the year. They get auditors to go through the invoices and all that. They check everything."

She made herself look at the dinghy again. The workmanship was amazing: a smooth, reddish-gold hull, bright fastenings – bronze and copper, Anna guessed, and it was obvious, even to a non-expert, that there were several different woods involved. The colours varied from a pale cream to a rich mahogany. All presumably chosen for their different qualities of flexibility and resilience, not artistic effect, but beautiful all the same.

Anna realised she was stuck with it. "It's…lovely. Thank you for bringing it, sorry, *her*, round here."

The girl looked totally practical. Short, springy hair – fair, not blonde – grey eyes, skinny and probably wiry, except she was wearing overalls so you couldn't see. There was something about her face that reminded Anna of someone.

Liam was going all round *Theodora*, touching her and leaning over to peer in and obviously wanting to climb aboard but knowing he couldn't because the dinghy was on land and also had been lifted up to have that work done underneath.

"Will I be able to have a go, Anna? I don't mind that there isn't an outboard."

Anna relaxed. If it made the kids happy…"Of course you can. Have you noticed she's got two rowing positions? You and Luke can be boy power when there isn't any wind and Vicky can steer. Where have you put my oars?" she asked the boatyard girl.

The girl stiffened. "Sorry," she said. "They are to follow. You are expecting *two* pairs of oars?"

"There are two sets of rowlock fittings," Anna pointed out. "But you don't need to worry; I can get my lawyer to check with the college what they promised to supply. My mother can call in sometime and pick them up. She's performing in a festival near there."

Heike realised why she'd thought she recognised Lottie Livesey. Her publicity photo was stuck all over Lowestoft. *Two* pairs of oars… to be made and varnished. All in her spare time, which she didn't have. And the money for the wood, which she had to earn.

"Don't trouble your mother," she said. "I will take care of it all. But I must finish now. The light is almost gone. If you have varnish I will begin the coats on the repair tomorrow. I have a little to make a start."

She was putting away her tools.

"How are you getting to the station?" asked Liam.

"I stay here tonight."

"Where?"

"I camp. It is not cold."

"You've got a tent?" he was excited. "Can I see it? Are you in that place where people go to have picnics? In the wood near where the radar used to be?"

"I'm not sure. I must go now."

Five night shifts this week. Then eight hours a day for her course and helping George whenever she could. The tiredness had been okay while she was working on *Theodora* but now she had stopped, it wasn't. She had to get away from these people. She had a sleeping bag and a bit of tarpaulin. If they would go away, she could sleep here, lying next to her precious dinghy. Not hers. Theirs.

"Where *is* your tent?" said Anna. "There's no overnight camping allowed in that picnic spot."

"I didn't say I have a tent. This is not your business. Please leave me alone. If you have varnish I would be glad for you to bring it in the morning. I have enough for a first coat only."

She lifted her rucksack on her back and picked up her toolbox. She could sleep anywhere. Allowed or not allowed. Then she noticed the dampness that was coming with the night. She should use her tarpaulin to keep the dinghy dry. It didn't matter what she had.

"You could sleep at our house," said Liam. "My brother Luke isn't there. You could have his bed."

In that enormous place with guards and Russians?

"No thanks," she said. "I will cover the dinghy and then I will find my camp."

Surely they would go now?

"Liam's right," said Anna. "You should sleep at ours. You won't be in the way at all and there's been a security alert. They might be a bit funny about random campers."

"No!" said Heike. "I'm okay!"

She opened her rucksack and jerked at the roll of tarpaulin. It came out with a rush and everything with it: the thick cheese sandwich she had packed, her tin of Red Bull, bananas, Pro Plus tablets, last few squares of chocolate, glucose, her sketch books, photos of home – the precious things that she kept with her because she was too afraid to leave them behind. Everything falling onto the gravel in the fading light.

The boy moved to help, didn't see a banana. Trod on it. Squishy muck all over his shoe. Almost stamped on the sketch books, though they were in plastic bags.

"Don't, please!" she almost shouted. "Why can't you leave

me alone? I will finish in the morning but now I have to sleep."

Anna used the torch on her phone to make sure they'd picked up every last item. It was like collecting evidence.

"*Theodora*'s my dinghy. I don't want you to work on her if you're totally buzzing with sugar and caffeine. Only if you've had a proper meal and a good night's sleep. You can come back with us, like Liam said, or I'll call a taxi to take you to the station."

It was a straight choice and Heike hadn't any strength left. She tucked the tarpaulin that would have been her groundsheet carefully round *Theodora*'s transom, re-packed the rucksack and walked with them back through the main gates and along the drive until they reached the house that was like a palace.

"Don't worry," Liam said. "We only have the top floor. Up there to the side. It's the brick bit looking out to sea. The rest of it's a school."

Heike struggled to show interest. "It was famous, in the war?" Her tutor had said something about the place when she'd asked permission to make the delivery trip.

Anna and Liam both began to explain but her head felt as if it was packed with wadding. Every muscle in her body was howling to lie down. This was the front of the house, white stone with a complexity of turrets and pinnacles. Lights came on, dazzling her. The front door was like a dark arch opening into a wide wooden corridor. There was a video cam and a screen.

A heavily-built man was arguing with a boy in the corridor. They were speaking Russian. She didn't want to hear. Did she know the man? She hoped not.

"Yuck-off," whispered the boy, nudging her. She was too tired for jokes but did her best to smile.

"We'll take the lift instead of the stairs," said Anna. "Your toolbox looks heavy." She'd suggested Heike leave it under the dinghy for the night but there was no chance of that. Not if there was a security issue. Those tools were the basis for her life as a craftsman. That – and a reputation for honesty.

If anything could have kept Heike awake it would have been the worry about Anna Livesey's lawyer checking what had happened to the money they'd paid for the oars.

But it couldn't.

Liam was practising guitar in the next room when Heike woke up. She listened for a while. This was his brother's room. She could have guessed it belonged to a boy, scattered with books and electronic stuff and jeans and trainers. Like Arvo's. It made her feel homesick.

The practising stopped at the end of a song and the door was pushed open very quietly.

"Are you awake?" Liam whispered. He was a friendly boy. Fair hair, reddish, sturdy, healthy-looking but not so comfortable with himself, maybe?

"Yes," she said, sitting up and beginning to wonder what the time was. "I like your music. My brother plays music but it's a different sort. More electronic."

"Is your brother older than you? Does he live near here?"

"He's at home in Tallinn, Estonia. He's older than me but he's still studying. He's at university."

"Do you miss him?"

"I miss all my family but I need to get on with what I'm doing. Then perhaps I can go home. When I have qualifications and experience. But there are not so many jobs with wooden boats where I live. Not yet."

"Anna came and checked on you in the night. She said you'd eaten all your food even though it had gone completely cold. She's gone out now, with her friend. She says to tell you she's sorry but she can't find any varnish. My dad would probably have some but he's the other end of the river."

"He doesn't live with you?"

"Not usually. Anna had the lift installed after he had his accident but he prefers staying on *Lowestoft Lass*. That's where my brother is. It's Saturday today and we're on half term."

"Sounds good but I must be getting up now. I didn't mean to sleep so late."

He took the hint and went back to his room and waited for her there until he guessed she was ready and he could take her to have breakfast. He accidentally filled her tea cup so full there wasn't any room for milk.

"That's okay. I like to have my tea black."

"That's what Zander does." A thought struck him. "Is Estonia somewhere in Russia?"

"It is NOT!"

She tensed up after that, ate her breakfast really fast and seemed like she couldn't wait to get out of the house. It was Liam's job to look after her so he just went along with it and tried to tell her things he thought she might find interesting. Like the house being the place where radar was developed in the war.

"Against the Germans?"

"Yes. Or anyone who wanted to fly at us over the sea. Radar

went on for a long time. There's a defence station here and that was against the Russians."

"But now you let them into your house. With their big cars and their stolen money."

"This isn't all our house. I told you. It's a school."

"For the rich people."

"I suppose so." Liam wondered why everyone got so angry. This girl was starting to sound like Luke. He forgot how angry he'd been, only yesterday.

"There's an old man I play my guitar to. He's probably Russian but he's not rich. He lives in a care home and nobody knows who he is."

"I work in care homes. Most people don't know who anyone is. Very often they are not sure who they are themselves. I need to get on now. I have plenty of work to do before I catch the bus. I am at work tonight also."

She hurried her breakfast. Liam offered to show her round but she didn't have any time to do any more than glance out of the window to the sea.

"That's Holland over there," he told her. "If you go straight across."

"It's the same from Lowestoft where I work. But if you go just a little bit north, before you turn east, then you find your way into the Baltic Sea and you continue to sail and you reach my country. And my country is a good place to be – when Russia is not taking it."

Liam walked with her down the long drive. They were to collect a dinghy park key from the security lodge. Iakov was there. Heike knew his bushy slicked-back hair, black eyes and scowling eyebrows but she wasn't certain why. He challenged the Suffolk man when he handed her the key to the dinghy park but the Suffolk man said it wasn't his business. Heike bristled like an angry cat but managed not to speak. Liam thought he heard her spit as they walked away, but he didn't actually see.

"There's a hole in the dinghy park fence," he told her. "From inside the Manor through the wood. I'll show it you if you like. Then you won't always need to get a key. Shall I stay and help?"

But she was a perfectionist at her work and didn't want him, and Luke was at Fynn Creek and everyone else was out.

Lottie had asked him to make sure he packed everything he was going to need for five days in London. They'd be leaving early tomorrow.

Liam went off on his own again. He spent a little while sitting on the beach, feeling the stones in case there was anything to replace the beauty he had lost – and maybe get back the luck that seemed to have gone with it. But there wasn't. He was also checking out to sea as best he could without the app but he couldn't identify anything. He might have to ask Anna if he could have his phone back and if there was maybe some way of adjusting the screen.

Possibly it was because Liam was thinking about going north and then east that he was mainly looking in that direction. Perhaps the visibility wasn't too good, though the day was bright and breezy with fair weather clouds coming up like cotton wool balls from the south and west. Whatever the reason, he didn't see the sailing vessel that was coming with them.

Liam felt depressed. There wasn't any point going to the cliff.

He went back to the house and fetched his guitar then he cycled to the care home, leaving a note for Lottie and Anna.

But it was lunchtime there and the staff were harassed. Some people were eating okay but others had to be fed, often two or three by a single carer. It was quite a mess. Liam saw a man wandering around wearing something that looked like a nappy and there was a lady spitting her food as if she was in a distance competition. The angry old lady in the wheelchair was banging her tray and shouting. Suddenly she reminded him of Vicky when she'd been a baby and they were being looked after at the Rectory. Those had been bad times before Donny came along.

Liam couldn't see his special old man. He asked for John but someone said they thought he was asleep. So he got on his bike again and pedalled back to the Manor. Realised too late he hadn't told anyone at the care home that he wouldn't be coming to play his guitar next week because he was having to go to London. Maybe it didn't matter. Maybe they wouldn't notice. They'd all got forgetfulness anyway.

Heike finished everything she could do until she had some more varnish. She stowed *Theodora*'s equipment neatly out of sight and carried her bags to the bus stop, where she sat on her toolbox, closing her eyes and trying to relax her shoulder muscles and breathe extra-deep. She mustn't sleep on the bus journey because then she might miss the station but when she was on the train it would be different. Lowestoft was the end of the line.

She didn't see the Chinese junk came though the shingle banks. She wasn't in the right place to watch it turn into the tide, furl its extraordinary sails and pick up a visitor's mooring just opposite the dinghy park where she'd been working.

If she'd seen it she'd probably have risked missing the bus, the train and even her night's shift to take out her sketch book and draw its spectacular hull shape. She might possibly have overcome her usual shyness to speak to the boy, only a few months younger than herself, who rowed swiftly ashore in a slate-grey Mirror dinghy and hurried up the drive to the Manor.

But she didn't.

CHAPTER FIVE

An expedition north

Strong Winds had left the Deben and was heading north for the River Ore. Donny had come ashore the previous afternoon to invite Liam for a few days' sailing instead of going to London.

"You and I have never been off anywhere without the others," Donny said, when he'd found Liam moping in his bedroom, not doing his packing. "I'll take my revision with me – it's exams again straight after half term. It's always revision and exams these days. I can't stand much more of it."

"Just you and me…on *Strong Winds*?"

"Yup. If you'd like it. Mum's gone to the Rectory to help Wendy and Gerald with the girls. I reckon we'll only get as far as Lowestoft but we could look about a bit on the way. Not do it all at once. The forecast's excellent."

Lottie was fine with the idea. So was Anna. Maybe they were relieved they didn't need to take him to London. Liam was too happy to care.

They'd had a big supper and all played cards together. It was the sort of game where everything was a bit random and people laughed and shouted at each other and no one really cared if they won or lost or couldn't see the numbers. Vicky played too and there was no Zander.

The bell on the haven buoy clanged flatly as it swung in the lazy swell. It wasn't a happy noise but Liam and Donny had no time to feel depressed. The tide and wind were hurrying them on. They were entering the River Ore. Donny'd reduced sail early but still there was this amazing sensation of speed, being carried forward, past more shingle banks, half-submerged, longer and somehow wickeder than the entrance to the Deben. Now Liam was on one of the boats that he'd used to watch from the shore when he and Luke had walked that far. Maybe someone else was watching him and thinking how grand.

Strong Winds wasn't like any other yacht anyone here had ever seen. If someone had a spotter's notebook they'd have to make a whole new page for her.

"Where're we going to stop, Donny?" The experience was making Liam feel breathless. They'd been less than an hour coming up the coast with the wind fair but the tide against. Donny offered to let him steer but he didn't want to. There was a buoy they were meant to be making for but he wasn't sure about it and he needed to be getting used to *Strong Winds*' ropes and equipment now that it was him who was her crew.

Immediately before they turned into the new river there were houses on the left-hand shore and people doing paragliding and jet skis. It was the right-hand side that fascinated Liam: a long bank of pebbles that they were rushing past. And beyond it, out of sight, more of the sea that they'd just left.

"Have to go a bit further before it's good to anchor," said Donny, privately relieved to be past the weirs and spits of shingle that shifted every year with the winter gales and didn't necessarily stay in one place during the rest of the summer either.

"But you'll need to come and hang on to the tiller while I get the anchor ready."

Strong Winds could virtually sail herself in these conditions but he thought it would be good for Liam to get involved. "Keep her pointing exactly as she is until I call to you to bring her round. Then do it quickly. I'll manage everything else."

When the junk was anchored and the sails were stowed, they didn't stop to eat or drink. They lowered Donny's dinghy, *Lively Lady*, from her davits and rowed ashore, taking a small anchor and a long line to secure her from the top of the sloping shore. It was so narrow, just like Liam had imagined, a natural wall made of pebbles and sand that had been heaping up there for hundreds of years and were getting held together by plants and bird shit. It was sheltered close in but when they'd climbed to the top of the bank, the wind came whistling across from the sea. Much stronger than it had seemed when they were out there.

"Weird place," said Donny. "Mum likes it for the birds."

That was what Liam had been hearing: the shrieks and protests of disturbed seabirds as they complained to each other about the human invaders.

"If we laid flat on our stomachs with our heads looking over the ridge, we could keep watch out to sea for hours without anyone knowing we was here."

"We could," Donny agreed. "But I wouldn't mind a walk."

The younger boy nodded.

"Which way d'you want to go?" Donny continued. "It gets a bit military further up. Wire and stuff. Me and Mum don't go there – she says bad spirits. And I'm pretty sure we're not allowed."

"Can we go back the way we've came?"

It took them most of an hour to walk all the way to the end of the spit. They were going slow with Liam staring at the ground, wondering if this was the day he'd find his new lucky stone. But he couldn't see one. A bit too much plastic and frayed ropes' ends and bird dung.

"Tide doesn't never come over here?"

"Don't think so. I chose some of this for geography course work and it's growing longer most years. Except where it isn't."

"Where's that?"

"Up by the lighthouse. Going to fall into the sea, that is."

Then, when they got to the end of the spit, opposite Shingle Street, where they'd come in past that clanging buoy, Donny started telling Liam the story of the bodies on the beach, where burned soldiers were supposed to have been found trying to invade England. The moment he stopped he knew he'd made a mistake. It was like that time, years ago, when he'd told Luke and Liam the story of Blind Pew in *Treasure Island* and given the little boy nightmares.

"The point is…it wasn't true," he added hastily. "You ask Luke's friend or any proper historian. It was just one of them spook stories, like UFOs and stuff. It's the sort of place that makes people think like that. But we ought to be getting back. We could walk closer to the seaward side and you can look right up the coast where we'll be going when we head for Lowestoft. I've brought a bucket for driftwood or sea coal. We get through so much in the winter that we have to keep collecting all year. Mum found some tiny pink tellin shells here. You could tell Vicky they were fairy fingernails. There's angel wings as well."

Liam was tired but he didn't say. Kept his head down, kept on looking. Picked up sea coal when he noticed it. Found one big white whelk shell in really good condition. Usually they had bits chipped off them or holes bored through. He held it up against his ear to check that the sound of the sea was safe inside and when they got back to the junk he checked again and it was still there.

The day was salvaged; the bodies on the beach forgotten. Donny got on with cooking them a panful of sausages before they crept up Butley River for the night.

"You know what, Liam, mate, you want to get your eyes checked." Donny was trying his best not to sound angry. Everyone knew that the upper part of the River Alde meandered around like the python in *The Jungle Book* when its coils got kinked. There were withies on most of the bends, long twigs sticking out of the water with red cans on top for the ones you needed to leave to port and green flags for starboard. At least, that's how it was meant to be but quite often the top-marks had come off or the twigs had got snapped and even missing one of them could throw you out of the crazy pattern.

Donny was used to relying on his mum's brilliant eyesight, so he'd stationed Liam forward to keep a lookout and shout instructions while he trimmed the sails and steered. They'd gone upriver really early with the flood tide and had breakfast at Iken. Donny would have tried going further but he was already losing confidence in his crew. Then the ebb had started running earlier than he'd expected and Liam's guesses had got wilder as he got more anxious on the journey back, and now they were hard aground completely the wrong side of a clearly marked withy and likely to be here for about the next ten hours until the ebb had finished stranding them and the flood risen high enough to let them get away again.

Aldeburgh, the nearest town, was a keen sailing place and because it was half term there were dinghies racing and people in every type of yacht and motor boat ready to enjoy themselves with their families in the fine weather.

"Seriously, when did Lottie last take you to see an optician?"

"I dunno," Liam was truly upset that he'd messed up. They'd had a great day yesterday, just mucking about: going ashore in the Butley River and searching for mushrooms up a green grassy hill. Liam hadn't seen any mushrooms but Donny'd found a gigantic one – about plate sized – and they'd eaten it with fried bacon. Then they'd played cards again and after that they'd sailed *Lively Lady*. If he went to have an eye test, they'd give him specs. That's what always happened to people. He'd look an idiot in specs. Everyone would tease him and he wasn't sure how much more stress he could take.

Donny didn't push it. If his great-aunt Ellen had been there (which she sort of was) she'd have told him it was his own bad judgement anyway.

Strong Winds was already rising out of the river like a creature from the deep as the tide poured away. The bank of mud they'd hit was quite firm and he had a bad feeling she'd go over and they'd be spending the rest of the day with her on her side and people gawping or taking photos. He needed to lay out anchors and do his best to balance her. And after that, he supposed gloomily, there'd be nothing to stop him getting several hours revision done.

⚲ PEBBLE ⚲

"Hey, Li! Just because *SW* isn't going anywhere doesn't mean we can't. Help me pull the chain out and shift the water carrier over this side and we'll float *Lady* out into the channel and go down to Aldeburgh for the afternoon. I've even got some money. You can sail her if you'd like. And I'll do lookout and instructions."

It was an easy, confidence-building sail and Liam had money, too. They found a safe place to leave the Mirror, walked to the cinema, sat right at the front and watched the latest *Star Wars* film. Afterwards they brought massive portions of fish and chips and went onto the beach to eat them. They walked almost as far as the Martello Tower and the wire fence that stopped people walking any further towards the places that used to be secret.

"D'you want to go and look round there some time?" Donny asked. "It's where they tested bombs. There's a boat crosses from Orford but I don't know how much it costs. I might be saving my money so we can get a takeaway from the Floating Lotus when we reach Lowestoft. There's mooring fees as well. But we could go if you'd like it."

"I've got forty pounds," said Liam. "Lottie said I should give it to you, but you wouldn't take it."

Just at that moment he didn't mind if they never went anywhere. His stomach was full, the sun was warm and he'd discovered that if he covered over his right eye and used his left close up, he could build a column of pebbles that got ten high. It didn't work at all the other way round but he put that out of his mind. You needed to choose really flat stones. He lay on his right side and searched patiently with his left hand for that perfect next pebble that was going to take him to eleven.

"We can go if you want." He wasn't going to say that he didn't want. "There was a missile at our place called the Bloodhound. They were going to fire it at the Russians if the Russians fired at us first. Luke and Anna think it's really interesting." Liam thought it was horrible but that was probably because he was a wuss. "Mainly, they were always watching out so they didn't have to."

His fingers had been busy all the time: finding and checking; selecting and rejecting. Now they'd found something different. It wasn't flat, like he'd wanted, and it wasn't a stone either – or it didn't feel like one. Sort of softer and a bit lighter. He rolled over and held it up, not too far from his left eye. It was a bit more than the size of an ordinary marble but it wasn't clear and round like a marble. It was lumpy and dull yet it felt good in his hand and when he held it up there was firelight caught inside and Liam knew immediately that he'd found his new lucky stone.

"I think that's amber," said Donny, sounding amazed. "Which is awesome, as all the amber round here comes from the Baltic and it's all to do with the currents and longshore drift and stuff. If you hadn't picked that up here it might probably have come rolling down past Orfordness and ended up in Bawdsey one day."

"When would it?"

"I have totally no idea."

No eye deer. Liam stayed a bit quiet as they walked back to *Lively Lady*. Donny had tried to show him the little scrap of something – it might have been a bit of leaf or a prehistoric bug – that was caught in the heart of his amber. Except the more he'd tried to focus the more difficult it got. Donny might be right, maybe he did need specs. Now that he had a new lucky stone to see him through, he could ask Lottie to take him to the optician, have the eye test, get the glasses, then stay cool until people found something else to laugh about.

When they were back on board *Strong Winds* they agreed that they'd finished with this river. They wanted to go out to sea and up the coast to Lowestoft.

"Probably only stay there a night or two – I've a bit of an issue with mooring charges," said Donny. "And maybe leave Orford Ness unless Luke and Anna want to go. Or when we see what money we've got left."

So, as soon as *Strong Winds* floated, they sailed down the river past Aldeburgh, past Orford – even though it was dark – until they anchored in the same place, just inside the shingle spit, ready to set out early in the morning. Liam had his whelk shell as well as his amber under his pillow. The shell was like his extra ear. It heard the river whispering past *Strong Winds*' wooden sides, the calling of the sleepless birds and the distant movement of the sea. It couldn't hear that clanging bell so he didn't think of bodies.

Sea on stones: pushing and pulling, retreating and returning, plucking and nudging at the land. That was music he could hear every night if he opened his window at home, but from *Strong Winds* it sounded different. It was further away because it was the other side of the spit, but it was growing clearer in his head because tomorrow they were going sailing again. A whole day. East a bit and then north, Donny had said. And that girl had said that if you went north a lot, and then east, you'd get to the Baltic which was her home sea and where his amber had come from.

Donny was sleeping the comfortable sleep of someone in his own bed and Liam must have been sleeping for some of the time but he was definitely awake when he heard the motorbike. Except he couldn't have been because it couldn't have been a motorbike. You couldn't have had a motorbike on that spit, it was protected. It wasn't making the right noise and it was further away.

And then he started having horrible thoughts and he hid down inside his sleeping bag and kept telling himself that the spit was like a rampart keeping them safe and the story of those bodies wasn't true anyway. Except it might be because they had been testing weapons here and it wasn't only in the war that people didn't say what they were doing and wouldn't tell you the truth if you asked them.

The noise came back later. Quite a long time later, but he didn't know how long because he hadn't been checking. He'd been holding on to his amber to keep safe and deciding that the whelk shell knew too much. He was going to drop it overboard before they left and let the river drown its echoes.

Now that Donny understood he couldn't use Liam as a lookout, he got him steering much more.

"You can do a lot by feel," he explained, once they were out of the river and past the buoys that marked the channel through the shoals. "I'm the skipper, so I'll set us a course. We've got a compass but you probably can't see that until you get your specs, so you need to concentrate on what the wind is telling you, and the waves as well. You can listen to *SW*. Gold Dragon used to get me to trim the sails with my eyes shut. Said it was good practice for night sailing and it would make me a better helmsman anyway."

It wasn't only that Donny's great-aunt's spirit lived on in every timber of her boat: he kept her ashes in a locker along with the salt-stained book that had come home from the Barents Sea and the papers old Nokomis had collected when she'd tried to find his father. The ashes were in a jar that was so tightly sealed that even if *Strong Winds* stood on her head and turned somersaults it wouldn't burst open. Skye would have taken it far out to sea and scattered the ashes to release Gold Dragon's spirit but Donny couldn't cope with losing her so finally.

"You've got your lucky amber now, you'll be okay," he told Liam.

Liam steering left Donny free to attend to some issues of his own as they sailed up the coast in the morning sun. He brought his revision folder on deck and sat for'ard most of the time, keeping an eye out for other boats and fishermen's pots. He fetched snacks and gave Li a break when he needed one. Mainly the younger boy stayed at the tiller, sometimes tweaking one of the sheets, occasionally letting *Strong Winds* fall right off course but getting her back again.

There was a moment off Sizewell when he seemed to get flustered and that was Donny's fault as he'd dozed off while struggling to memorise statistics on the population of Brazil. He was woken suddenly by the sound of the engine.

"What's up, Li?"

Strong Winds' foresail was backed and the wind spilling from her mizzen. Liam had pressed the engine start and was using full throttle. They were totally off course.

"There was…I might have hit a yellow football."

Donny looked around them, then quickly checked *Strong Winds*' hull for damage. He couldn't see anything wrong and he'd set the course so they weren't too near the sets of beacons which marked where the seawater went in and out round the power stations, cooling them. Anna had told him the statistics about how many tons of water were rushing round every minute but there wasn't anything you'd notice, except that fishing boats and fishing birds liked the warmer bit where the water had come out again. Lottie had been saying something about extra monitoring being done in advance of the festival but Donny couldn't see that there was anything different from when he'd been here before.

He looked up at *Strong Winds*' sails, flapping and cracking in confusion and at Liam's face, which was white with panic. He turned the engine off and stood beside the younger boy. Spoke as calmly as he could.

"Maybe you did. But there isn't any harm done. Sometimes things blow off from beaches. I caught an inflatable green crocodile once. Gave it to Baby Ellen. Major success. But what you need to do now is pull the tiller towards you and get some wind back in that foresail. She'll soon settle. We'll save the engine for when we get there."

Had Liam dozed off as well? Donny offered to take a turn at the steering but the younger boy shook his head. Maybe what he ought to do was cook them both another meal: they still had a long way to go.

✿ PEBBLE ✿

Donny needed to think about their entry into Lowestoft. He wasn't too worried about getting into the harbour. He'd done that when it was really rough. Conditions today were perfect. It was more an emotional thing. Lowestoft had been one of the first places he'd seen Gold Dragon in action outside her ship, and Ai Qin at the Floating Lotus was the only person left who'd known about the life his great-aunt had led before she came back to England. Donny wasn't sure what he was hoping for: a glimpse of the wider world maybe?

He also needed to work out what they were going to do once they were in the harbour. There wasn't anywhere to anchor or tie up for free but he'd done a search and they were going almost as far in as they could, almost to Oulton Broad and then were going to berth for the night on the Mutford Mariners' pontoon. It was the cheapest and the man had sounded friendly when he'd called him from Lottie's phone. But he'd also said that there might not be anyone around to help when they arrived.

Although Donny loved *Strong Winds* it was no good pretending she was always easy to manoeuvre in tight spaces. Not by him anyway. He'd decided to motor.

Liam had done really well all day but for the last few hours the junk hadn't been sailing so freely and Donny took over the steering with secret relief as they approached the harbour entrance. He'd explained about fenders and ropes and what they were going to need to do once they found their berth. Then he switched on the engine. Loved its solid *chg chg chg*.

There was no power. Donny checked it was in gear and pushed the throttle as far forward as it could go. Noise. Plenty of noise. But no power.

Strong Winds was being pushed sideways. Those concrete pierheads were coming closer. There was shallow water beyond the channel. People got wrecked here.

The three green lights were showing. They should be going in.

"Mainsail up, Li," he called, "quick."

He'd taken it down as they approached, wanting visibility and not too much speed. The mizzen and foresail weren't enough. Not if he needed to swing her round against this current. Please Liam, be quick.

"It's right to your hand. Don't look. Just pull!"

Liam didn't query, didn't try to look: he grabbed the halyard and pulled. Donny hardened in the sheet. The battens swung flat to the wind, the junk answered grudgingly and turned against the powerful cross-setting tide. She was nail-bitingly slow and they passed so close to the port pierhead he felt he could have reached out and given it a shove.

Then they were through and into the harbour.

"Lower away," Donny called. "Then stand ready with your warps." They needed to edge across to the pontoon where they could wait until the road bridge opened – and until he'd had a think about what could be wrong with the engine. And maybe with his steering as well.

The harbour master had seen their skewed approach, was calling them on VHF. Donny hadn't answered, he'd been concentrating.

"Yacht *Strong Winds*, Yacht *Strong Winds*, this is Lowestoft Port Control. Are you in difficulty?"

Once they were safely tied up alongside the pontoon, Donny had time to reply, explain about the loss of engine power,

❧ PEBBLE ❧

confirm that he was waiting for the bridge to open and was booked to moor for the night at the Mutford Mariners' Club. He assured the port control official – with a confidence he did not totally feel – that he was okay to proceed under sail.

The evening conditions were fine, really fine, he told himself. They had the tide with them now and the breeze was steady. He did know how to manage his boat. He could do it, even in a relatively narrow space and a strange environment.

He had to. He wasn't admitting to anyone else that there might be something wrong with *Strong Winds*.

CHAPTER SIX

A snorkel and a face mask

There was an egg-shaped man sitting on a white plastic chair when they reached to the end of Lake Lothing and nosed into a space on the outermost mooring pontoon. Donny'd never seen such a bizarre collection of vessels as they'd passed on their trip from the swing bridge to this cluttered far corner. Many appeared to have been dumped, others designed for very specific tasks which he wasn't sure he understood. Dive boats, wind farm boats, abandoned fishing vessels, relicts of two world wars, small ships, dredgers, schooners, survey vessels, submersibles, unfinished projects. His antique Chinese junk was positively mainstream.

Except that *Strong Winds* wasn't feeling good at all. She was slow and reluctant. The sluggish handling that he'd noticed on the last few hours of their trip hadn't been Liam's fault. It was hers. If she'd been a person he'd have wondered whether she was ill.

Anyway, they'd made it and the man was nodding at them. He was probably smiling but he had such a mass of facial hair it wasn't easy to be sure. He hadn't got up to take their lines as watchers often did.

"Heart," he explained, wheezing slightly. There was a sheen of sweat over the top of his balding head though the evening was quite cool. Everything else about him was camouflaged by the mass of brown hair and beard and a jutting belly. "I'm George.

Secretary here, though I can't do much. Welcome to the club. That's a very fine vessel."

"Thanks," said Donny. "Is it you I have to pay? And are there passcodes and things?"

"Yes," said the man called George, "I was waiting for my young apprentice but she's probably working late. Or early."

"Oh," said Donny. Now their voyage was over and *Strong Winds* was safe, he desperately needed a wee. He could see a tiny brick bungalow that might be the clubhouse but in marinas you usually had to have a passcode to go anywhere.

"Are there, like, facilities in there?" He knew there must be. He needed to get to them.

"There she is," George spotted the person he'd been looking for. "Finished for the day or just starting another one? Show these visiting yachtsmen into the clubhouse, would you, Hetty?"

They followed her up a concrete path and into the small square building. Donny dived for the gents and Liam was left with the girl. The skinny shape, short hair, dusty overalls were familiar.

"You stayed in our house. Your name's Heike, not Hetty."

"Yes I did, thank you. George isn't strong on names. He's a kind man and it doesn't trouble me. If you've come to collect the oars, however, I am sorry, they are not yet ready."

Obviously he hadn't even thought about oars. "You said you worked in Lowestoft, but I didn't even know I was coming here then. I thought I had to go to London with Lottie and Anna. I'm here with my friend Donny. That's his boat. It's a Chinese junk."

The kid's friend owned that! Heike disliked this Donny already. Sure to be a spoiled brat.

His junk though, was something special. She'd never seen

anything like it and she badly needed a closer look. The kid was okay. She remembered waking up to the sound of him playing his guitar.

"I'm studying at the Shipwrights' College. It's next to this. George lets me live on one of the boats here if I help sometimes in the club."

"There's something gone wrong with our engine. We nearly crashed into the harbour wall when we were trying to get in."

"But we didn't because you were such a brilliant crew." Liam hadn't noticed that Donny was back.

"This is Heike, Donny. She made Anna's dinghy that I showed you."

Donny held out his hand to her. They were about the same height, same colouring. "That's amazing. It's an amazing dinghy. So totally cool. I heard you tried to cut the corner coming into the Deben?"

She'd come straight from work. Needed a shower. Didn't shake his hand.

"I was stupid. My chart was out of date. I didn't know the entrance changes every year. Fortunately there wasn't too much damage. I have the repairs in progress."

Donny wondered what country she'd come from. Probably wasn't polite to ask.

"Stresses me out every time, entering that river. Do I need to do any paperwork to moor here?"

She fetched the pad. "Your boat details and your name and address and how long you're planning to stay."

"It was going to be one night. I'm not sure now, because of the engine."

What would he do if it needed some major repair? He hadn't got any money. Go engineless for ever? He didn't think his skills were up to it. Especially if *Strong Winds* was in some sort of sailing sulk.

"I could take a look?" It wasn't what she enjoyed but she'd done a basic marine engineering course and it would get her on board. "Or there are many experts around the harbour…"

"I couldn't afford them. It only happened as we were coming in."

"These happenings are always at the worst moment. Like my problems." She sounded a bit friendlier now. "I can come to you in the morning. I have to clean up now and go to work."

"What work's that?" Liam asked.

"Night staff in care home, I told you."

"Oh, yes. But not in the one where I go, where the old Russian man lives?"

"No, it's here in the town. I will see you in the morning when I have finished my shift. You make me breakfast and I look at the engine, okay?"

She didn't need sleep: she needed to get on board that boat.

The next problem for Donny and Liam was that their new mooring was so far from the rest of the town. It was almost Norfolk. Also Donny realised he wasn't sure exactly where the Floating Lotus was. Except that it was near where they'd moored before, which was the opposite end of the harbour. Near the sea and the yacht club, not here.

They used the showers in the club, checked they had enough money and decided to give it a go. First they walked along a path round the edge of Lake Lothing but there were too many fences coming down to the water, so then they followed the railway line and that was okay until it stopped. Which was where Donny admitted he was lost. He'd been with Gold Dragon before, bobbing along in her wake. Then the second time his friends Xanthe and Maggi were in charge – and they'd had mobiles. Liam wished he hadn't chucked his phone at Anna. Or he'd accepted when she tried to give it him back.

They asked people but people didn't seem to take much notice of Chinese restaurant names. They were sent to Gold Pandas, Jade Emperors, Blue Dragons, Lucky Stars and when they did find the Floating Lotus it was only a takeaway, not a restaurant any more. There was no Ai Qin.

Donny tried asking for her but the man behind the counter didn't speak much English and didn't look friendly. Donny didn't try too hard, because if something bad had happened to the beautiful, welcoming lady in her crisp, white shirt and embroidered waistcoat he didn't want to know. He remembered the chef with his face scarred by old knife wounds and the flock of giggling girls who'd come to peep at *Strong Winds* the first time they'd moored here. The Floating Lotus had been a good place then. It didn't feel like that now.

But Donny and Liam were hungry. It had been an early start and a very long day. They bought cartons of noodles and spare ribs and chicken balls and they got given a bag of prawn crackers. Then they went a few dark streets further and ate their food by the Easternmost Point. They listened to the whirring of the gigantic turbine and the slap of the waves on the sea defences.

"I don't know how much longer I can stand going to school

and learning about the world from a textbook," said Donny suddenly. "And I'm fed up with never having any money either."

Liam didn't say anything at first. There wasn't anything much he could say because he'd only been to the Floating Lotus once and hadn't understood anything about the network that had been operating there. Also he had 'Old Maui' on a loop in his head. So, if he was thinking at all, which he wasn't, he was running down from the cold Kamchatka Sea and spreading his ragged sails to the arctic gales.

"I know what that noise was last night," he realised suddenly. "It was a jet ski. That's why I thought it was a motorbike and it was revving and stalling because it was hitting against the waves. They do that off our river, too."

Donny didn't know what he was talking about and he was thinking sad thoughts about losing the last person who had really known his great-aunt. So he didn't answer and Liam went back to singing shanties in his head.

"There's an old man who lives in a care home near us," he told Donny further on. "They call him John, but that isn't his name. And when I played my guitar to him he sort of woke up and sang. But then he cried. It was horrible."

There was space for a joke about Li's guitar playing but Donny didn't make it.

"I reckoned he might have been a sailor," Liam went on. He might try telling the old man about their voyage, when they got back, except he probably wouldn't understand. "He knew the song words in English but when he tried speaking, it sounded like another language."

"I reckon long-ago sailors did know songs. It was how they worked together."

As they got nearer to *Strong Winds*, Donny's mind returned to his worries. "I don't know what I'm going to do if the engine's broken. Gold Dragon and Defoe both showed me a bit about maintenance but not if anything's badly wrong. Which is sure to happen someday and it might have happened now. And all I know about engine parts is that they're expensive. Gold Dragon left Mum her savings but Mum needs them to live. Lottie tries paying her as often as she can and so does Rev Wendy but Mum won't take it usually. I need a job but there aren't any. Or I don't know how to get them."

Liam couldn't answer any of that so he clutched his lucky amber and felt its warmth in the palm of his hand.

Donny and Liam were still asleep when Heike arrived. She'd been up all night looking after people who were so confused they didn't know the difference between night and day. She hardly knew it herself. Except her body sort of screamed in envy when she climbed down into *Strong Winds*' cabin and saw them sprawled across the bunks.

"Good morning," she said.

Donny was sitting up and struggling to get alert, brushing his hands through his hair and blinking at her.

"Sorry. Hi." He needed to think if he had clothes on. Yes, he'd fallen asleep in his T-shirt and jeans.

"Sorry," he said again, disentangling his legs from his sleeping bag. "Late night."

"I didn't have one. I was working."

He stopped himself from saying sorry again. He guessed it would annoy her. "Can I make you some tea? Thanks for coming, by the way."

Liam was curled deep into his bag, under his blankets, only the top of the back of his head visible. Donny felt he needed to explain.

"We were trying to find somewhere – a Chinese restaurant – and we got a bit lost. It was all wrong anyway. The person we wanted wasn't there. Liam isn't ten yet and it's his first trip away. I should have left it."

"He's a good kid. I stayed at their house when I was working on the dinghy."

"The big place?"

"Yes."

"So, would you like tea? Or breakfast? We've finished most things but there's toast. I need to go shopping later. If I've got any money."

But he might not have. He put the kettle on anyway. Hoped she didn't mind that the milk was long life.

"I've had enough tea. I drink it all night. And coffee."

"Did you say you knew about engines? This one completely lost power. I turned it on when we were coming in and there was nothing there."

"It turned on okay then. Did you check the exhaust? Was the water coming through? What colour was the smoke?"

Donny didn't know. He'd been trying to avoid being swept past the harbour wall and onto the shoals.

He made instant coffee for himself and a couple of slices of toast and jam for them both. There wasn't any butter, but she didn't seem to mind.

❦ A SNORKEL AND A FACE MASK ❦

Then they set to work.

Heike was someone who asked questions in a logical order and connected one thing with the next. It helped Donny realise that he did understand more that he'd thought about the engine. Maybe he'd only panicked so badly because he'd always been able to take it for granted. "Starts every time," his great-aunt had said on that first day they'd met.

Heike couldn't find anything wrong. Except that it obviously wasn't right. It sounded wrong and when they tried to motor off from the pontoon they weren't going anywhere, except down the harbour with the tide. Donny pulled them back in quick, Liam stayed asleep.

George turned up. He was driving a motorised buggy which couldn't get onto the pontoon, so he stopped at the end of the concrete path and Heike went to talk to him about what they (hadn't) found.

"George says that if the engine's working but the boat won't go, there must be something stopping it. We must look at the propeller."

Donny and Heike tried lying down and looking from the pontoon but they couldn't see anything. Then Donny lowered the dinghy and pulled it close in to the rudder and leaned over the side and stretched as deep as he could to touch the propeller. There was something there that didn't feel normal. Something hard and soft and knotty and unidentifiable.

"Haven't you got a face mask?" Heike asked.

He had. And a snorkel. The Lake Lothing water was murky and unappealing. Donny stripped off his jeans and T-shirt, put on the equipment and went over the side in his swimming shorts.

"You don't have a wetsuit?"

"No."

He felt awkward with her watching him but he needed to concentrate on getting a good look at *Strong Winds*' propeller. It was about two feet below the water line. The snorkel wasn't going to be much use. Donny took a deep breath and went under. Even with the face mask he couldn't really see. But there was something bunched round the shaft and over the blades, tight and lumpy and hard to his touch.

He came up and blew the water out of the tube, hard.

"There's something – lots of it – but I don't know what. Could be wire."

George had been right. Even though he was sitting on a buggy on the concrete path nowhere near *Strong Winds*.

"He is what you call a Legend," said Heike, affectionately.

Donny went under again. It was a relief to have found something. Now he had to get it off.

"Can you cut it?"

But even Gold Dragon's mega-sharp knife that she'd bought here in Lowestoft all those years ago wasn't making any impact as Donny went under again and again, hacking at – whatever it was.

"I can't shift it at all," he said to Heike. "And there's something else. Some sort of… something, attached."

She went to talk to George again.

"He says we can warp *Strong Winds* round to the slip and sit her into the cradle. She's too heavy to be winched up but if we're quick she'll be in there when the tide goes. Then we can get a proper look."

They woke Liam and hauled the junk round with just a

breath of wind in the foresail and all three of them on lines, with Donny steering too. George watched from the concrete path. Then, when she was safely within the small metal cradle, they secured long ropes from her bows and Donny took an anchor out astern.

"That's belt and braces too, that is," George said. It sounded like a compliment.

There was some shouting from inside the club, as if there might be an argument happening. George drove away in his buggy and Heike followed in case he needed help. She wasn't away for long.

"It's a man they call Jake," she said. "George won't have him in the club."

Donny and Liam looked at each other. That was a name they hated.

"Is Jake…a policeman…like, gross…?" Donny asked. Ex-inspector Flint was surely still in jail.

"No. He is dark and angry and he watches all the time. He has bad friends and he is a Russian," she said it with hatred. "I think he has been at your place too," she added to Liam. "I saw him at your gate."

Not Yuck-off! Couldn't be. He'd have to be with Zander and Zander was in London. She must mean one of the others who had come from London with the Ivanovs. Liam wasn't going to ask because he didn't want to know.

And Donny didn't know anything about the security issues at Bawdsey Manor, anyway, so they sat in *Strong Winds*' cockpit and ate biscuits and drank squash and talked about other things while they waited for the tide to go down.

"Don't you have to go to work?" Donny asked Heike. "Or to sleep," he added, remembering she'd already been at work, all night.

"It's okay," she said. "I have some cleaning to do in the club. I like to help George when I can because he allows me to stay here."

"Where?"

"In a small boat that isn't used. Possibly he is keeping it for someone. George only tells you what you need to know."

"He looks like he ought to be in *Lord of the Rings* with that amazing beard."

Heike smiled, for about the first time. "For me he is like my *Vanaisa* back home, my grandfather. He had a beard like that. And his hair grew long and it was grey like an old wolf. I loved my grandfather; he told us stories, Arvo and me."

"What sort of stories?" Liam asked. When she said 'wolf' something had made him think of something that Luke had said.

"Usually they were fairytales, but sometimes they were stories of his life."

"Did he die?" In Donny's experience that's what usually happened to anyone old who you loved.

"I don't know. Probably. He got confused and then he went away. My father thought that he had gone to seek his death. I don't know…he was also a bit obsessed. Always searching for my cousin who is lost. Searching in England, even." She gave herself a shake and sat up straighter. "Have you talked to George about paying for your boat on the slip?" she asked Donny, "Usually it's only free for members."

Donny's stomach lurched. He had not.

"I'd better go and find him."

"You can have my money from Lottie," said Liam.

"Thanks, mate. I reckon we might need it." Donny felt tense. Why did he never have any money?

"I thought he would be rich, with a boat like this," Heike said to Liam after Donny had gone to find George. So he tried to explain to her about Donny and his mum, Skye, and Gold Dragon, who was dead, but it probably all sounded a bit complicated. Then she started asking about his family and the big house where they lived.

"So Ms Livesey and her sister are rich but the rest of you are poor?" Heike wasn't being rude; she was trying to understand. "But what about that car your mother has?"

"She's not my mother. She's my step-mum. My brother and I mainly have to live with her. But she's okay," he added hastily. He didn't want to talk about his mother being dead, or his dad and Lottie not really getting on anymore. She's called Lottie Livesey and she's a singer and she's starting to get famous. That means she's earning lots of money and she gave me some to come on this trip. She's a very kind person. So's Anna. Anna's kind too."

Heike didn't say anything. She disliked Anna Livesey, with her lawyers and her Russian friends – and *Theodora*, which Anna obviously didn't appreciate.

Could she talk to George about the oars? she wondered unexpectedly. When she was a little girl in trouble she would have talked to her *Vanaisa*. He would have helped her.

Heike had accepted that her grandfather was gone but she was certain that he would never deliberately abandon his beloved yacht, his *Ra'*. He wouldn't have gone overboard unless he was certain *Ra'* was safe. So the yacht must be somewhere, even if he wasn't.

She liked what she had understood from Liam about this beautiful *Strong Winds* being passed to her new friend Donny by his great-aunt. She liked Donny, too. It helped now she realised that he wasn't rich.

Her father had done his best to help *Vanaisa* prepare for his voyage. He'd put tins of food and some drink on board. But the old man had taken no money with him. Just a list of their names which her father wrote to help him remember that he had a family.

She wasn't going to think that they'd been wrecked: that *Ra'* was gone forever and her grandfather was lying at the bottom of the sea, his bones scavenged by crabs. She preferred to imagine that he was strapped to his helm, all sails set, him and his yacht, gaunt ocean ghosts, travelling on forever, seeking the lost child, her cousin Vanya.

CHAPTER SEVEN
A bowl of chicken soup

Anna had never imagined anything like the London house where Zander and his family lived – when they were not living in one of their houses somewhere else, or cruising on their superyacht.

She and Lottie were staying in a cheap (for London) hotel near the museums where she'd thought she and Liam might have gone: the Ivanovs had a whole mansion in a square that had been closed to traffic. Anna felt tense and self-conscious as she was buzzed through the entry system then directed towards for the broad steps and the marble pillars and the reinforced front door.

Probably this was how some people felt when they came to visit her.

Inside, the house was beautiful – at the least the parts where she was taken. There was apparently a whole basement full of cars which had been dug even deeper to make room for a full-size swimming pool and a gym where the staff worked out. Zander's father used it but he and his mother weren't so keen.

"I like to swim," he told Anna, "But it's my mind I am most frequently wishing to exercise."

The rooms where the family lived were luxurious and elegant, full of books and newspapers in several different languages. On the top of the house, with big windows overlooking London was a private concert hall, decorated in white and gold. The lift that took them up was glass with a velvet bench running all the way round so people didn't have to stand, even for that short time.

"Perhaps your mother would like to come and sing here for us?" Zander's mother, Raisa, said to Anna. She was warmly dressed with hennaed hair and a sharply protruding stomach that was uncomfortable to look at. She walked with a stick and one of her feet turned slightly inwards. Anna knew she had been a talented cellist but she had to give up her career because the bones in her hand kept breaking.

"My husband and I have a research foundation to help others who have the same condition. We are always running fundraising events. This room is not a private luxury."

Anna wanted to like Raisa. It was just that she sighed so much and looked sad most of the time.

"Sasha – Aleksandr – tells me you are interested in research. So you know it always needs money. We have a clinic here which is not only for my treatment and we are funding a new hospital suite."

Maybe this wasn't so different from the time long ago when Anna's own home, Bawdsey Manor, had been a research centre in the walls of a rich man's house. They hadn't had to do fundraising, though.

"Don't you get a grant for the clinic? Doesn't it help the NHS?"

Raisa's body was tired and stiff but her dark eyes were expressive.

"We are exiles from our country," she said. "Very rich exiles. Everyone is glad to take our money and the money from our very rich friends. We raise funds for treatment as well as for research." She walked slowly across the room to one of the windows and looked out across the city. "But in Russia, with our government, it is very difficult. I don't go there. Arkady Nikolayevich must visit sometimes but London is our home now, I think…" She didn't sound certain. "If your mother would like to sing here I will gather her an audience. They will be rich but the money they will give will help others who are not. There are panels, you see, that fold across these windows to make the acoustic good. But please only ask her if it is something she would like to do."

Anna gazed at the room and thought how different this would be from the vast stages and screens and amplifiers and huge audiences that was Lottie's singing life now – or the folk clubs and pubs where she'd started her career.

"Have you heard her singing? She's not classical."

"Sasha has told me she is good. That's all I need to know."

Zander shrugged slightly. "It's obvious she will be a big star. The record companies will see to that but possibly she has contracts that don't allow her to choose charity events."

"I wouldn't let her sign anything like that." Anna maybe spoke too sharply. "She wouldn't anyway. My mother has strong principles."

Lottie ought to do that care home concert she'd been talking about to Liam, Anna thought suddenly. For all the people who couldn't afford to go to Luminal. Yes. That would be good.

"Would I be allowed to see the clinic?" she asked. "And do you mind being asked about your illness?"

"Talking about my illness is my job now. It's almost all I do," the older woman answered. "And living with it."

"Hey, Mama, you have me! And you have Papa, too!"

"And all the worries you both give me." For the first time Raisa looked a little brighter and led the way back to the lift to take Anna to inspect the clinic area before insisting they must eat. The cook was making them a special chicken soup from her special family recipe.

"With matzo balls?" asked Zander greedily.

"Of course."

Matzo – wasn't that what Jewish people ate?

Zander's father, Arkady, came in to lunch with them. Anna had met him when he and Raisa had come to the Manor after the security scare. She'd been asked to join their meeting that night as she, not Lottie, was responsible for the top-floor flat. She'd been impressed by Arkady Ivanov's refusal to be angry about the guard who'd run.

"I knew Dimitri when he was with the fleet. His note says that 'as a father' he must ask me to understand that he has to go. Whether this is because he is a father or I am a father or whether he is referring to our professional relationship – I cannot say. He gives no detail. But 'Father' – it is a strong word."

"Like President – or Tsar," Zander had muttered. He sounded resentful. Maybe he'd got attached to Dimitri. Maybe he was in a bad mood. Maybe he didn't get on with his father. Anna couldn't really work out what it would be like to be Zander. Maybe it might have made a difference if Dimitri had delivered the note himself. Instead he'd used her little brother.

The principal of the language school had asked the Ivanovs whether they wanted to talk to Liam but Arkady had waved the suggestion aside. "It's late at night and it would perhaps frighten the small boy if we bring him in as if for questioning.

He was asked to deliver a note and he did so. We leave it at that."

Zander's father was a tough-looking man with a smooth grey suit, made of something really expensive, and wire-rimmed glasses – except it probably wasn't wire, more likely titanium. Anna could believe he had worked in Intelligence before the world had changed. And now he was a stratospherically rich man with newspapers and other businesses across the UK, Russia and the world. Yes, Liam could well have found it alarming to be questioned by this man. Anna had been glad when her part of the meeting was done.

Zander didn't look like either of his parents. He was taller than both of them and looked more like a poet, with his dark curly hair, high cheekbones and pale skin.

Today Arkady kissed his wife, hugged his son and shook Anna warmly by the hand. "Welcome," he said in Russian, and Anna was glad to be able to answer in the same language. She was more pleased still when he switched back to speaking English. Zander had told her that his father had spent several years in London when ordinary Russians weren't allowed to travel. She guessed that that might have been the time he had been connected with Intelligence.

A pair of bodyguards had come in with him and there was a maid bringing the chicken soup and a boy with her carrying more dishes. Anna tried to say hello to them, too, but they didn't make eye contact and the family acted as if they weren't completely there. She'd noticed Zander trying to treat his replacement bodyguard that way but he hadn't succeeded. It was a big relief that Iakov had stayed in Suffolk to oversee the new security installations and wasn't here, watching and scowling from across the room.

❦ PEBBLE ❦

The soup looked like a total meal, full of veg and meat and tiny noodles and these whitish balls that Zander was getting so excited about. He wasn't waiting for anyone else to get served, had a spoonful already on its way to his mouth, was taking a deep long sniff to get the aroma and smiling across at his mother who was watching him as if he was the only person in the room.

Anna was watching too – mainly because she needed to know what was the correct way to eat such a bowlful; did you shovel it in and start chewing or tip the spoon sideways and suck politely? She saw Zander's face change, look less certain, but, knowing it mattered to his mother, ate the big spoonful anyway, consideringly. Ate another, not so sure.

Arkady spat, violently. Lumps of half-chewed chicken and vegetables sprayed back into his bowl.

"Stop now," he ordered Zander. "Go at once to rinse your mouth. Purge if you can. Fetch the cook," he told the bodyguards. "And more bowls. I want to see him eating this. Annushka," he said to Anna, "You will not touch it. Nor you, *Zolotse*."

Raisa laid her spoon down. She seemed completely calm. "The cook is new, *Papotchka*. Perhaps unfamiliar with the recipe. There will be an explanation."

"There will need to be."

It was excruciating. The cook was fetched, then he and all the staff were forced to eat bowlfuls of the rejected soup while Arkady watched them for signs of hesitation and Raisa asked practical questions about the way her recipe had been followed. Zander had left the room and didn't come back for a long while. Anna sat watching, wishing she was anywhere else.

Eventually it was established that a mistake had been made with the type of salt that had been used. The mess was cleared away, the cook left the room and very soon afterwards they were eating caviar and blinis while they waited for a new main course of salad and herring, then a gorgeous marshmallow pudding.

Zander had returned but seemed to be finding it hard to talk to his father. Anna felt stunned. Raisa did her best to normalise the atmosphere, asking her husband about his meetings for that day and trying to draw Anna in with questions about the history of Bawdsey radar and her great-uncle's scientific work.

"A great man. Our people tried to turn him, of course," said Arkady, who seemed to have regained his good temper, as if the incident had never happened. "We had heard he was a pacifist so hoped to persuade him that sharing his knowledge would be for the good of the world. But he didn't listen."

"Do you mean that you met my great-uncle?"

"On formal occasions – and there were not so many of those."

"And you wanted him to work for Russia?"

"The USSR, as we were then. He was older, of course, and no longer involved with the active service. But still, he would have been a very great prize."

"My great-uncle would never have become a spy!"

"You think this is shameful. But what is a spy? There was bitterness between our countries but between scientists there is sometimes a different understanding. If West and East could have worked together the world might have been a safer place. I hope it's better now, but I don't know…"

He was quiet then before he made a very obvious effort to listen to Raisa and get involved in her suggestions for ways Zander and Anna might like to spend the afternoon.

Anna was amazed by this conversation and by the lightening changes in Zander's father. He seemed so open, warm and genial now – not the man who had been spitting his food and shouting for the cook. She did her best to answer his standard parental-style questions about her studies and her hopes and where she might apply for university. Which all used to be so easy but weren't any more.

She was glad when the meal was over and she and Zander set out to visit an exhibition of photographs. But they couldn't just walk there, they had to be driven and then collected and with a bodyguard never far away as they walked round.

"Is it better when you're at school?"

"That was the idea. That Suffolk was safer than London so I would be more often at liberty. But I hate it – except when I'm with you, of course," he added. "They want to send me back there tomorrow before my father leaves for Russia. He has a meeting with the president and he's paranoid right now. The president has been re-elected and they are pressurising my father to do things that he is not willing to do. I am ignorant what this is. He tries to keep me safe by not telling me anything."

"What happens if he doesn't do…whatever it is?"

"Now the president has returned to power, no one can say no for very long. People have been put in prison or they get beaten up or they die unexpectedly. One of my father's friends was poisoned. Here in London."

Maybe that explained the scene at lunchtime.

"Your father had better do it then, unless it's very bad."

"He thinks he can negotiate. He and the president served

together when they were younger. My father knows things that the president knows that he knows."

That didn't sound totally reassuring.

The photographs in the exhibition had been taken in Afghanistan. They showed gun emplacements and lookout points high on bare mountains. You couldn't call them beautiful but they would stick in the mind – like the concrete constructions on her own bleak stretch of coast.

"Couldn't we go to the cinema instead?" she suggested, opening her phone and scrolling through. "But definitely NOT James Bond."

"Let's go back to the house and play some chess. My mother likes it when we are all together. And if you can charm my father a little more perhaps they'll let me stay longer. You could say you need to attend our concert tomorrow, to check on the acoustics…"

Anna needed to think about that. She had exams next week.

Liam's pillow was wet. He'd been crying in his sleep. He turned it over and tried to get a grip. "Man up," he told himself. Hoped Donny hadn't heard him.

They'd worked so hard yesterday. They'd got *Strong Winds* onto the cradle, then, as the tide went down, they could see a mass of neoprene and wire wedged hard around the propeller shaft. When the water drained away further, they discovered a sort of box attached to the wire, which they must have been dragging with them as they sailed. None of it looked much like the yellow football that he thought he'd hit, but Donny pointed out the shredded remains of some rope and said there'd probably been a marker buoy attached.

"It wasn't you who was meant to be on lookout, it was me and I'd got sent to sleep by the population of Brazil. It used to be a hanging matter, falling asleep on watch," he added.

"In a care home you would be dismissed," Heike agreed.

When Donny had finished disentangling and cutting away the cable, Heike put it and the box into a thick white plastic sack that should never have been floating around the harbour and carried it all into George's office.

"There are so many companies operating in Lowestoft now," she explained as she bagged up their finds, "some of them are very good, very high tech, but there are others that are what you would call chancers. But this set-up is for science, I think. Perhaps there may be a reward if one of the good companies has lost it. Whatever it is, George will know. And you should use the pressure hose to clean your ship's bottom."

Liam had got that job, for a while. He liked the feeling of the hose juddering into life when he squeezed the trigger, the blur of wet mist and the hissing impact as it struck the hull of the junk, sluicing off swathes of mud and weed and colonies of barnacles. His aim was quite bad, so Donny took over for the last bit, clearing all the places he'd missed. *Strong Winds'* hull was smooth and bare. She'd sail better now.

"Your ship needs antifouling," said Heike, and with a sinking heart, Donny admitted that was true. Antifouling had to be paid for and, even at members' rates, it took every penny they had left, including all Liam's holiday money. No more fish and chips, cinema tickets or takeaway noodles. No more anything – except the tinned food, rice and dried pasta that were already on board. Donny didn't dare check the amount of diesel they had if they needed to use the engine on their journey home.

Then Heike had gone away to get some sleep. She said she'd help them float the junk back onto the pontoon but Donny and Liam were certain they could manage. They asked her if she'd like to come and eat tinned supper with them, though they expected she'd be working and would say no. Instead she looked pleased and explained she was doing a day shift the next day, so for once had an evening free.

It had started okay. Liam played his guitar while Donny was cooking and it turned out she sort of knew some of the shanty tunes though she didn't have the words.

"I think my grandfather used to sing them but I wasn't speaking good English then. His father had sailed on the clipper ships."

"Your English is amazing. Did you do it in school?"

"Yes, and German."

"But your family speaks Russian?"

"ESTONIAN!"

"Sorry."

She calmed down. "You English people take your independence for granted, but we were occupied by Russia against our will and forced to speak their language – and not allowed to travel or to sail or to communicate with the world outside. Many people died of their hardships. Or were killed."

"Was anyone in your family killed?"

"My grandfather lost almost everyone. His mother, his father and his three sisters. People say we should forget. I don't ever forget."

"What happened?" Donny wasn't sure he wanted to know. Liam didn't speak.

"Too many things. It was the war. Estonia was an independent country but Hitler had told Stalin that it would be okay for him to grab us. Then whole families are taken away into Russia and never heard of again. They are slave labour and they die."

Strong Winds' cabin was a place where other bad stories had been told but not when Liam had been listening. Heike didn't notice how he was feeling.

"My great-grandfather – the old seaman who was my grandfather's father – and his wife and their three daughters are all loaded onto a truck in the early morning and they are gone and never seen again. My grandfather was sleeping down in the harbour when it happened. There was a friend, Dr von Hagemeister, who had asked him to take care of his yacht – a beautiful yacht, the *See Adler* – because he had been resettled back to Germany. He had been kind to my grandfather so *Vanaisa* was glad to help. But, in the morning, his family was gone. Just gone."

"Um, were they Jewish?" Liam managed. He'd learned about the Holocaust.

"No. They were ordinary Estonians. Like it could be you. Except those things don't happen in England. In Estonia it was 25 percent of the whole population who was taken or died. If there are three of us here, it mean that already one has gone: we won't see them ever again."

Liam curled into his corner and thought of Luke. He couldn't eat any more. Donny got up to make cups of tea. Maybe Heike realised, but she couldn't stop. Drawing her stories was usually enough but tonight, somehow, she needed to tell. She needed Donny to know.

"So my grandfather went to Hamburg where his friend the doctor now lived. First, he worked in the shipyards there – but then he joined the German navy, the *Kriegsmarine*. Because by then Germany had invaded Russia and they were fighting to get the Russians out of Estonia. Of course, it was only because they also wanted to take our country for themselves but my grandfather would support anyone who fought the Russians – and I think he didn't truly realise how bad the Nazis were."

"What happened to the *See Adler*?"

"Our city, Tallinn, was bombed. By the Germans first but then much worse by the Russians. Whole areas burned – and the yacht burned, too. All of our shipping and boat-building industry was gone, all of our good people taken away. But anyway the kind Dr von Hagemeister didn't survive, even in Hamburg."

She paused.

"You'll probably think I'm insensitive," said Donny. "But I'd like to talk about something different. Or could we just play cards?"

As no one had any money they had played for matchsticks but the cards had gone blurry and Liam was too tired.

And now he had woken up with a wet pillow.

"Bad dreams, Li?"

If he answered he'd probably start crying for real.

"Bad feelings, then?" Donny had known Liam when he was quite a lot younger. "Look, mate, how would you feel if we pushed off home? It's well early but I've checked the bridge opening times. We could leave now. We should write a note for

♋ PEBBLE ♋

George. Apart from that, there's nothing stopping us. Heike's working today, she said. We'll see her again, for sure. Something about oars for Anna's dinghy...?"

All Liam could safely do was nod. He was out of his sleeping bag and pulling his clothes on before Donny even had time to fill the kettle. *Strong Winds* was floating; all they needed to do, Donny said, was write that note and run up to the club for one last trip to the facilities. Then they could slip their lines and go.

CHAPTER EIGHT

An unfriendly seal

The sea was metal grey and shifting randomly as if it were muttering in its sleep. There were work boats starting early, some peeling away to the wind farms in the north, others heading east where the sun was rising peach and gold under flat, grey clouds.

As soon as they were clear of the shoals, Donny turned the junk towards the south. There was hardly any wind.

"Could be a slow day," he commented. "Have to save our diesel in case we need it later. You can get your head down again if you like. I'm okay to stand this watch."

But Liam would rather bring his sleeping bag and pillow up from the cabin and prop himself along the side of the cockpit. It was very, very slow but Donny had explained they'd have the tide with them for most of the next six hours and the wind ought to pick up as the day went on.

"Could we go all the way to Fynn Creek? Get to Dad and Luke? There won't be anyone at the Manor except the school."

"That'd be getting towards midnight. Not sure about taking the junk up Fynn Creek in the dark with just the two of us. Luke says the channel buoys are out of position and the new owners haven't bothered correcting them. We could anchor in the main river and go up in *Lady* though. It'll be well late."

Long beaches passed, low cliffs, eroding coastline, scattered houses, some perilously close to the edge. They ate odd meals as they drifted south: the pasta they hadn't finished last night, tins of tomato soup, tea and biscuits. Liam hadn't ever liked tea but it tasted different out here.

They didn't talk about Heike – or her stories – but there was a moment, not so long after Southwold, when the tide had turned against them and the wind still hadn't got up and it almost felt like they were about to be going backwards, when Donny said unexpectedly, "Makes you think, doesn't it, about that battle where they captured the lion. The one between the English and the Dutch where they just drifted all day hammering each other with their cannons and no one could really see anyone because there wasn't enough wind to blow away the smoke. That was about here and about now – this time of year, I mean."

"Suppose so." Liam didn't usually think so much about the history. The stuff that had happened to Luke and Angel was bad enough.

"I try and keep a lookout from the cliff at home," he told Donny, "But the horizon's been getting blurry."

"Maggi's started wearing contacts. She says she never realised there was anything wrong with her eyesight but now everything seems sort of two sizes bigger. She doesn't get so many headaches, either."

Liam was holding his piece of amber. It felt warm and the sun was out and everything was looking better. If he did wear contacts he could probably play football, though he wouldn't give up guitar.

"You ought to meet my old man at the care home," he told Donny again. "Even if he might be Russian."

"Don't let Heike near him!"

Liam laughed and felt more comfortable. It was late morning

next time he looked around. They'd reached the place off the power station where they'd had trouble on the way. The wind had died. The sea was like a mirror. Donny had anchored, opened his textbook and stretched out in the sun. Liam knew enough to understand that they must be waiting for the tide to turn. It was a beautiful day but there wasn't anybody sailing. They couldn't without any wind.

There was something black and rounded breaking the surface of the water. He nudged Donny and pointed.

"Is that a seal?" he whispered.

"It's a diver. Look, there's a dive boat over there. See their flag? I wonder if they're looking for the thing we found. Heike said there could even be a reward…but if they're offering one George should get it. He let us have so much for free."

They lowered *Lively Lady* and rowed across. There were two people drinking beer in the boat and a diver in the water alongside them. He was Liam's seal. Donny stopped rowing and called hi.

"Have you lost something?" he asked.

"Not your business, laddie."

"It ain't a treasure chest."

"We're not the pirates of the Caribbean, neither."

Donny realised suddenly that the men in the boat were talking like that because they were drunk. The diver pushed up his face mask. His face was red and he had black, hairy eyebrows. He pointed to the Alpha flag.

"That signal is telling you to keep away." His accent wasn't English.

Way back in Year Eight, Donny had done a few sessions of a sub-aqua course with his tutor Mr McMullen.

"You've got shape signals up," he answered, "and I'm approaching on the side you've marked as clear. If you were investigating something and didn't want anyone near you at all, you should have cordoned off the area with marker buoys."

"You have swallowed the COLREGS?"

"There was something here we picked up a few days ago. We thought someone might have lost it, that was all. We were coming to tell you…"

"You will describe it."

If the diver had only said please.

"It was just a bit of rope. We cut it off okay."

"So why you have come bothering us?"

"They told us at school that people who lost things at sea sometimes left something to mark them and then came back later. It made me wonder about the bit of rope."

"Its colour was?"

"Bright pink. We could have picked it up anywhere, really. It didn't have to be here."

Liam was glad that Donny was lying. He had recognised the voice. They were quite close to the dive boat now. Liam couldn't make out the jumble of stuff on her foredeck but Donny could. He swung *Lady* round and started rowing back to the junk.

"You are certain the rope was pink?" The diver was shouting after them. "There was nothing attached?"

Donny paused as if he was thinking, backwatered a few strokes, "There was some plastic. A sort of black and slime-green eyelet which might have been part of an inflatable. Like a blow-up Kraken, maybe? Is that what you lost?"

"We have lost nothing. You are wasting our time with your blow-up toys."

"Sorry, I'm sure." Donny rowed rather fast back to *Strong Winds*. Liam wasn't sure whether he was upset or trying not to laugh. He knew how he was feeling – and that was worried.

"That diver was Yuck-off. He's Zander's new bodyguard. He's Russian."

Donny wasn't convinced.

"But if it was him, he'd be in London guarding Zander. Did he look like him?"

"I couldn't see properly. And he was wearing that suit."

"They were all idiots. Anyone who gets drunk while they're working a dive boat is an idiot. They had a whole crate of beer on board."

"But I think he might have been," Liam persisted. "You heard what Heike said. She said George was having trouble with a Russian who was trying to get into his club and she'd might have seen him at the Manor. Although Heike is a bit obsessed…"

"Maybe it was him," Donny conceded. "I just thought they were cowboys. They'd got a yellow surface buoy on deck marked ENVIRONMENT AGENCY – as if it was official – but they totally weren't. That's why I changed my mind about saying anything."

"I hate Yuck-off."

"Why?" Donny was surprised. Liam didn't usually hate people.

"I hate him because he chopped down my tree."

"The wild apple on the corner that you and Luke use for getting over that fence?"

Liam nodded.

"Bastard," said Donny. "I hate him too. But we're nowhere near Bawdsey, What's he doing trying to get in the club at Lowestoft? Or diving off Sizewell?"

"Nothing good, if it was him."

"That's for sure. Let's risk some of our diesel and head out of here."

"My dad'll have some you could borrow."

"And we'll use Luke's phone to ring the club in the morning. Then George can decide if that dive boat's scummy and whether I should have said anything that would help him get a reward."

As they motored southwards, they were followed by a drone. A gunmetal grey quadcopter that lurked and hovered above them. It buzzed them for about ten minutes. They guessed it must be filming.

"Smile and wave, smile and wave," Donny muttered to Liam. "And we'll call down to all those other people who are in our cabin. Sound excited! Pose!"

It was sort of quite funny, acting for the drone, but they were glad when it was called back to the dive boat and gladder still when the flood began to run and they finally got a favourable breeze to hurry them back to the Deben through the long, light evening. Then up the winding river to drop anchor off the Fynn Creek entrance in the late, dark night.

When Donny spoke to George the next morning he learned there'd been a break-in at the club. Money had been taken from the bar plus several bottles of spirits and crates of beer. The main effort appeared to have been to pull the place apart. Every

♆ AN UNFRIENDLY SEAL ♆

store cupboard that could have been emptied had been emptied, every box of equipment tipped out.

The box they'd dragged in on *Strong Winds'* propeller hadn't been there because George had already taken it to a friend of his, whose name he wasn't mentioning. Or couldn't exactly remember.

"Do you want me to come and talk to the police?" Donny asked. "Tell them about that dive boat and the people on board?"

He didn't want to but he knew he should. It was his fault this break-in had happened. *Strong Winds* was so noticeable; probably everybody around Lake Lothing had seen her sailing up to the club that first night. The harbour authorities would have known she'd had engine trouble and anyone with business at the Oulton Broad end could have seen her on the slip. He remembered someone staring at them through the Members Only gate when they'd been antifouling. A dark-haired man. He'd rattled the gate and pointed as if he wanted to come in, but they'd told him to ask at the club for the code. Maybe that had been Iakov?

Obviously, no one could have seen them close up disentangling the wire and taking off the box or they wouldn't have been there searching with the dive boat the next day. But his own impulse to row over and offer help had flagged up the connection. He wished he'd never thought about the reward. They'd guessed that he'd been lying about the pink rope and the Kraken. It was a nasty feeling.

"I wouldn't come rushing," said George. He sounded stressed and wheezy. "I might know that dive boat you're describing and they'll all have alibis. Wouldn't mind not getting any more involved, meself. Ain't feeling so good this morning."

"What about Heike? Is she okay?"

George's voice was like a punctured bellows. It was hard to understand what he said.

"Got herself in a mess," was what Donny heard. But it was something about oars and a dinghy, not about the break-in.

"Someone ought to tell her to be careful." Heike'd said that she lived on a boat at the Club. He didn't know which one it was but she'd be there on her own when she wasn't at work. "Does she know about the people off the dive boat?"

"Did me best," was all Donny could understand from what George said. "You try talking to that Henrietta sometimes…"

Donny knew what he had to do. He had to get back up to Lowestoft, find Heike and warn her. Maybe she could live somewhere else for a bit. She and George had welcomed and helped him and all he'd done was tow trouble into their quiet, friendly harbour.

There was trouble in Fynn Creek, too. The new owners had started to turn the lagoon into a hardstanding area they could use to park the lorries and the earthmovers and the containers that would be the workmen's base when the real constructions began. There wasn't anything much there now, only some reeds and birds and a derelict yacht that had been wrecked by storms. The plan was to block the lagoon entrance, pump it dry, clear it, then start the infilling job.

Unfortunately, the digger driver whose job it was to begin shifting hardcore to block the entrance had cut through the main electricity supply. Things like that happened, people knew, but the new owners weren't making any attempt to get electricity available to the creekies. They'd installed a generator which managed their own supply and extended to the few (very few) posh yachts that they hoped would stay and berth in the new marina. They told everyone else they'd need to make their own arrangements.

They were also offering scrappage deals. The old boats that were people's homes could be sawn up and used as part of the infill that would make the lagoon into a car park. They seemed to think this was quite a generous offer. They gave people estimates how much it would cost to have their boats destroyed commercially. Appeared to be missing the point that most people had been getting along quite happily and didn't want to get rid of their living spaces.

The lack of electricity gave Bill particular problems on *Lowestoft Lass*. He could use gas for cooking and torches or candles for light and he and his boys could wear extra clothes and pile lots of blankets on the bunks. But the fishing boat leaked when the tide was in and Bill needed electricity to run her pumps. Otherwise she'd sink.

It was hard to do hand-pumping from a wheelchair. Luke had been helping to keep the water down all week and Bill had bought a small solar panel and a rechargeable battery which they were trying to install. They hadn't yet succeeded and half term was almost over.

Bill was always short of money but he immediately offered Donny the train fare to go to Lowestoft to warn Heike. Donny'd be doing him a favour, he said. He could collect some paint he'd had ordered and save the delivery charge.

"I ain't giving in here. I said I'd get this old girl looking good again and so I will."

"I wish I could help."

"You've got yer own problems. Anyways yer mum'll be wanting you back. Not much of the holiday left now."

"It's exams on Monday," Donny agreed gloomily. "I'll try and do some revision on the train. I've got to go, though. To warn Heike."

"Course you have. And you can tell the young lady she'd be welcome here if she's needing to make herself scarce. Only wish we had more suitable accommodation."

That was a great idea. Donny had been wondering what he could actually suggest to Heike. Warning her was one thing, but presumably if the club had been vandalised she already knew she had a problem.

"Thanks Bill. She doesn't look as if she'd get fussed about the lack of full-length mirrors and ensuite spa. Except she has to work…"

"Heike won't want to come to the Manor because that's where Yuck-off is – and Zander." Liam wasn't all that keen about going back himself but he knew he'd have to. He wasn't any help here. As soon as he could talk to Lottie and get his specs it would be different.

Luke had been on his phone again. "Anna says Zander is being driven down from London today and so's she. Lottie's got to stay longer. She'll tell the driver to come here so he can collect you as well. She's like Lady Muck when she's with that Russkie," he added, savagely.

"Ain't you coming back with us?" Liam asked him.

"Gotta help Dad, haven't I? Get that panel fixed up for the pump. Then I promised Angel I'd spend a night round hers if

LL's pumping alright. I'll be back to Bawdsey tomorrow – but I won't be taking no lifts with the Soviets."

He and Heike would get on well, Liam thought.

"I don't mind," he said, "if it saves trouble."

Donny had left by the time the big Mercedes squeezed up the narrow lane to the Fynn Creek boatyard. Liam was waiting at the entrance with his bag and his guitar. There were only few holiday events that he was planning to answer questions about but Anna wasn't saying much and when Zander spoke to her it was in Russian. The driver said nothing.

Back into the town, round the head of the river, then a slow, depressed trip along the narrow country roads. Liam hung onto his amber and tried to think good thoughts about how his life was soon going to get better.

Iakov's powerful motorbike overtook them as they drove through Bawdsey village. People were chatting in the sunshine or going to the shop. They turned to stare at the noise of the bike, then at the heavy car with the bulletproof windows. Zander took no notice, Anna and Liam were glad no one could see them through the tinted glass.

The bodyguard was waiting at the entrance to the Manor. "You should keep me better informed," he said to Zander – in English so it was insulting.

"*Zdrást-vuî-tye*, cheer up!" said Anna in Russian. She wondered why Iakov was scowling with such intensity at Liam. Then he stepped back and waved the car up the final approach to the house, following on his bike.

"He'll need to get in a bit of practice before he gets selected for the Olympic meet-and-greet squad," she joked. Zander managed a smile but Liam looked glum.

"What's the problem?" she asked him when they were back in the flat, making toasted sandwiches. Zander had been escorted immediately to the school section.

Liam couldn't work out what he should say. She was his sister (step-sister) and she was so clever, but her arriving in the car with Zander made them seem even more like an item.

"Dunno."

"Was the holiday okay? Where did you go? And where's Donny? He might have waited to say hi."

"When's Lottie coming back?" he asked. "I need her to help me get an eye test. I didn't see one of the beacons when we were coming back from Iken and that ran *Strong Winds* on the mud when the tide was going out."

"And I suppose everyone stared and took photos. Poor Donny!"

"They would've but we went off down to Aldeburgh and had fish and chips and I found a bit of lucky amber."

He showed it to her and she admired it and told him stuff about prehistoric gum that he already knew and other stuff about the amber mines in Kaliningrad and the Amber Room, which had been some sort of wonder of the world but which got bombed and burned in the war.

"Like the *See Adler*." Then he tried telling her about Heike's grandfather and what had happened in the war but he got a bit muddled and guessed she wasn't really listening. So he went back to the question that was really on his mind.

"Could we ring Lottie and ask her if she'd book it?"

"Opticians? Could do…it's still Saturday."

But Lottie was with some journalists and couldn't talk. So Liam asked Anna if she'd take him into town on the bus but she said that it probably needed to be an adult – and also she totally had to get on with revision for her AS exams. She'd missed two whole evenings going to concerts with Zander.

Liam knew he couldn't ask his dad for help because Bill needed to stay watching the pumps on *Lowestoft Lass* and it was often difficult getting into places with his wheelchair.

"Is it okay if I take my guitar onto the beach then?" Obviously he wasn't going to be any use as a lookout until he had his specs. He just didn't want to stay in the flat. Or anywhere near where Zander and Yuck-off might be.

"As long as you accept your phone back that you chucked at me. I've kept it charged. I'll probably do my revision in the garden. It's always lovely weather when it's exams. It'll break as soon as we're finished. The Luminal organisers have taken huge insurance against the festival being a washout."

"Your mum's big breakthrough. Gets to be a mega-star."

She looked at him. There was something in his voice she didn't like.

"Are you grudging her, Li? Because if so, don't. Luminal's not all about money for Lottie."

And there was something in her voice that shut him right up.

CHAPTER NINE

An item of early evening news

The drone kept hovering where Liam was sitting in one of the ripples of shingle, finger-picking his guitar. It made it hard to concentrate. The tide was quite low and there was lots of space but when he got up and walked along the beach towards the cliff it followed him. It looked like something out of *Dr Who*. Liam had a carrying strap so the guitar was okay on his back while he scrambled up. He planned to get out of sight in the bushes at the top.

But the bushes had gone and there was only heaps of brush drying in the sun and some places where bonfires had already been lit to get rid of the gorse and the brambles that had been dragged out. It wasn't only his wild apple that that had been cut down now. There was about four metres either side of the wire that had been cleared all the way as far as he could see. It made the Manor look like a military installation.

The drone left off following Liam and buzzed along the inside of the fence until it was almost out of earshot. Then it came buzzing back along the outside as if it had given him a personal demonstration how it could keep surveillance of the boundary with the former defence station.

"Why would I want to go inside there, anyway?" Liam felt like shouting at it.

It had been the nesting season. He couldn't see the smashed

nests and dead or dying chicks but when the drone had buzzed off there was a creepy silence. He hadn't realised how much he'd got used to the rustle and chatter of unseen communities when he'd been sitting up here keeping lookout. There were only a few sad isolated cries, as if survivors, searching.

He had to remind himself hard that this was *not* Anna's fault. Like she had said, it was only the top flat at the Manor that was hers. She had been away in London and so had Zander. Liam didn't doubt that it was Yuck-off's orders and something to do with Russian money and security paranoia. Why should they care about small birds and wild apple trees?

He forced himself to send Anna a text: 'Walking to East Lane'. Then he set off as determinedly as if he was walking all the way back to Lowestoft. At East Lane he could turn in past a farm and his school and the care home. He'd like to visit the old man if it wasn't too late.

He wondered how far the quadcopter would follow him. How long could these things stay in the air? He was going to drain its battery by not doing anything except walking. Because if the drone was following him that meant it couldn't be bothering anyone else.

Liam didn't understand anything that was happening. He felt like some scrap of shingle being rolled every which way by the tide. But he'd rather be a scrap of shingle than a smashed-up baby bird.

For the first bit of the walk he carried on along the path between the fence and the edge of the cliff. It got narrow in places where the cliff was crumbling and it occurred to him it wouldn't be difficult at all to burrow your way under the fence if you were like a giant rabbit or something. There were plenty of holes and scrapes and real rabbit droppings. It was tempting to stop and call into the bigger burrows then pretend to get an answer back.

After a while he got used to the drone being there. He couldn't resist waving occasionally. It was like having company. Saddo.

It stayed with him for more than an hour. Battery life that good must make it top of the range. He supposed super-rich people would have better ones than anyone else. By the time it gave up he'd come down from the cliff because there wasn't any cliff left. He'd passed old pill boxes that had crashed down onto the beach in random chunks of concrete, and blue plastic drainage pipes dangling from the exposed earth like giant worms that had lost their way.

This far up there'd been a major break-in by the sea. They'd been taken to look at it by the school because of the thousands of tons of rock that had been shipped there from Norway. The boulders were huge. They were called rock armour. They were all different angles and you could dare each other to jump across them but with Liam's dodgy eyes he wasn't doing that today. Not with his guitar on his back. Once he had his specs it would be different.

Then Anna called him. She was angry.

"But I texted you!"

"Like when?"

"Like…maybe two hours ago. I said I was walking to East Lane. I've got there now and I'm on the road."

"I've been checking all that time and worrying."

"You should have asked your friend Iakov. He's been flying a drone after me."

"He's *not* my friend! You should have texted. I need to work, not waste time worrying."

"I did text."

But when she told him to look and see that he'd used the right number his message was still there. It seemed like he hadn't noticed that he hadn't pressed Send.

"Li," she said more kindly. "If you give it me when you get back I'll show you how to make the font size bigger."

"I'm going to see my old man in the care home first."

Lottie was on TV when he was let into the care home lounge. It was the early evening local news and they were focusing on Luminal, now only three weeks away. Her PR team had released the news that she'd be singing her new song 'Light up our shores' from the top of Orfordness lighthouse on the morning of the summer solstice. The new album would be on general release after the festival but the whole event was going to pick up on a theme of welcome and living without fear.

The festival organisers were asked (again) about their controversial decision to hold the event so close to the nuclear power station. Were they getting subsidised by the nuclear industry? There were protestors and denials and the whole discussion was getting angry till they cut back to Lottie.

"You have to remember," she said, "that the people who are working at Sizewell could be our neighbours and our friends or our family. Why should they feel that we turn away from them? And even if they've come to work there from abroad, that's okay. We don't want secret economies in Suffolk."

Liam felt worried then. He thought she might be going to

start talking about the hidden workers and the gangmasters that she'd lived with before. Plus other things he was trying to forget. Instead she said a bit about environmental monitoring, then started on about Sizewell being the place where two Dutchmen had landed in the Second World War. They were fleeing the Nazi invasion of their country and coming to Britain to fight for freedom and they had crossed the North Sea in a kayak.

A kayak! thought Liam. Like Luke's friend, Angel, when she'd paddled bravely away from the kidnappers...except the kidnappers had been Dutch. That was confusing.

"Think of it," said Lottie. "One hundred miles across the North Sea in wartime! While knowing that if you got captured you'd likely be shot or sent to a death camp." There were some black and white sea pictures with mines, and searchlights and boats appearing in the darkness. World War Two music and an explosion with water going up.

The care home staff had been watching the TV programme. Some of them were probably planning to go to the festival.

"Nē," Liam's old man had been parked close to the TV. "Nē... nē..."

"Only one in ten of them made it," added Lottie sadly and the picture cut to a modern memorial on Sizewell beach. "And there are still people fleeing from war or from oppression or from poverty. And sometimes the ones who haven't made it are washed up on the beaches of the world. We're going to carry them with us, in our hearts. That's what's going to make this festival special."

Liam hadn't ever heard Lottie talking like that. Normally, when she was at home, it was more about whether he'd remembered his sports kit. Even when he'd gone with her to the studio last year it had been technical discussion, like about the amount of post-production work she did (or didn't) want. This interview was explaining why she'd got so obsessional about Luminal. It almost sounded as if someone he didn't know was talking.

"And what about your own family history?" the interviewer was asking now, "Are there aspects that make you feel a personal involvement?"

A couple of the care workers were smiling at Liam. He felt a bit sick. But Lottie was talking about her own family – which wasn't his – and Bawdsey Manor and its history and then the Cold War. She even mentioned having a quarrel with her mother about bombing and how she was sorry they'd never made it up.

"We let the sun go down on our anger," she said, "both of us. But on the early morning of the summer solstice, I'm going to be singing from the Orfordness lighthouse as the sun rises. That lighthouse is going to be taken by the sea, very soon. We must all make the most of the time we have… At least, that's what I think," she added disarmingly.

Some of the carers were clapping, even though it was TV. Then the news was over and the weather forecast came on. Liam felt a bit drained. His old man was still staring at the screen.

"Nē," he was saying, over and over, like a child. "Nē… nē…"

He didn't respond when one of the carers tried to comfort him. Didn't seem to hear. *Was* he a Russian, Liam wondered? Maybe Anna should try out her language skills on him. Meanwhile the carers were offering squash and cake and suggesting everybody might like a quick singalong before bed.

"We're lucky to have you now your mum's so famous," one of them said and for once he didn't say 'step-mum'.

"It's my dad who learned me the shanties," he told them instead. Then put his fingers willingly to the strings of his guitar.

But the old man wouldn't join in.

They're starting to turn up in pairs, Bill noticed. It made him feel nostalgic for those days when he'd first been one of a couple. There'd been young Anna and her princeling, then Luke with his friend Angela, now here was the lad Donny introducing a skinny girl in overalls who was carrying a hefty-looking toolbox and an outsize backpack. Donny had collected Bill's tins of paint, which were in a box, and also had three large bin bags tied around him. They'd trudged two miles from the station and almost fell into the wheelhouse.

The little boat in Lowestoft where Heike slept (when she did) had been gutted. Completely trashed and all her possessions heaved overboard. She'd been right to keep the things that mattered in her rucksack – her sketchbooks, tools, coursework, passport – it was only her bedding and her clothes and her few cooking things and food that were muddied and soaked in Lake Lothing. And her phone. That was stupid. She should have kept her phone with her – except she'd have been tempted to call home too often. Then they'd have guessed she wasn't as happy as she'd always tried to pretend.

George wasn't at the club – he was at home, on oxygen, someone said – but the police who were investigating the break-in had come and taken photos of her boat and had advised her to go away for a few days, leaving them her mobile number of course, which wasn't any use anymore.

"And what sort of permission do you have to be here?" they'd asked. So she showed them her passport and her certificate of registration onto the diploma course. Also the receipts that proved her course fees were paid up to date. They'd asked her for a visa but she told them she didn't need one. "I come from Estonia. We are an EU country."

"You're working here?" They still seemed more interested in investigating her than the damage to her possessions. So she'd given them the agency number and the agency had confirmed that she had been working for them on the night of the break-in.

But when she went round later, to get her next shifts, they said they hadn't any work for her.

"They think I'll cause them trouble," she told Donny. "They're busy people, they don't like trouble. They didn't like it when I asked them for some payment in advance. They must have everything done correctly. They are afraid of being fined."

"Do they owe you any money now?"

"Yes, and I'm sure they will pay – they are not crooks – but I won't get it until the day it is due. And if they don't give me any more work… I will have a bigger problem than usual."

"What about the college?" He'd arrived after the police had gone. She'd salvaged most of her stuff, chucked away everything that was ruined, and now she was using the club laundry to rinse and wash and dry her clothes and bedding.

"It's closed for this week but I have paid them all I owe. I'm so near the end now. I can finish the course – as long as I can eat. There are other agencies that will give me work but I have to find a new place to sleep, which is not perhaps so easy when you have no money. I need to move away from the club. George is my good friend but these are some bad people we have stirred up."

"And all because Li and I were looking for somewhere cheap to moor for the night."

"You didn't know what you were bringing."

"I still don't. All I do know for sure is that we picked it up off Sizewell and there's a dive boat that might have been looking for it too. Liam thinks that one of the men we saw is one who's meant to be guarding Anna's friend Zander. And he might even be the one you call Jake."

"He is a *Russian!*"

"Yeah, yeah." Donny had steered her off as quickly as he could by getting her back to the issue of her sleeping space. "The only problem with you staying on *Strong Winds* is that I have to take her back to the creek where I live in time for school on Monday. There's no problem about space on board – we've a whole empty cabin – but it'll be really difficult for you to travel from there to Lowestoft for your course."

"There are trains?"

"Not from Gallister Creek. But come anyway. We'll talk to the Allies and see how we can help."

"What are your Allies?" She didn't sound as if she liked the word.

"They're my friends. It's what we called ourselves when we were younger. You might meet Maggi but Xanthe's totally Olympics-dominated now."

"Ms Anna Livesey – is she one of your Allies?"

Donny didn't hesitate. "Anna is the Best," he said. "She's the first friend I ever had and she's completely brilliant. Anna can always think of something."

But it was Anna's step-dad, Bill, who had come up with the answer.

"The junk won't do," he said to Donny. "They'll have her marked. Even if you convinced them you're innercent. You go back and get yer head down into yer books, exactly like you said. Luke'll need to get home ter Bawdsey and keep an eye on little Liam. Which leaves a bunk free here and me in need of a handy shipwright." He didn't look directly at Heike in case the idea repulsed her. "I'm disabled, as you see, and I ain't got a lot of money but you can work yer keep till you finish yer course and see where you're headed after that. There's probably a bit of help I can give with yer train fares to start off with."

She didn't answer straight away. Her face, that was usually so pale under her freckles, had gone red, and now it went pale again.

"You are another George," she said. "But I'm afraid if I accept I will bring trouble to you too."

"You don't want ter worry about that," Bill was trying to lighten things up. "Donny and the others will tell you I'm well capable of diggin' me own holes and jumpin' in with both feet."

"They probably only wanted to get you out of Lowestoft." Donny was sure Bill's idea was good. "And me and Liam too. You couldn't skip your course for another few days, could you? So they really think you've gone?"

"If I don't get my diploma, then everything has been for nothing. All the money and also my dreams. But I will talk to my tutor. I don't want to bring trouble to them as well."

She sounded really depressed. All they could do was offer tea and food and ask her if she wanted to have a sleep.

"Do you know what I would most like to do?" she said. "I would like to be making a pair of oars that I can supply to Ms Anna Livesey. She is Donny's greatest friend and she is your daughter..."

"Step-daughter," Bill put in. "And it ain't a relationship I like to push."

"...but every time I meet her all I can think is that I have stolen from her and she will hear from her lawyers and find me out."

Of course they didn't understand what she was talking about, but it didn't take too long to explain and Donny almost had to laugh.

"Anna wouldn't have hesitated for a moment. She'd have sold those oars before the varnish had dried if she'd needed to, and she'd have got a better price as well."

"But now she has a beautiful dinghy which she cannot so easily use. When the wind was weak and the tide was against me, I could go nowhere without oars."

They knew that this was true. Little sailing dinghies without engines needed oars.

"They don't have ter be beautiful, they only have ter work...?" Bill asked.

"But *Theodora* is so lovely. She was my diploma project. I earned a distinction with her."

"You already got yer marks for the oars?"

"It was almost our first assignment, after we made toolboxes."

"I got an old wood pair, come with me dory. I ain't never going to row again. Got a metal pair as well, for the boys. They'd come up okay if you was to spend a bit of time on 'em. The oars I mean, not me boys!"

He told Donny where he could find them and the oars were brought into the wheelhouse and examined. They were grey with age and had not a shred of varnish left on their dry, cracked surface. But the cracking was only superficial. Underneath, the wood was sound and the size would be about right and Heike began to smile and mutter about oxalic acid, sewn leather and the merits of copper banding as against epoxy and e-glass. Bill and Donny simply nodded and agreed.

It was the end of another long day and Donny needed to get back to *Strong Winds* to catch the tide in the morning. They cobbled together some supper and sat around for a while, too tired and relieved to move in a hurry. Heike took out the sketchbooks that were her most special possession and showed them some more of the drawings she'd done when she was younger, helping herself sit still as she listened to her grandfather's stories of his life.

She showed them submarines, warships and explosions. Her drawings gave Donny the worst nightmares he'd had since he was about twelve:

The explosion…the searching…that white face with its desperate appeal… Down, breathless, down into the darkness, crushed by the weight of the icy sea…

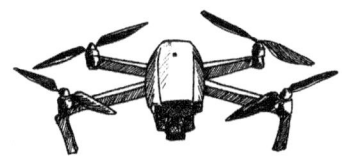

CHAPTER TEN

A human mollusc

Anna and Zander arrived to collect Liam from the care home in the Russian car. Anna said she thought he'd sounded tired and the driver didn't have anything else to do. Arkady Ivanov had left for Russia and Raisa had all the help she needed in London so Zander's parents had decided that the driver, whose name was Oleg, should stay around the Bawdsey area until Arkady's return. He'd be supporting Iakov with security.

"Did you realise at all how far you'd walked?" Anna asked Liam.

"*He* could have told you. His bullies have been spying on me." Liam knew he was being rude to Zander but he hadn't asked to be collected like a parcel returned to the depot. "And they spied on me and Donny when we were on *Strong Winds*."

Anna had come into the care home lounge: Zander had stayed in the car. He'd made it obvious that he was only there because of her. Anna had been very charming. It was one of those times that she seemed so like Lottie and much older than she really was. You could tell people were glad to meet her. They asked questions about her mother and about Luminal, said nice things about Liam. She'd tried her few simple Russian phrases on the old man but without response. All she'd been able to tell Liam was that no in Russian was *nyet*, not *nē*.

But even charm had worn thin on the short drive back to the

Manor and it was a struggle to say thank you. The driver didn't seem to expect it anyway.

Anna had tried asking what he'd meant about spying on *Strong Winds* but Liam wasn't answering. The next day Zander – who never normally spoke to him – started asking the same questions. Suddenly he was being friendly: offering to teach him to play chess, wanting to know about the junk, the holiday, Donny…

Liam got away without saying much – though he might have liked to learn chess. Sunday was as lonely as Saturday had been: Anna stressing about her revision, Lottie still in London, Vicky at the Rectory. He'd pinned his hopes on Luke getting back; thought that was going to make such a total difference, but all Luke wanted to do was chillax and play Nintendo.

"C'mon, Li, we're back to school tomorrow. Let's have some brother time. Crack open the nachos. There's dip in the fridge."

Liam wanted to be with Luke but he didn't want to play screen games and he wouldn't explain why.

Once they'd got home the previous evening and he'd had time to think, he'd made a deal with himself that he wasn't going to whinge on about his sight problem until after Luminal. Now he'd watched the TV programme he could see it would be selfish to take time that Lottie was wanting to give to other people. He could leave getting his specs until later.

He showed Luke his lucky amber that he'd found in Aldeburgh, which had come from the dinosaur age and probably from the Baltic Sea. But that mainly got Luke going on about Pokémon Amber. He and Angel had got this obsession. When Liam was telling him about being followed by the drone, all Luke could think of was throwing a Poké ball at it. That was how you captured things in the game. He tried showing Liam, but Liam couldn't see it.

Liam had to leave Luke then because he knew that, until he got fixed up with specs, he couldn't throw or kick or skim, either with electronics or for real. Screens were too small and, when he went to the beach, the shapes of the pebbles had gone. He played a few songs on his guitar then wandered outside. The thought of school tomorrow made him feel sick.

He told Anna he was going to the quay to buy an ice-cream and then hang around to wave if *Strong Winds* went by. He was pleased with this idea because it sounded like something he'd normally do. There was getting to be a gap between other people's Liam and the new, secret, person. There would be people thinking that what they saw was him but that would only be a shell. Sort of like hibernation until the Festival was over and he could ask Lottie for help.

He forgot he didn't have any money. Didn't notice the new CCTV camera over the front door. The flowers were dull but the sun felt warm and there was a breeze and the smell of mown grass as he walked carefully down the long drive. This was okay, he was coping.

Then he heard the drone and his insides went to jelly. He wanted to run; wanted to get away. But he felt so wobbly that, if he ran, he was sure he'd fall. Why was this happening to him?

The gatehouse at the end of the drive stood immediately inside the belt of trees that screened the Manor from the public road. They were tall, solid trees with big flower bushes in between them. Liam couldn't remember what the bushes were called but they were as tall as he was with dark shiny leaves and amazing bright flowers. People paid to come and see them on charity open days. Even Yuck-off and his men couldn't have their bonfires in here.

Liam hurried round the back of the gatehouse and almost fell into the shelter of the trees. He pushed his way through the bushes towards the fence and grabbed it. Felt his way along the mesh until he found the loose edge where a lower section of wire had peeled away from its neighbour. He felt his hands sweating slightly as he pulled hard to bend the wire towards him and open up the gap. Then he crouched down and wriggled through.

The burst of sun as he emerged in the dinghy park was like a bucket of warm water dashed into his face. Instinctively, he looked up towards the sky. The drone would find him, he was sure of that. So now he was looking down again, being careful, using his hands, picking his way through the rows of small boats and abandoned gear and empty trailers until he found what he was seeking.

Theodora. Heike had turned her upside down and raised her more than a foot above the ground, propping her securely on old car tyres and balks of timber. She was warm and silky. She was home.

It was Sunday morning and lovely weather. Liam knew he was lucky that there wasn't anyone else nearby. He clutched the amber in his pocket gratefully and slid underneath Anna's dinghy.

Now his world was dark again and safe. The mast and fittings were there and he could feel the smooth, tough groundsheet that

Heike had spread out to keep them off the earth. He touched the small mainsail in its clean bag and shifted it to make himself a pillow. *Theodora* was like his shell, keeping him hidden from that spy in the sky. He didn't have to pretend to anyone. He could just exist.

The life of a mollusc was intense. Not seeing where people were or what they looked like concentrated every impression into the sounds they made, their feet and voices as they walked past the enclosure on their way to the beach, or came inside to collect or return their boats. The listening ear that was Liam shrank if they came too close, relaxed as they went away.

There were other sounds too: dinghy rigging tapping against metal masts, cars coming and going from the quay, a whole orchestra of engines on the river and, as Liam's hearing got more and more skilled, he caught the rattle of sheet winches and flap of canvas as sailing boats manoeuvred in the narrow space. Then the special bamboo snap as the fully-battened sails of a junk tacked smartly across.

That would be Donny heading home to Gallister Creek. Liam wanted to run out and wave. He was stopped by a knocking on the hull directly above his head. It wasn't a knocking: it was a pecking.

The human mollusc became stiller than still. Those were footsteps, claw-steps. A seabird strutting, beak-boxing. Liam smiled at his own joke.

Splat. He knew what that was! That seagull better be long gone before Heike came again.

He'd turned his phone to silent but now he felt a text arriving. Wriggled to pull it out, maxed up the brightness and the font size.

A HUMAN MOLLUSC

"Where are you? Why are you not back? Do we need to fetch you? Don't dare ignore this."

Big sister was watching him.

Liam sighed. He checked the time.

It explained why he was hungry.

The drone picked Donny up as he was pushing the flood to get out of the river. The channel was narrow between the mounds of shingle. They were high this year, masking the wind. He'd got extra diesel from Bill and was using the engine to make sure he kept control through the occasional rips and eddies.

He thought of his friends. Wished he'd got down the river sooner with time to stop and call at Bawdsey. Maybe make some plans with Anna for after exams. It hadn't been a great holiday with Liam: they'd stirred up trouble they didn't need. Maybe Li would have been better off going London – and he should have stuck to his revision. Done nothing really, except fall asleep on his books. He wouldn't have met Heike if they hadn't gone to Lowestoft. Though it didn't seem like she and Anna were heading to be friends.

Donny altered course for the second of the three small buoys which marked the channel. He hardened his sheets. Didn't matter that he had the engine running: he was still going out of here like a sailor.

That fat buzz. Like a fly off a dung heap. It hung above his head. There was a large yacht close behind him and two more heading in. Plus a scatter of racing dinghies and jet skis.

The breeze came free on the sails as soon as *Strong Winds* was away from the river mouth. Donny switched the engine off gladly.

♞ PEBBLE ♞

It would be a brisk beat back to Harwich. Then he was heading up the Orwell to collect his mum and maybe eat a late tea at the Rectory. Was this sky-spy planning to follow him all day?

He remembered how Gold Dragon used to chuck firecrackers at anyone who annoyed her.

Donny waited till the other yachts were well out of the way. The red and white Woodbridge Haven buoy twinkled in the sun. *Strong Winds* was steady on her course. "Don't worry about me," she murmured. "I can manage quite well by myself."

He scrambled quickly down into the cabin and checked the shelf of curios his great-aunt had collected on her world voyages. There was the powerful catapult she'd used in the South China Seas, before she sacrificed her hand. She'd replaced the elastic when he and Skye had come to live with her and made sure they learned how to use it.

Ammunition? Donny was back up the companion way, catapult in one hand and the other diving into the bucket of sea coal. A hefty lump. Fitted the sling exactly.

He strolled back to his place by the tiller, checked *Strong Winds'* wake was straight and turned to smile up at the quadcopter, as if he were posing for a photo.

Then he had the stem of the catapult firm in his left hand, the sea coal loaded in his right. He braced his feet steady on the deck, aimed, pulled back the elastic to its maximum extent and launched the projectile. He could almost hear Gold Dragon's gleeful cackle.

The quadcopter's frame was smashed, its engine stalled and the pricey little gizmo was knocked out of the sky and down into the sparkling waves.

A HUMAN MOLLUSC

Donny looked down into the cabin and gave a quick thumbs-up to the locker where he'd stowed his great-aunt's ashes. Then he decided to take a long board out to sea before heading into the Orwell. He felt liberated, triumphant, quite extraordinarily happy.

It was hard coming out of his shell into the sunshine. Liam's eyes couldn't adjust to the brightness and he felt bombarded by the sounds, the scents, the breeze on his face. He put his hand in his pocket and clutched his amber to steady himself.

He heard voices and small wheels. Guessed it was a family manoeuvring their dinghy back though the gate into the compound. Thanks, lucky stone. Liam turned towards them and found his way out. Then he knew where he was. This was the reinforced path that had a sort of rubber mesh sunk into the pebbles to make it easier for people to pull trailers along.

Liam followed the path to the quay, found his way through the parked cars and crossed the road carefully towards the Manor. The red and white entry bar made a firm line against the dark background of the trees. He knew that if he kept to the side of the green space which was parkland, while following the dark grey hardness that was road, he'd reach the front door. Then, once he was in his room, he'd be safe again.

But there was Zander's voice asking for him at the gatehouse. Zander not in a car, not with a bodyguard, Zander on his own.

"Hi, Liam. I was looking out for you."

Zander was walking beside him. That was a surprise.

"You didn't bring anyone."

"No. I have given them the slip."

Liam had noticed that Zander sometimes spoke as if he'd learned his English from a phrasebook. They walked a little further together.

"Where's Anna?"

"She has taken her books into the garden and is not to be disturbed."

"That's okay. I can get myself some lunch. And Luke's there."

Even if Luke was still obsessed with his Pokémon, Liam could go sprawl on the bed beside him, munch some nachos – if there were any left.

"You are a lucky chap, Liam."

"Why?"

"Because you are part of a family." Zander sounded sad.

"Don't you have any brothers or sisters?"

"No. It was a problem for my mother to have me. I am sure she would have liked many more children. And my father, too. They would have loved a daughter. And I a sister. Or a brother."

"Me and Luke used to fight a lot. And Vicky cried like all the time when she was little. And Anna wouldn't talk to any of us for ages."

"Anna sent me to find you. She was worrying about you."

"I'm okay."

But he didn't mind Zander walking along beside him. It was unexpectedly helpful. All he needed to do was keep pace. Liam began to think that following other people might be a good way to get through the next two weeks until he had his specs.

"Your brother doesn't like me but perhaps I could meet with your little sister sometime – Anna needs us all out of her hair while she is studying."

Liam imagined him and Vicky and Luke and Zander all burrowing about in Anna's flat, black locks. He knew that wasn't what the older boy had meant. He was trying to be friendly, be a bit more normal than usual.

"Me and Vicky walk to school in the morning if Lottie's got breakfast meetings. You can come if you like. But not in that car. And not with Yuck…*Iakov*. Or his drone."

"I accept with pleasure. What time should we meet?"

"Bout twenty past? Luke and Anna catch the bus at eight but we're way too early if we go with them. I didn't used to mind being early."

But that had been in the days when he'd met up with his mates and they'd played football before school. Now people had to be almost in his face before he was certain who they were.

"Vicky's got this thing about fairies. Lottie gave her a picture book about them living in flowers but she spots them everywhere. She thinks of stories too. They're sometimes quite good."

He wasn't going to have Zander sneering at his little sister.

"In Russia we have stories of magic – and in music too, which is my personal interest. I will be waiting for you both from eight fifteen. Though it may be I need to ask my driver to collect me if I'm not to be late for lessons myself."

"Whatever. But Lottie always takes us if it rains or if she thinks Vicky's too tired. Then she cancels her meetings or does Skype. Vicky's her proper child. Like Anna."

He knew that Lottie would cancel her meetings for him, too, if he told her that his eyes had got so rubbish. But he wasn't going to say anything. Not till after Luminal. So if Zander wanted to walk to school with them that would be quite useful, if a bit surprising.

"Okay. I will look forward to it."

They'd reached the Manor entrance. Liam went into the lift and felt for the button. Zander turned away to find Iakov and report his success.

CHAPTER ELEVEN
A hard place

Liam was lying on the ground, shielding his face, curled like an embryo. The place where he was lying was hard and dark and he was frightened. Twisted into a tiny knot of misery.

Everything hurt.

How much of him was broken? Liam didn't dare to move and wherever he was, it was dark. He stayed curled and completely still until he got control of his brain. Then he thought his way round his body: from his toes, which could still wiggle, through his legs, where all the muscles were still working – as far as he could tell without daring to do more than clench and unclench each one – hips and ribs, only uncomfortable because the ground was so hard. The surface was rough, a bit gritty. Dark.

His feet rubbed themselves together as if they were comforting each other. He'd lost his shoes when he was running: twisted out of one and kicked the other off when he'd stumbled. Stiff new school shoes. Lottie'd ordered them via the internet when she'd realised there wasn't any time to go shopping.

His school bag was gone. Had he thrown it?

He'd thrown it at Zander!

But he'd missed.

Zander had taken his guitar. Wouldn't give it back. Said Iakov would break it, string by string, if Liam didn't tell him what he needed to know. Liam didn't even understand what that was.

He'd lunged and leapt at Zander but the Russian, who was so tall, had held the guitar high above his reach, refusing. And insisting.

So Liam had charged at him and head-butted. A direct hit. Right in the centre of his elegant stomach.

Zander had doubled up. The guitar came down from a height. Hit some dumped hardcore by the side of the road. Liam had heard it twang and crack inside its carry case. Then Zander had lost control. He straightened up and slapped Liam on the left hand side of his face.

Liam was trying to reach down to grab his guitar. He was clumsy. He couldn't get it. The slap knocked him off balance and he fell at Zander's feet. Would he get kicked? The older boy jumped back and pulled out his phone.

Liam didn't wait to see him jab the alarm for Iakov. He got up and ran.

Zander had been walking with him to school, like he usually did these days. Normally Vicky would have been with them but today she'd got a costume to carry so Lottie had taken her in the car. Liam could have gone with them but Zander had seemed so disappointed.

Zander had been teaching him chess in his head. Liam had thought that they were friends.

The quarrel had happened by the entrance to the old defence station. Zander had suddenly begun asking him questions and talking as if Iakov was talking through him – going on about the trip on *Strong Winds* and where he and Donny had hidden the thing they'd dragged up. Calling Donny a liar. Within seconds, it had turned into threats and a fight.

Then all Liam could think about was getting away.

There wasn't any detail in what he could see but he'd sensed that the gate into the old defence site was open. Had started running upwards towards the sky, along a track that could be taking him in the direction of the sea.

Hadn't dared stay long on the track. That Russian car could be coming or the scary motorbike. He'd swerved sideways onto the grass. Went on running uphill. His face stinging and swelling where he'd been slapped. Ruined buildings. Incomprehensible shapes.

The morning had been getting darker all the time and his course was more erratic; his leg muscles were aching, his breath searing. He had to keep running. He was a footballer.

"Well done Liam! Keep going, mate!" Voices from another world.

His head was spinning. He couldn't hold his balance.

A change of surface had caught him out completely. He tripped and lurched and fell. Flung out his arms but they were no protection.

Zander pulled the site gate shut and arranged the chain so it didn't look as if it had been opened but it wasn't locked. Liam would be able to slip out once the danger had gone.

Now it was Zander's job to get rid of the danger. Which wasn't himself.

He hadn't called Iakov. He'd pulled out his phone because that was a taught reflex. Threat/mob/snap. He'd resisted it, hadn't mobilised assistance, hadn't taken a photo.

The tracking system was still in passive mode. That was default: he knew that he was monitored 24/7. He played no games with Iakov as he had with Dimitri. Dimitri had been a bodyguard employed by Zander's father; Iakov was an SVR agent, *Sluzhba vneshney razvedki*. The SVR reported directly to the Russian president and Zander's father was still in Russia. The president had the power to issue orders to the SVR without consulting anyone else. Zander knew that if Iakov told him to jump, his only possible response would be to ask how high.

This was a chess game where he couldn't know his opponent's moves. His options were limited all the time by his fear for his father's safety and his utter ignorance of what was going on. Almost the only advantage he possessed was his awareness that the International School didn't realise that the Dimitri/Iakov replacement hadn't been like for like. Having an SVR agent operating on their premises among such an elite bunch of students from other nations would be completely unacceptable. The moment Zander revealed Iakov's true identity he would be expelled.

Zander longed to leave. Apart from Anna and her family, there was nothing for him here. His English was already good, he wasn't interested in sport and sea views and for someone who had spent most of his recent years living in a London house with a private concert hall, the weekly coach trips to local theatres or the guided tours through the public rooms of stately homes were totally tedious.

The principal was already angry. She'd said that she'd be seeking a meeting with his father as soon as Arkady was back in the UK. Fine by him, Zander thought. He was only staying because he assumed that was what his father wanted him to do.

His single success had been to resist Iakov's instructions to plant a detector directly on Liam. The agent couldn't get near the boy. Liam disliked him too obviously. There'd already be devices inside Liam's guitar and school bag.

Zander finished rearranging the chain round the metal gate. He took a clean handkerchief from his blazer pocket and wiped his hands. His right hand, the one that had slapped Liam, was red and sore. He had hit him hard. He was ashamed to have done such a thing.

He collected the guitar case and the bag and carried on walking towards the village, hoping that the pause in the journey would register within the bounds of normal on the GPS tracker. Their walks this week had always included stops to accommodate Vicky's frequent requests to reach up for a wild rose or collect bunches of the wayside weed that she called fairy lace. Zander had helped her willingly. He hadn't met anyone like Anna's little sister before; he thought she was sweet.

Now, as he walked, he dialled the primary school, apologising unintelligibly to the automated system for Liam's impending lateness. He could only hope the younger boy would still go to school. It would be a safe place for him.

Zander would deliver Liam's bag and guitar case to the school. If the bags were bugged – which he was certain they were – then Iakov might assume the younger boy was where he ought to be. But he wasn't certain what Liam's school would do when they noticed he wasn't there. Maybe if he didn't call his driver to collect him but carried on walking people would assume that they were still together.

Whoever had smashed Iakov's drone had done him such a massive favour.

℘ PEBBLE ℘

Liam couldn't see anything. Could anything see him? There wasn't a chink of light. The ground was hard. Concrete? He must have fallen into some sort of underground pit. What would happen if he tried to move? Would someone push him down again?

"Zander?" he ventured, quietly. "Aleksandr?" Zander was a bully. Zander was Russian and rich and stuck up. He and Zander had had had a fight. But Zander was his sister's friend. And for the last few days Liam had been thinking that he was his friend, too.

"Zander?" he tried again. But there wasn't any answer and Liam became more certain that he was on his own. Didn't want to be on his own in the dark in this underground pit. Liam felt hot tears coming as he squeezed himself smaller and tighter and lay completely still.

Then, after a while – he didn't know how long – he began to wonder. It seemed as if he could hear a bird. Not a hawk or a seagull ready to swoop down and peck at him but a high-up-singing-in-the-sky happy bird. Its name was lost in his aching head but somehow it reminded him that he'd been outdoors too, he'd been running in some wide space.

Standing up – or even sitting – seemed impossible in this darkness. If he even thought about it he felt giddy and likely to be sick.

"Take it easy, mate," he told himself. When you were down on the pitch you sometimes needed to give yourself a moment. It wasn't like he was faking. Liam shifted his left arm to give a bit more cushion to that side of his face which was on the concrete. It was horribly swollen and so sore. He guessed it was bleeding.

Then he asked his right arm, the upper one, to move as quietly as it could, stealthily even, and check out the area closest to him.

His arm sent out his hand, like a scouting party. It went down from his body first, creeping out across the hard, gritty surface, confirming that's what it was. Concrete. And it wasn't damp or cold. Almost sun-warmed. The scouting party sent a message back asking him to consider that he was outside. Not in a pit. That he was lying somewhere that was open to the sky.

The side of his face that was upturned tended to agree with the scouting party, confirming that its sensors (his skin) detected warmth and breeze. His brain, which was their High Command, was angry because sunshine readings didn't make any sense when everything was totally dark. It told his hand to get back out there and only come back when it had something more useful to report.

The hand tried not to mention that it was grazed and sore where it had tried to break his fall. Obediently, it carried on its search of the surrounding area, using fingertip technology. There was a crack in the concrete surface, perhaps something growing from it? Liam's hand, moving carefully along the unseen line detected tiny leaves and stems and possibly … petals? Too small to register. Next came something that was tufty then sharp. Moving further, something that stung! Liam's hand leapt back to base.

He allowed it to stay for a moment, his thumb like an anxious platoon leader, checking the other digits for damage. "Permission to report. Nettle attack suspected. Possible additional threat from miniature thistles, seeding."

The fingertips weren't expecting sympathy. They were immediately on patrol again, tingling and wary. They were certain he was in the open, lying on concrete and in a natural location. Not a car park or a playground. You wouldn't get a line of plants like that if there were spray-guns about, or wheels, or feet.

The patrol brushed over a scatter of small round balls, too light, too regular for pebbles. Liam's brain was listening now. His other hand was asking permission to stop supporting his aching face and burrow down into his left hand pocket to touch the lucky amber.

The request was noted but permission refused. If his left hand wanted to reach its pocket he would have to roll over from his left side onto his back. Or sit up. But was that safe?

Instead he made his right arm stretch upwards into the darkness and circle around, feeling for walls. It could detect nothing. Except warmth and space and thistledown and that same light breeze that blew happiness to birds and sailors.

Liam's memory was coming back. The fight with Zander. Himself running across grass. Rough grass. In a place that was high up and open. No trees but ruins and brambles; bent, rusted metal, destruction and abandonment. Was it perhaps a dream?

Liam's fingers and thumb picked up another of the small round objects that were too light to be pebbles. Rolled it experimentally between their pads, collecting data to send back when his puzzled brain was ready to process it.

If he was lying outside, in the sun; if he'd been running across grass and tripped onto concrete, surely he ought to be able to see where he was? Even if he'd banged his head.

Liam strained to open his uppermost eye. Nothing happened though he could feel his face muscles doing their best. Dreams could be like that when you weren't quite ready to wake up. It could seem like you were forcing your eye open but there was nothing coming in.

Liam's mind went back to his fingers. Or his fingers sent a message to his mind. They'd come up with a suggestion about the object.

He sat up to attend to them better. This released his other hand to touch the left side of his face. It was so swollen where Zander had hit him that his left eye had completely closed up.

The round thing his right hand fingers were holding was about the size of a pea but it was dry. His fingertips were certain that it wasn't a dried pea. It wasn't dense enough. And they'd already rejected the idea that it was a tiny stone – the sort people called pea shingle. Too round, too light too regular. You'd never get a scattering of pebbles that were all identical like this. Not that the round things were totally smooth. They weren't like the pellets of a BB gun. They were more like something (chewed grass was suggested) that had been balled together, processed and dried. Liam's fingers had come up with the suggestion that they were rabbit droppings.

He was holding a pellet of poo.

That wasn't the problem.

If he was outside in a place where there was sun and breeze and birds and little plants and rabbit droppings but it was completely dark, then the darkness wasn't in the place, it must be in him. He could understand his left eye not being able to see because it had been slapped shut. But if his right eye couldn't see then either it was also closed or…

Liam dropped the pellet of poo and felt around his right eye with both his hands. Pulled the lids apart as wide as they would go. Stared so hard that it felt as if the eye ball would pop out.

There was nothing. That eye was
Blind.
He was
at this moment
blind.
Liam's brain blacked out.

The skylark stopped singing when the young gamekeeper took a shot at some rabbits. He killed one and went to retrieve it. Then he hung it up by its back legs in the shade to be collected when he was collected later. He was mainly employed to keep an eye on the site, report any vandalism and check for breaks in the fence. He wasn't there every day. There were plenty of other odd jobs that needed doing around the farm.

Hamish didn't get paid much but the farmer was happy enough for him to take as many rabbits as he liked and sell them via the wild meat dealer. There wasn't anything else in season, except pigeon and squirrel. He'd been horrified by the carnage those people from the Manor had made all along the boundary fence. Ignorant townies.

They'd told the farmer it was to do with some security scare; one of the rich kids under kidnap threat, or so they said. Hamish thought the farmer should have made more fuss – except he'd noticed a bit of disturbance around the old bunker entrance. His little dog had got herself in there which she shouldn't have been able to do. It wasn't a good place.

He was lonely now without her.

Lottie didn't pick up the truant call till lunchtime. She'd gone up to the Luminal site for another meeting with the organisers. It was personally vital to her that the festival shouldn't have a bad impact on the environment so she tried to attend all the meetings on green issues. It added a huge amount to her workload, but it felt as if it mattered. This was about the future and a better world for the next generation.

"Liam! Not arrived at school today?" she repeated. "But I saw him set out. He was with his friend Zander. They were walking together. I saw them." A cold feeling caught at her. "Where's Zander? Has there been any attempt…? Zander has personal security."

But the primary school secretary couldn't tell anything about Zander, didn't of course know much about Russian oligarch families and their kidnap fears. All she could tell Lottie was that there'd been a message left by the older boy to say that Liam would be late. No reason given, only that there had been 'a problem'. That had been almost four hours ago. The secretary had been trying to contact Ms Livesey since break. She'd left a message on Mr Whiting's phone as well.

"Vicky? Is Vicky still in school? I dropped her off myself!" Yes, Vicky was fine. It was only Liam.

"It's a beautiful day, Ms Livesey. A couple of boys together… They might have been tempted…?"

If it could only be that, thought Lottie. Smiling and warm as ever, she thanked the secretary for ringing, asked her to call immediately if Liam turned up, and assured her she was heading back at once to discover what had happened.

"Liam's bag is here, and his guitar," the secretary added. "They were propped inside the gate. One of the playground supervisors noticed them at morning break. I've got them in my office, when you come."

His guitar and bag…left by the gate. Lottie didn't know what that information meant…what she should think…

"There is one other thing," Hadn't the bloody woman said enough? "The guitar seems to have been damaged. The playground supervisor thought it didn't feel quite right when she picked it up. So we took a look inside. Perhaps we shouldn't have done? But it's certainly suffered a bit of a crack."

"I think you should be ringing the police!" Lottie burst out.

"Do you Ms Livesey? Mightn't that be over-reaction? It's such a lovely day… you don't think they've gone to the beach? Very naughty of them but they wouldn't be the first. And we have been a little worried about Liam recently. Since he gave up football. Older boys can be a powerful influence…But if you feel the police should be involved…"

She didn't. Of course she didn't. There must be a simple explanation. She was only jumpy. Because of…things. Didn't want police. Not yet.

What could she do? Ring the language school principal, obviously. And gate security at the Manor. She didn't have the numbers in her phone. She took a few moments to find them because her fingers were shaking. She was desperate to be driving home not sitting forty miles away making phone calls.

Lottie didn't for one moment think that Liam and Zander would have bunked off to go to the beach. It wasn't in their characters. Not that she knew Anna's friend so well…

Should she ring the police? Start a proper search?

Lottie wanted to ring Anna, her trusted, her competent daughter, but she knew Anna had morning and afternoon exams. She tried to ring Bill, the children's useless dad.

Not his fault, she kept telling herself. Bill a good person in a bad situation.

She couldn't get through. As usual.

Not his fault, she repeated. Everyone knew there wasn't any phone reception down in Fynn Creek. You had to walk up beyond the gate to the top of the drive if you wanted to make a call. Bill couldn't manage the hill in his chair, needed the buggy. Probably having trouble keeping it charged, now that the new management were making electricity access so difficult. Not his fault. And the paperwork to get a Motability car was taking so long. Not his fault.

So why was he living on that stupid boat in the first place? Why couldn't he just settle in the Manor, which they'd got all specially adapted, and at least help her keep an eye on the children?

Lottie knew she was being unfair. She had loved Bill once. He was Vicky's father. Luke and Liam's dad. Her life had moved on and he'd got left behind.

The principal returned her call. No, Aleksandr had not attended his morning classes. Her students were assembling for lunch but she'd checked and he was not there. She told Lottie that she'd contacted Mr Dzerzhinsky, the personal security operative, and had learned that his charge had 'gone for a walk'. Zander carried a GPS locator on his phone as well as a tracker in his wristwatch.

Lottie felt a surge of relief. She didn't much like what she'd seen of Iakov, but the man obviously knew his job.

"Could you just ask him to call Zander, please? Make sure that he's still got Liam with him?"

The principal had already tried ringing Zander. Repeatedly. But he wasn't picking up. And, while they were having this conversation, the principal felt she needed to say that she wasn't happy at all with the current situation – both the time being spent with Ms Livesey's daughter and this new friendship with Liam.

"I was content, initially, to give permission for Zander to help you in this way – I do realise you have a great deal to think of just now, Ms Livesey, but Zander must keep up with our curriculum and his example to the other students is not good. I won't ring his mother because of her health."

Lottie took a very deep breath. And another. When had she ever asked for help? Liam and Vicky had been managing fine getting themselves to school. They'd have told her if there were any problems. Wouldn't they?

She thanked the principal and asked if Iakov had mentioned where, exactly, Zander had gone for his walk?

Towards the beach and heading north. Mr Dzerzhinsky had agreed that he would follow and assess the situation and would be in contact if he judged it necessary.

"Judged it necessary! Liam's been missing, probably with Zander – but we don't actually know – for more than FOUR HOURS!" Lottie knew she was losing it. She needed to be driving now. Not talking.

Terrible thoughts began running through her head and she was driving too fast to stop them.

She realised how little she knew about Zander, how she'd sensed he was not a person at ease with himself, however sophisticated and arrogant he'd seemed. How she'd begun to wonder whether Liam was worrying about something…

How could she have left them alone together? A seven-year age gap. Or was it more? It couldn't be a healthy relationship. It would have been so easy to have popped Liam in the car this morning, safely. And how had his precious guitar got broken?

Oh Christ! What would she tell Bill – and the others – if anything dreadful had happened? How could she bear it? Her sweet little boy. Because he was her child, just as much as if she'd been his biological mother.

Lottie stopped suddenly and phoned the care home. Just in case.

Liam wasn't there. It was the middle of a school day. The only place he should have been was safely in the lunch hall, or his classroom, or the playground. She fought back the impulse to ring the school again and ask them if they were sure they'd checked everywhere… he couldn't have got stuck in a cupboard or a toilet?

This was a small village primary school with tiny classes. Sixty pupils and a family atmosphere. Of course they knew where all their children were. Which was more than she did.

CHAPTER TWELVE

An unidentified object

Zander sighed as he climbed the steep, uneven steps up onto the sea wall. Why would people walk for pleasure? He was fed up, his feet were aching and he knew that he was going to be in trouble when he finally returned to the school. He hoped it would only be school trouble. In his head he was sure that there wasn't anything Iakov could do to hurt him here in England; in his heart he wasn't so confident.

There was a small piece of fence across the path. It had a crosswise step and probably some particular name he hadn't learned. It would stop the motorbike coming after him. There were waves splashing against the wall on the seaward side and small lagoons inland. Ponds. They were nothing compared to the lagoons at home. Those were like inland seas.

Though Kaliningrad wasn't his home anymore. Nor was St Petersburg. His family had houses in several place but no home. Always exiles.

Zander wished his father was back. Had to talk. Had to make him listen. Tell him how he hated it here.

He hated himself, too. How could he have hit a child who had trusted him? Zander disregarded his own sore stomach – he knew he'd pushed Liam too far, holding his guitar out of reach, threatening. Behaving like Iakov.

Zander trudged along the wall. It was a sunny day, waves

dancing, seabirds calling. He wasn't wanted. This was a Keep Out coast. There were walls and rocks to Keep Out the sea; Martello towers to Keep Out the French; concrete gun emplacements to Keep Out the Germans and on the site behind his so-called school there'd had been nuclear missiles to Keep Out the Russians.

For one wild moment Zander considered really talking to Anna. Not just making conversation, but explaining his feelings, asking for her understanding.

No chance of that now he'd slapped her little brother.

Zander hunched his shoulders and tried to ignore the bruising on his stomach and the blisters on his feet. He'd ring for the car once he'd stayed away long enough.

A jet ski came snarling in from the sea. Its engine cut out and there was his bodyguard mounting the wall ahead of him. Zander looked back. He could see the glint of the sun on the roof of the Mercedes. His driver was over the gate and jogging along the path to catch up with him. There was someone else beyond that. Some 'goon', Zander thought, using a word he'd learned from watching old films. Unless he chose to go swimming he was trapped.

He stood still, pulled himself up straight and waited for them. They were employees, he reminded himself. Though it didn't feel like that. Not at all.

Lottie had done the right thing. She hadn't gone straight to Bawdsey, she'd driven to Fynn Creek. Parked her car and run down the slope to *Lowestoft Lass*.

Bill was there. He'd pulled himself onto the low cabin roof and was sitting with a girl. They were discussing something with intense concentration, their heads close together. For a moment

Lottie stopped. Shocked. Then she recognised the girl from the boatyard. The one who'd delivered the dinghy. She and Bill were looking at an oar.

"Bill!" Lottie called as she hurried across the gangplank and along the side deck. She reached out to take his hands. "It's Liam. He's missing from school." She burst into tears.

Bill went pale. Dropped her hands and put his arms around her.

The girl stood up sharply. "Li-am?" she repeated.

Lottie remembered she was foreign.

"Our son...I mean his...my...our younger son didn't turn up to school today. His bag and his guitar are there. But the guitar's been damaged. He was with Anna's friend, Aleksandr. She's concentrating on her exams and they've been walking together. With Vicky as well, but this morning I took her in the car. And I didn't take Liam! He chose to go with Zander."

Lottie wasn't talking to the girl, she was talking to Bill. She'd pulled back from his embrace, was holding his hands again, staring into his eyes, frantic to make him understand and quickly.

"You left him with the *Russian*!" said the girl. "Did you know nothing of the danger?"

"What in hell's name are you talking about?" Lottie swung round at her.

Bill started to say something but the girl cut in: "Liam and his friend Donny came sailing into Lowestoft but they had picked something round their propeller. I was able to help them remove it with my friend George from the club. It was a box – some form of equipment. We don't know. George took it away and we thought nothing more – except when Donny said they had picked it up off Sizewell. That is your nuclear power station, yes?

And when the club was vandalised and my boat was trashed and all my things were in the water, then we guessed it was because I had helped remove the thing they were seeking. So Donny came to fetch me and I am hiding here."

"*Helping* here," Bill corrected. "But Liam…? What could have happened to Liam?" His face was anguished as Lottie's. All their past troubles rushed over them like a tidal surge.

"I don't know. They rang from the school. It might be nothing." Lottie took a deep breath and wished she had a tissue. "I can't cope with this on my own, Bill. Not anymore."

"A-course you can't, my love. I shouldn't never have let it go on. Now help me up and we'll be on our way. Young Heike will hold the fort this end."

The girl nodded, pale beneath her freckles. For a moment she reminded Lottie of someone.

"Thank you," Lottie said to the girl, smiling and meaning it. The girl looked reliable, though Lottie had no idea why Bill's old fishing boat was a fort needing to be held. Was there something to do with pumps?

"We are expecting Luke and his friend after school," Heike reminded Bill.

"I don't want Luke coming here." Lottie reacted immediately, "I want him at home. I want us to be together."

"A-course we do," said Bill. "An' that's what Luke'll want as well. Though I'm hopeful all we're going to find is them two lads have been skiving off along the beach for the day. We can phone young Angela's parents as we go. No need for standing around now. Our Vicky'll be ready for collecting by the time we're down that end of the river."

Heike's care home work had made it easy for her to learn the techniques for getting Bill neatly into his wheelchair and across the gangway onto the path. She pushed him at the run all the way up the slope to Lottie's car.

"You will tell me if there is news?" was all she asked, as Bill pulled himself in and Lottie folded the chair. "Though I don't know how."

"Best I leave you my phone," said Bill. "Lottie an' I'll be together so I won't want it. Only works up here, you know."

"Check it now," said Lottie, suddenly hopeful, "Just in case…"

But there was only the recorded message from the primary school secretary several hours old.

Hamish bagged a couple more rabbits before he noticed Liam. He pushed them into his canvas game bag and hurried across. All he could see was a small huddled form. Not moving. Asleep? Shouldn't be there anyway.

Young lad. 9ish? 10ish? Unconscious. Been badly sick.

Hamish put his gun and bag to one side and knelt down to examine the boy more carefully. Glancing round every so often. The place had never felt more empty and yet crowded. The boy was lying on concrete that had been a launch base for the nuclear missiles.

Hamish wasn't normally an imaginative lad. He was observant. Very. Didn't usually think much about wars. He watched this wide area going back to nature, like the moorland where he'd lived before they had to come down here. It was better for the birds than an agricultural space because there wasn't, in general, anyone disturbing it – except himself maybe and his little dog.

Still couldn't believe that she was gone.

If Hamish *had* been imaginative he might have wondered whether this was some sort of sacrifice or a ritual. As he wasn't, he satisfied himself that the boy was still alive and concentrated on the large bump on the side of his head. The left eye was shut and what looked like a separate bruise was spreading like a storm cloud across his forehead. It didn't matter why he was here. What mattered was getting him looked over by a doctor. He wasn't a good colour. It could be urgent.

Hamish remembered he'd left the gate open because he was expecting a visit from the bird conservation people. They were planning a census of the larks. Hamish thought they should be getting the law onto the vandals who'd been brush-clearing down the side of the Manor fence in the nesting season.

This lad needed an ambulance. Hamish scrambled up and hurried towards the gate where he could get reception to call 999.

If he'd still had his dog he'd have left her with him. The memory made him feel sick: those weeping sores, that blood she'd puked up and out the other end as well. There was nothing the vet could do, so they'd said goodbye. Couldn't be seeing her suffer like that.

As he ran to get a signal for his phone, Hamish passed the entrance to the bunker that he'd had to close up after the break-in. Noticed one school shoe, then another. Must belong to the boy. Had he been responsible for the break-in?

Whatever he'd done, he needed help now. Hamish picked up both the shoes and hurried on his way.

"I can't tell you anything because I have nothing to tell. Why should the child know where this thing has been lost?"

Iakov had ordered the goon to take the jet ski back to wherever he kept it. He, Oleg and Zander were together in the car and he was putting Zander under pressure.

"Because that boy and his destructive friend picked it from the sea. Perhaps, to start with, an accident, I don't know. Then they took it to Lowestoft where the girl and the fat man helped them take it off. Afterwards it has vanished. And so has the girl. The fat man has a big heart attack, is not expected to survive. The trail there is cold. Those two boys were laughing at us."

Zander couldn't manage a suitable response.

"We believed then that the instrument was in Lowestoft. Now we are not so sure. The fat man is very sick. Has left his club and the girl has gone too. So what if it was on board that boat? What if it is still on board? That's possible, but we don't know where the boat has gone. We try to follow but the big lad, he has smashed the drone. It is from Finland. Not so easy to replace. He was sailing to sea."

"I've heard that he has an uncle, in Holland." Zander offered. He'd never met Donny but Liam liked talking about him.

"If we find that boat, we take it to pieces quite."

There was a silence in the car.

"So the small boy. He is here, so he is our hope. First we try this easy way, we use you. If you can't help us, then we take him. He will know where his friend with the boat has gone. Then he will tell us."

"What is this instrument? If you tell me then perhaps I can discover more."

Iakov took no notice. He was scowling at his own thoughts. "I don't like that older boy on his foreign boat."

"The boat is correctly called a junk. It's Chinese."

"CHINESE!" That had really got to Iakov.

"The father of the young boy lives in a hidden place," put in Oleg. He was an Ivanov employee, not SVR, but he didn't like the Chinese. "I was instructed to collect him when you were returning from London with his sister."

"This was after the return of the Chinese boat. It had delivered the small boy to his father. And what else could it deliver?" Iakov was working himself into a treasure-hunting frenzy. "Then it sails for Holland, we think."

Zander didn't think anything of the sort. He yawned slightly.

"You can drive me home now," he ordered Oleg. "I have completed my exercise for today."

"You have once again failed," said Iakov. "This will not be helpful to Arkady Nikolayevich. I think we go wait outside the school. We pick up the boy together with his small sister. Then I get to ask the questions."

"*Pizdets! Mudak!* I have to study!"

"So why this country walk, young master? I begin to wonder if you are treacherous. And your father, too. Okay. We don't stop at the school. We go back to where I have recorded that you stopped this morning. By the missile site. Then you will experience learning of a different sort."

Zander felt himself beginning to sweat. He couldn't help it. Iakov was a trained interrogator. And very likely an assassin.

"You are not completely mistaken," he said, struggling for his usual arrogance. "We stopped because we quarrelled. I was threatening his guitar. I have learned how much he loves it. I told him that I would break it unless he described in detail the voyage back and anywhere they stopped."

"And?"

"At first he didn't believe me. So the guitar…suffered." He should keep as close to the truth as possible. "He won't walk with me again – and neither will his family allow him."

"But what did you discover? We flew the drone behind their ship for as long as its battery allowed. They didn't stop."

"Perhaps it was later," Zander said. "The child is very young. I don't consider him worth your time. So now I was walking on in order to investigate further. There are many possibilities."

He gestured vaguely towards the coast. All those relics of old war. They would surely appeal to Iakov?

"I have recorded that he has walked this way," the agent conceded. "But as you say, he is a child. The most likely place where he and his friend would have met with adults is the creek where his father lives. I have read the files. The father is not a rich man. He may sell what he knows for money. We go there first. Now."

Alone in Fynn Creek, Heike felt a longing for her family. She wished she could pick up Bill's phone and Skype them. But it wasn't a smart phone; it was a pay-as-you-go – and prehistoric.

So she went back to *Lowestoft Lass*, pumped a few strokes though it wasn't necessary and put a final coat of varnish on *Theodora*'s oars – transformed from the greyish pair that Bill had handed her five days ago.

She wondered what had happened to Liam. Why hadn't he gone to school? His parents had seemed really worried. Too worried? It could be the effect of living in that big place.

Wherever Russians were, there was trouble.

She'd taken a photo of the box that Donny had disentangled

from *Strong Winds*. She'd thought she might show it to Arvo or her father next time she called. Ask them what they thought. But the photo was on her phone, so that was gone. Like the Thing.

Maybe she could draw it? She'd need to sort out a Skype session soon or her parents would be anxious. Heike fetched her sketch book and sat in the sun on the raised cabin roof. It wouldn't have been a cabin, originally, it would have been a deep fish hold.

It didn't take long to sketch the box with its wire and the remains of the neoprene that had been stopping the propeller. She was being careful only to draw what she was sure she remembered, not add anything. It wasn't a very satisfying sketch. There were some swivels and shackles she knew she hadn't got right. And the frayed blue rope going nowhere.

She started drawing *Lowestoft Lass* instead. Imagined her in her working days at sea with the fishermen on board pulling in their nets as she pitched and rolled, buffeted by the waves. It made her angry to think that this boat could be hacked to pieces, her timbers crushed flat beneath a car park. It would be like building on bones.

The manager had called on Bill again this morning. He told him that the draining of the lagoon had been completed and tried once more to persuade him to give up *Lowestoft Lass*.

"There'd be no charge for the scrappage. You've obviously no idea what an offer this is. You're pouring your money and effort into something that's obsolete. This old hulk's finished. Cut your losses and find yourself something that'll get you out and about. Something to enjoy with your children."

Bill hadn't said much – except no – and Heike had made sure she was very obviously busy, looking as much like a professional ship restorer as she knew how. The manager had gone away, shaking his head. That didn't, unfortunately, mean that Bill's problems had gone away with him.

She kept worrying about Liam. Could he be in danger or had he just bunked off school. She didn't really know any of these people.

It was much too soon to take the phone up to the top of the track. She cleaned a paintbrush that had gone hard when Luke had left it in a tin with no white spirit and then she decided to go and take a look at the drained lagoon. She put her sketchbooks in her backpack, closed the forehatch, locked the wheelhouse.

As she drew near she could see a digger and men with hard hats standing round a yacht that was lying on her side. She was so old she was almost skeletal. An area of reed bed had been cleared and the ancient hull fully exposed. The old yacht looked exhausted and defeated. Resigned to her fate. Someone revved a chainsaw.

Heike couldn't believe what she was seeing.

"Stop!" she shouted, running forwards. "That's my grandfather's yacht! Where is my grandfather to give you his permission?"

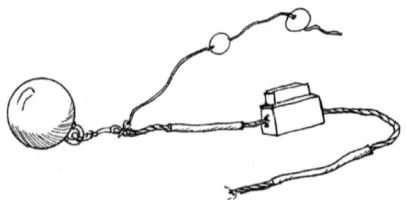

CHAPTER THIRTEEN
A newly varnished oar

Heike pushed through the cordon of men and flung herself against *Ra*'s bare and blistered planks. The layers of paint applied so diligently over ninety years had weathered away as she lay trapped and dying in this lagoon. Still, they had continued to protect her for as long as they were able.

"Where is he? My grandfather. The owner of this yacht."

The workmen stood bewildered. The man who had revved his chainsaw ready to begin, took off his ear defenders.

Heike repeated her question.

"This?" He turned to stare at the old boat as if he hadn't looked at her before, then he turned back to Heike. "There's no one owns this. It's just a wreck. Now stand aside, please. We've a job to do."

"If you say she is a wreck, then you have notified the Receiver?"

The man looked blank.

"Everything is the property of someone," Heike explained. "This yacht is the property of my grandfather. If my grandfather has died, then she belongs to my family. If she has been wrecked you cannot steal her from us. You have laws about wrecks in this country. They are very clear."

Heike mentally thanked God or fate or whatever power had arranged that she attend the college where they had taught these things.

"The Receiver of Wrecks must be notified in a correct way. Then they have a legal responsibility to find the owner. You will need to inform them that I am here on behalf of my grandfather. There are also special protections for wrecks of historic value. This yacht has that value."

But how had *Ra'* got here, so far to the top of the creek, beyond the boatyard and the moorings? What had happened to *Vanaisa*? Heike felt her emotions welling up. She must stay steady. If her grandfather was gone, she had a duty to his ship.

The men were looking uncertain, resting their heavy equipment. Someone was approaching wearing a suit with his hard hat. The site manager. Her breathing was a little fast. She dropped her shoulders to relax herself. She wasn't going to show that she was nervous.

Other mooring-holders were leaving their boats and coming to see what was going on. Some of them just happened to be carrying a boathook or length of chain as they squelched across the fallen reeds. The manager noticed this too. One at a time, that was his strategy.

He faked a smile at Heike. What was she? Some Boats Rights activist? He'd seen her on some other old hulk. He needed to get her off the scene so his men could begin work. Any more delays and the project fines would be building up.

He looked at the boat-shaped heap of rotten wood that she was claiming. That's all it was, dead wood. They'd struggle even to get it burning decently. The keel and underwater sections of the old yacht had been awash in the water twice a day before they drained the lagoon. They were sodden, salt-impregnated, covered in dry slime and withered bladderwrack.

Heike followed his gaze. The sight that repulsed him gave her hope. If *Ra'* had been lying all this time in mud and salt water her timbers would still be preserved. But how long had she been here? When was it that *Vanaisa* had developed that crazy certainty that he must search again for Vanya? Four, five years maybe?

"Good afternoon," she said to the manager. "This yacht belongs to my grandfather. Do you have his permission in writing for her to be destroyed?"

If he said yes she would know that he was lying. Her grandfather could speak and understand English and he had managed, with help, to read the appeals for information that the Englishwoman had written all those years ago. But he had never been able to write in the language and with the illness destroying his mind he certainly wouldn't have learned to do it now. When he'd left them he hadn't even been able to speak reliably. He had struggled to tell her and Arvo those same old stories. There were great jagged holes in his memory and no logic to pin them together.

"If you'd like to come with me to the office, I can show you the relevant files," the manager answered, suavely dodging her question. "As long as you have correct identification? And documentation of your right to be here." He'd picked up on her non-English accent.

"You have a file for my grandfather?"

"As I said, come with me to the office and I can show you."

He glanced quickly at the foreman and gave him a nod.

"Don't you trust him, girlie," one of the creekies called out. "The old man didn't leave no papers. Soon as you're out the way they'll get going. Then it won't matter whether you got rights or not, poor old boat'll be sawed up."

"You knew my grandfather?" This was unbelievable!

"Poor old beggar. Hut in the woods he had, once he couldn't stay on board this no more. Used to help Miss Grace with her cows. She called it rent."

"So where is he now? Is he …?"

"Haven't seen him since the fire. I heard he'd got attacked. Only person that'd know for sure would have been Miss Grace."

"He's avoiding his mooring fees, wherever he is" the manager could feel his advantage slipping away. "I certainly do have a file in my office for your grandfather – a file of unpaid invoices. If you're claiming ownership of those I'll be happy to accept settlement. With accumulated interest and our legal fees."

"Do *you* know where he is?"

The manager shook his head.

"So where have you sent your invoices? If this is your idea of a mooring, I wouldn't be paying you. I can't believe my grandfather signed any contract for this!"

The creekies put aside their homemade weapons to give her a round of applause.

"Company don't provide no services, company can't expect no payment," one of them said and all of them nodded. Then some of them returned to discussing Heike's grandfather and his yacht.

"Old boat were down on the jetty. Broke free in the storm. What were that – four year ago?"

"October. It weren't the Great Storm but it were doing its best. Poor old beggar only just arrived and he were that out of his head. Couldn't ha' tied his warps properly."

Heike was about to object that her grandfather had sailed the world, could have cleated off his mooring warps round the handles of his coffin. Then she thought again about the illness. "Forgive me," she said instead. "My family believed that we would never see either my grandfather or this beautiful yacht again. This is such a moment for me. I can't describe…I need to hear everything that you can tell – but if there is anyone who knows where my grandfather is now – or if he is even alive – then you will understand that that, above all, is what I want to hear."

She looked round at them all, hope dying in her face as one by one they shook their heads. "But you did know him once, before this fire?"

"Used to see him around. Didn't speak as such…"

"Weren't that much left to know…"

"Felt bad about it after, if I'm honest…"

"Maybe we could've done more…"

"Never thought of him having family…"

The manager had been liking this. "So your grandfather lost the mental capacity to manage his own affairs? How very distressing. And you can't show appropriate power of attorney? I thought not. Perhaps in the circumstances my company will authorise me to renegotiate the debts. Come along to my office and I'll see what we can do to help."

She wasn't going with him. She had no idea what she should do. Except stay here and protect *Ra'*.

Then she saw the big Mercedes purring down the drive. Two men and Zander emerged and headed towards *Lowestoft Lass*.

"You're okay with that?" she asked the manager. "Those Russians going to Mr Whiting's boat? Don't you have any security on your gate? How can they just drive down here?"

The manager had also noticed the car. Everything about it spelled money. He had visions of a superyacht nosing up the creek. Of his unbuilt apartments being bought *en bloc*.

"How do you know that they are Russians?" he asked her.

"Her old grandad, he was Russian too. Always hunting for mushrooms and that. Used to howl like a wolf to the moon."

"He was *so* not Russian!" Heike flashed. "He was Estonian, as I am Estonian and this yacht is a part of our history! Please, will you keep her safe for me as I have been trusted to keep Mr Whiting's boat safe for him? Please!"

"Where's Bill then? He don't go nowhere."

"His son is missing. He's gone to look for him. I must care for his boat now. Those people shouldn't be here while he is not."

She didn't wait to see what would happen to *Ra'*. She was running to *Lowestoft Lass* with her bag bumping on her back. The creekies didn't hesitate either. They walked past the digger driver and the men with the chainsaws and the blowtorches, then turned and faced them in a line.

They'd had enough of being pushed around.

The manager had had enough as well. He knew his directors would hate the publicity of a brawl. He was going to get rid of this eyesore of a yacht – and most of the other hulks as well. But that would have to happen another day. For now he needed to ensure that the angry girl didn't upset the owners of that seriously expensive car.

Iakov had lifted his booted foot to smash open the wheelhouse door. Heike didn't notice how glad Zander was to see her or

⚜ A NEWLY VARNISHED OAR ⚜

intensely he'd been trying to persuade the SVR agent that it was not acceptable to behave like this, that his parents would not countenance it and how could Iakov assume that this was what the president would have wanted.

"He is our president, of course but he's not the president here in England. This is not acceptable. It will make trouble. I won't cover for you. I will tell the English police."

"But your father is in Russia right now. And as you just said, our president is the president in Russia. Do you and your mother want your father to come back, or not?"

Zander heard Oleg, his father's loyal driver, grunt with the effort of keeping his mouth shut.

"It's got nothing to do with breaking in to someone's English home. Why are you doing this?"

Heike came hurtling across the gangplank. She seized her newly varnished oar and swung it at them.

"Get off this boat!" she shouted, in English, for everyone to hear.

Oleg ducked, the oar hit Zander hard on the side of his head; Iakov, the trained professional, grabbed it with both hands, twisted it from her grasp and hurled it far into the creek. Then he had her arm wrenched up behind her back.

"Open the door."

"No!" The pain shot agonisingly into her shoulder. Then the site manager arrived, completely uncertain what was happening or what he should do. "Good afternoon," he called out nervously.

"Good afternoon." Zander answered as politely as anyone could who had just been hit on the side of the face with a six-foot oar. "I apologise for the intrusion. Our friend, it seems, is out." His hand came up to feel his cheek.

"So, leave," said Heike. "And don't come back. Ever."

Iakov had dropped her arm when he saw the manager. She wasn't sure she dared to try and move it yet.

"You have no permission to be on this boat," she hissed at him. "Just get off now. But maybe I also call the police and I ask them to take the fingerprints and send them up to Lowestoft to be checked against the vandalism there."

Iakov shrugged. "You are one silly, hysterical girl," he said. "You should be sent back where you can cause no more trouble."

The site manager agreed with that. He stepped back to allow the Russians to file back across the gangplank onto the path.

"I'm sorry you've had a wasted trip," he offered. "It's unusual for Bill Whiting to be away. If you'd like to come and wait in my office I could perhaps show you some of our development plans."

"Bill's looking for his son. Liam has gone missing. His parents are desperate with worry." Heike spoke in English and watched the Russians.

The two men looked carefully blank: Zander went white. "But Liam should be in school," he said, with difficulty. "I walked him this morning.

"*All* the way to school, Aleksandr Arkadyevich? Or possibly not?" Iakov's deep voice was like a growl.

They'd forgotten that Heike might understand them.

"If you think you know where he might be," she carried on talking to Zander in English. "Then we have to ring his parents."

"Of course," Zander managed to say. He pulled out his phone.

He could scarcely swipe the screen. "Please tell me the numbers. I have only that for Anna."

"This is not your problem." Suddenly Zander's phone was in Iakov's hairy hand, then pushed into his pocket. "If some small boy runs off from his school for the afternoon, it's for his parents to sort out. We don't get involved in their business."

"But I am involved," said Zander. He was speaking to the boatyard manager and to Heike. He was holding his cheek again and seemed to be struggling with his speech. "You are attending to what I say? This man," he gestured towards Iakov, "has forced me to pretend to the child that I am his friend because he wants information. I was threatened and I am weak. I hate myself. On the way to school this morning we quarrelled. Liam butts me and I… hit him. On the face. Not as hard as you hit me," he looked at Heike. "And with my hand only."

"Enough," shouted Iakov. "We don't want your children's fights."

"I drive you back now, Sasha," said Oleg, kindly. "We will go and find the boy and you will make it up to him."

Zander hadn't finished. He was ignoring his countrymen, needing to get his story out. "He ran off. I was ashamed. And so I tried to lead this man away. I left Liam's possessions at the school because I hoped that when I had removed myself, he would feel able to continue." His lower jaw seemed to have been knocked out of place. Pain was washing over his face in hot waves as he struggled to continue.

"Where did he run away?" Heike didn't care if Zander was hurting, her arm was throbbing too.

"Defence site. Gate was open."

"Then that's where his parents should be looking for him."

"Yes." His jaw was clicking and sticking. He closed his eyes.

"I call them now!" Heike brought out Bill's phone. "Oh! The stupidity of this English system. In Estonia we are having 3G, 4G everywhere. Here we must climb a hill for any signal at all."

The site manager had wi-fi and a signal booster in his office. Once again he offered hospitality. This time it was sincere. He had young children. He wanted Bill Whiting to know where he should be looking for his son.

Oleg and Iakov followed him along the towpath with them, one ahead of Zander and the other behind. No one was talking.

When they reached the Mercedes, Oleg swung into the driver's seat while Iakov opened the rear door and pushed Zander in. The powerful car raced away up the track while the manager ran for his gate immobiliser button. They heard the sheering-off of metal as the car burst through the barricade and hurtled on its way.

"S-guard, S-class," said the manager. "Armour-plated!" His gate had been smashed by something so top-of-the-range that he'd only read about it in magazines.

As soon as Heike had stepped into the site office a text arrived from Bill:

"Liam has been found and taken to hospital. We are following him there."

And then another, sent later:

"I will not be returning tonight. I am staying with Liam. He cannot see. We expect transfer to London 2mrw. Please continue to look after LL if poss. Yrs, Bill."

Zander had admitted that he'd slapped Liam. He'd tried to make out it was nothing much, but this text said that Liam couldn't see. She hadn't thought it would be possible to hate the Russians any more. But it was.

She wished she'd hit Zander harder. She wished she'd knocked off his handsome head.

She handed Bill's phone to the manager.

"Poor little lad," he said, reading the message. "But it's amazing what they can do these days. At least he's safe."

He asked her if she needed anything while she was staying on the fishing boat. She asked for electricity.

"We have hand pumps and I have fixed their solar panel but it does not make me confident and the work of restoration will be very slow if only hand tools and batteries can be used. I have the skill to manage this."

"But why does Bill Whiting want to keep spending all this money? He's not rich and there's his... disability. He could move into any one of our range of contemporary steel widebeams, for rental or purchase. With finance. We've made the same offer to everyone."

Heike had seen the type of boat he meant. They had about as much character as a floating sardine tin.

"His family were fishermen. Maybe *Lowestoft Lass* helps him feel connected to his heritage?"

That brought them both back to their quarrel.

"At least Mr Whiting pays his bills."

She didn't want to talk about money. "If you'll excuse me now, I need to send a text to my family in Estonia. And then I think we try harder to look for another missing person. Which will be my grandfather. And you don't smash up anyone's history to make a car park."

℘ PEBBLE ℘

"You move it then! That wreck's not history, it's junk. I've got the concrete ordered for two weeks and if that's not gone, I'm running the bulldozers over it. I won't have that thing in my car park. Your grandfather had no contract. He left no address and I'm not going to let your sentimentality run this project into penalty payments. What right had he to be here anyway?"

Heike didn't have any more energy to argue. She sent her text and left.

CHAPTER FOURTEEN:
A private ambulance

The long spell of fine weather broke that night. Spectacular sheet lighting lit the sky, jagged forks flashed and sizzled, thunder rolled and crashed and the sound of driving rain was so normal that it came as a blessed relief.

Lowestoft Lass was leaking badly and tossing as the tide rose. Ever since she could remember, Heike had been terrified of thunder. She knew it was irrational. She wasn't able to be rational. The electricity seemed to fizz along her nerves. The great trees in the wood above the creek stood tall against the blinding sky. At any moment there would be one struck and crashing down onto the helpless boat. Heike wanted to crawl under her duvet, hide her head and whimper.

But she couldn't. She had to keep pumping. And going outside to check the warps. And trying not to look up at the sky. How much longer would this go on?

When Zander and Anna – the two people in the world that Heike was most certain she disliked – tumbled through the wheelhouse door at almost two in the morning, Heike was so glad to see them that she almost broke down in tears. And they were as glad to be there. Both were soaked, Zander pale with sea-sickness.

To begin with everyone could only gasp and drip. Then Anna got her brain in gear and began chivvying the others into dry clothes. The thunder was reduced to muttering, the tide had turned and the water was draining away from the creek. *Lowestoft Lass* had stopped tossing and begun to subside into her mud hole. Even the rain was easing. Anna put the kettle on then went below and came up with a selection of Bill's garments from which she ordered Zander to choose.

"We're tolerating you. That's all," she told him.

"I'll take a turn at that pump," she said to Heike, "if you've anything dry that you wouldn't mind lending me. Total respect for that fantastic dinghy, by the way. I thought she was going to take off and fly when we were coming up that river!"

"I didn't know you were a sailor," was all Heike could think to say.

"I'm not. But Donny and the Allies made me learn and I do find the balance of forces interesting. Even deadweight Zander had his uses when the wind got right behind us."

"It wus hijuss," mumbled Zander. He was getting out of his Hugo Boss boxers and into Bill's old jeans as if he'd forgotten the whole concept of self-consciousness. The mumbling made Heike look at him more closely, now she'd dried the rain and tears from her eyes. The side of his face where she'd hit him was sort of bulging the wrong way at the bottom.

"Could be broken; could just be dislocated," commented Anna, towelling her black hair dry. "We tried to keep the swelling down with ice and ibuprofen but being sick in the dinghy didn't help. I'll use one of Bill's handkerchiefs to give it some support. If he makes it to London he should probably see someone."

"Is that where you're going? I'll fetch you some clothes. Everything I have is still in bags. I didn't have much anyway."

She and Anna both got changed and then Heike opened some tins of soup. She rummaged in her workbox until she found some completely clean tubing which she gave Zander to suck through. The gratitude in his eyes warmed her heart for a moment. Then she remembered he had slapped Liam.

Anna made hot toddy. She grumbled a bit at the absence of spices on board but seemed to know where there was whisky, honey and some lemon juice to squirt out of a plastic fruit. "This is as far as Bill's self-medication goes," she said, handing everyone a mug and telling Zander he'd need to rinse his tube. "You're supposed to drink it as hot as you can manage. There's some science in it somewhere."

"Please tell me what's been going on," said Heike. "I need to know about Liam."

Anna's confidence vanished, she looked stricken. "Liam's lost his sight. I'd like to blame Zander, but I can't. By hitting Liam he might even have done him a favour."

"*Nyet*," he muttered, wincing.

"The side of his face where Zander slapped him is so swollen that Liam can't see out of that eye. It's okay. It'll go down. He also fell badly and hit his head on concrete. But what it's shown is that the other eye isn't working at all. And Liam's been asking for help for weeks and none of us have been listening."

She twisted away as if she was about to break down.

"It isn't something you would expect," said Heike. She'd only thought he was clumsy. Hadn't wondered why.

"If we'd been listening, we would have heard."

"So now what?"

"The doctors at the hospital were talking about migraines

– but the symptoms don't fit. He's suffering from concussion but it's not that either. This is some condition that's already there and getting worse. It's why he wasn't connecting properly at football, why he complained about screens being blurry. And when he came back from sailing with Donny he even asked me whether I'd take him to have an eye test. And I said I was too busy."

She took a deep breath: "I don't know whether I can forgive myself. Ever. My mother feels the same."

"It was only a few days …"

Anna took no notice. "They've done blood tests and brain scans. But the cause is not obvious. So now they're referring him to Moorfields. It's a specialist eye hospital in London but they're not making him wait for an appointment. They're sending him as an emergency. Which proves," she added bitterly, "That they think time matters."

"I am very sorry," said Heike. Everything else that had happened that day seemed, for a moment, not to matter at all. Then she came back to her senses. "Why are you here?"

"Helping Zander to escape."

"From those men? Why? They are all Russians together."

She could see he was trying to protest. Anna spoke for him.

"Oleg, the driver, works for Zander's parents but Iakov is an SVR agent. That means he works for the president. There's something nasty and political going on. We assume that's why Dimitri – that's Zander's former bodyguard – was got out of the way so Iakov could take over."

"And Iakov's the man who was in Lowestoft? Who wants whatever it was that Liam and Donny found – the box that I gave to George?"

"Seems like it. Zander's father is in Russia at the moment and his relationship with the president is probably not good."

"Um going to my muvver."

"Iakov has the front entrance to the Manor and the drive and the gatehouse under surveillance. He'd be tracking Zander too if he hadn't lost his temper and grabbed his phone. And he also overlooked that I have a key to the beach gate. And a key to the dinghy park and, thanks to you, a dinghy. So our plan is to hole up here for a few hours – if that's ok? Then Zander can catch the early train and I'll be on time for school. I've got an exam," she added, almost unnecessarily.

"And *Theodora*?"

"The dinghy?" Anna looked surprised. "I was going to leave her here with you. Liam's not exactly going to be having the summer sailing fun I'd thought I was offering him."

Suddenly, thought Heike, I am in charge of three boats – no, four, I have Bill's dory too. She wondered whether anyone would remember that she was a college student with a diploma to finish.

"You don't know how long Bill will be away – ?"

"It's such a mess," said Anna. "But first we need a few hours' sleep and then we can get Zander out."

"Do you know what the thing is that's causing all this trouble?" Heike asked Zander.

Anna looked hard at him too. He shook his head.

"I made some drawings," she told him. It seemed like a lifetime ago. "You should probably take a look. Or I could make you a copy. So you could show your father when he comes back."

"If he...issallowed."

There it was. Out in the open. His fear.

It was still night outside the wheelhouse. The storm had passed on. In an hour or two the first birds would start to sing. They all needed sleep.

"I must tell you something," Heike said. They were her friends, these people she didn't like. "Four years ago, my grandfather sailed away from our home in Tallinn. He was very old and he had dementia and his yacht was as old as he was. But today – here in Fynn Creek – I found the yacht. And people who had seen him, although they don't know where he is now. I think it means that there is always hope."

They were too tired to want to know any more, but they heard what she said.

The hospital was full of noises. Bin lids flipped, nurses walked, children moaned or whimpered, machines hummed, clicked, pinged. Doctors and nurses talked; children woke up, frightened, their parents woke up too, tried to settle them to sleep again. But then there would be medicine rounds, trolley wheels, nurses' feet, being helped to sit up, given things to swallow.

Liam was given painkillers mostly; small plastic cups held to his lower lip, the nurse's arm around him, head tipped gently back and sweet, sticky liquids poured into his mouth. He was urged to drink water, asked whether he needed the toilet. He felt them checking the dressing on the side of his head; wrapping the sleeve of the blood pressure monitor around his upper arm, applying and releasing the pressure; putting a clip on his finger and removing it again; fingers parted the hair around his ear when they were taking his temperature. He heard the nurses' voices and his father answering them.

A PRIVATE AMBULANCE

Everyone kept telling him to sleep. How? How could you sleep if you couldn't shut your eyes? Or if it didn't make any difference whether your eye was open or shut, because it was always dark anyway and that made everything else so loud.

Liam clung to his father's arm. Strong, solid arm, soft shirt. They'd parked his dad's wheelchair next to the bed. Offered him pillows and a blanket which Bill didn't want. Liam could hear him breathing in the darkness. Asleep.

Liam couldn't believe he would ever sleep again. His dad's arm was the only thing. He wriggled round to rest his blind side on it and hung on with both hands as if it were a floating timber from a wrecked ship.

Some of the other children in the ward woke up in the thunderstorm, parents and nurses soothed them. There were tears pushing their way out from underneath the dressing which covered Liam's closed eye. The tears weren't taking any notice of the dressing. They were running over the top of his nose and down into the other eye where they joined up with the tears that were pouring out of there. Liam didn't try to stop them. He didn't really feel connected to his body anymore, only to his father's arm.

An ambulance had been booked to take them to London in the morning. But it didn't come. The storm had knocked out power lines and then there'd been flooding caused by the sudden downpour of rain after so many weeks of dry weather. Some people had been injured, others trapped. All the ambulances were needed for emergency work.

"If my son were an emergency last night, why ain't he still one this morning?"

"We're doing our best, Mr Whiting. You have to bear with us. We need to find someone qualified to travel with you."

"Because I'm a cripple?"

"Because of Liam's concussion. He hit his head hard when he fell on that concrete. There's still a risk of brain bleed. If it were just the sight loss, you and your wife could take him yourselves in the car. He needs to get to Moorfields quickly but he has to get there safely, too."

"Sorry," said Bill. "I weren't thinking."

"It's been a shock for you as well," said the ward manager kindly. "We're all doing our best to get you to London as quickly as we can."

Bill and Liam were like in a limbo now. The nurses helped Liam out of bed and then they washed and dressed him, offered some breakfast which he didn't want, then sat him and Bill in a waiting area. There was nothing more that could be done, except carry on taking his blood pressure and his pulse and asking him if he had a headache or felt sick. Sometimes they told him they were shining a torch into his right eye to check if the pupil was responding. He could feel their fingers but there wasn't a glimmer of light.

That did make him feel sick. How could the eye have given up so completely? And what was going to happen when the swelling went down from the left?

He and his dad sat gloomily, lost in their thoughts. Or trying not to think at all.

"Li-umm!"

The voice was thick, amazed, uncertain. "IsssZandr."

Liam shrank close to his dad. It didn't matter that his dad was in a wheelchair.

"You're the lad that walloped my boy? What've you come ter say for yerself?"

"Mmsssrry"

"I should think so. Though this trouble ain't all down ter you. What's the matter with yer face? And... ain't that my T-shirt?"

"Ihvvvprrrblms."

"Sounds like speaking's one of them. Well, we got problems too."

"Mmvrysrry, Liumm"

"I head-butted you."

"Srrrrvedmeright."

"You had my guitar."

"Srrrrrrrrry." Zander sounded as if he might cry.

"Were you being bullied by Yuck-off?" Liam turned his face where he thought Zander might be. "Did he make you bully me?"

"That what got yer sore face? Broke yer jaw did he, this Iakov?"

"WssssHeike."

"Good girl," said Bill. "Yer'd better sit down and tell us about it. We don't seem to be going anywhere much."

"NeedtttgttterLondunnnn. Notrnnns. Noffffffone."

"London? You and us both. We're waiting for an ambulance. And if one don't come soon I might be gonna clock someone. My boy needs help and it feels like they've forgotten the meaning of urgent."

"Mmmthersssammbulance. Hvfffone?"

Bill lent Zander Lottie's phone, which she'd left with him. Zander texted Raisa and in a remarkably short space of time there was a fully equipped private ambulance waiting for them outside the hospital with a qualified paramedic to drive them.

"Swear you're not tricking us." Liam felt a sudden lurch of fear.

"Sssswr."

"Swear on my stone." He had the amber in his pocket still. Held it out. Felt Zander take it. There was a gasp.

"IssBalllticumber. Issswr."

Lottie's was an iPhone. As the smooth, fast ambulance whisked them to London Zander typed out his story for Bill and Bill retold it for Liam.

There was the incident on *Lowestoft Lass*, Iakov and Zander's return to the Manor, his conversation with Anna when he'd poured out his troubles and heard the shocking news about Liam, their escape up the river in the storm. Borrowing the clothes and those few hours' sleep when Bill's old fishing boat had felt like the most luxurious palace in the world.

Zander and Anna had left Fynn Creek early but when they'd reached the station they discovered that an electrical failure in the signalling system meant there were no trains running. All the station taxis had been taken but there'd been a bus which was scheduled to stop at Ipswich Hospital so they'd made a really quick scheme that Zander should go there, to the hospital, a public place where Iakov was very unlikely either to find him or to snatch him. Anna would go to school and try to remember whether it was maths, physics, chemistry, biology or computer science she was taking and then, later, she would ring Raisa and reassure her that Zander would be on his way as soon as possible. He had his credit card.

♆ A PRIVATE AMBULANCE ♆

Zander had been desperate to see Liam, if he could. He was full of guilt about what he'd done. Getting smashed in the face by Heike and half drowned in the dinghy by Anna was nothing to the beating up he was giving to himself. Being able to organise the private ambulance was a tiny first step towards shifting his misery. He could never do enough, he thought, to try to make amends to Liam, protect and thank Anna, get revenge on Iakov.

Zander typing and Bill telling helped their journey pass quite quickly but then Liam's head began to ache again and he began to feel frightened about what might happen to him next. His grip tightened on his father's arm. Bill and Zander noticed and as the ambulance got closer to London no one said anything at all.

CHAPTER FIFTEEN

A well-filled sketchbook

Anna's second exam of the day finished before the rest of the school came out. She'd already decided what she was going to do next, so she phoned Lottie to tell her that she didn't need collecting and set off to walk back to Fynn Creek.

Fitzgerald School was about as far the wrong side of town as it could be and she was already tired. The long walk was okay though, she wanted to be away from everyone else's emotions and she needed time on her own to think.

She'd had a message that Zander had reached London safely, together with Liam and Bill. That was a big relief. Raisa could sort her son's jaw, which had looked quite bad this morning and Liam would get the expert medical help he needed. Her little brother's sight loss made her feel guilty, helpless, frightened but there was nothing she could do to help him.

What she should do was try and get her head round whatever was going on. Liam was like collateral damage in someone else's war. So was Zander, possibly.

When Anna had been with Zander's family for that lunch, there was one sentence that had stuck with her. "We tried to turn him, of course," Arkady Ivanov had said, casually, referring to Anna's great-uncle and the Cold War time when spy forces on each side were playing their dangerous games with ordinary people's futures. It had given her a feeling that there were people who thought everyone else could be manipulated, shifted around like pieces on a chessboard. Maybe that sort of game got addictive. Maybe it was a game that was still carrying on.

What about Zander? People treated him as if he was somebody special but it was pretty obvious that he was no more than a pawn. Maybe he was a pawn that might one day become a queen, which pawns could do if they reached the back line, but for now he was little more than bait – or a human shield.

Anna wasn't sure how she felt about Zander on a personal level. He was clever and different and good-looking (before the Estonian girl had rearranged his face) and definitely a bit troubled. But as she walked through the busy end-of-the-week streets of the small town, downhill towards the river, she began to think that it wasn't Zander who was in play now. And it wasn't Liam any more. It was Donny. And probably the girl as well.

She must stop calling her that. Her name was Heike.

Couldn't they all keep out of it? Walk off the chessboard? Whatever Donny and Liam had blundered into was nothing to do with them. But when Zander had come to find her, after his traumatic journey with Iakov in the car, he'd been quite certain that the agent planned to find the junk and 'take it to pieces' and that *Lowestoft Lass* was staying on his radar too.

Bill's fishing boat was trapped. She couldn't go anywhere. *Strong Winds*' anchorage in Gallister Creek was beautifully remote but the junk was too distinctive to hide for long. What was this Thing and – more important – why did the Russian agent want it? Heike'd made a drawing: she should look at it.

Anna had reached the embankment round the top of Fynn Creek. She looked across to the space which had been a tidal lagoon but was now drained, dried, enclosed and waiting for hundreds of tons of infill rubble. There was the old yacht; stranded, drying to death. It didn't look all that appealing. She could understand the site manager's eagerness to clear it away.

What had Heike said last night, about her grandfather? "Today – here in Fynn Creek – I found his yacht. I think it means that there is always hope."

Anna remembered the time in her own life when she'd refused to believe her mother was gone. Maybe Heike was right to be stubborn.

There were two men with boathooks seated beside the wreck. A third man walked across from the moorings, carrying two mugs which he put on an upturned oil drum. One of the seated people looked at his watch, then got up and left. The new arrival took his place. A guard system!

Once she'd crossed the top of the creek she turned downstream onto a path that was still muddy from the rain. For a while her view was blocked by the trees but then she saw the yacht from the other side. Someone had built a walkway out across the mush where the reed bed had been. Heike's grandfather, even? It was tempting to explore the old boat but it wasn't her business. Anna carried on until she reached *Lowestoft Lass.*

Heike was pumping. She'd also been painting: the wheelhouse was glistening white, with a band of bright blue around the door. The old fishing boat was immaculately tidy except for a line of clean washing, which Anna recognised as her and Zander's clothes from last night. She wiped her muddy shoes.

Both the dinghies were made fast neatly to the outer side. The tide was up and they were floating, ready if required. Anna glanced at her golden *Theodora*. For the first time she felt pleased she was a boat owner.

"Did you know they've set up a guard system by your grandfather's yacht?" she asked.

Heike was flushed with the exercise. "I don't need to pump so much but I am building the battery reserves. Yes, I know about the watchers. A man from the moorings came to tell me. They understand that I cannot leave here because I am caring for Bill's boat. I can't risk the Russians coming back again."

"No. I see that. Aren't you scared for yourself?"

"If I see the enemy I am to sound this." She showed Anna a seriously loud bull-roarer foghorn. "My new friends have loaned it."

Anna struggled to imagine a detachment of creekies charging the Ivanovs' armour-plated Mercedes with their boathooks, urged on by the sound of an antique foghorn.

Heike was still talking. "Perhaps they regret they didn't take my grandfather to their hearts. They didn't know that he was a man with a family who loved him. And there may have been some jealousy about a special mooring arrangement. I didn't understand that. There have been people coming to visit today who tell me about him. That they thought he was strange. They say he was always looking for a boy named Vanya. Then I know for sure that was my grandfather."

Hadn't Luke said something …? When he'd been here before? Or had it been Liam?

This discovery must be a big thing for Heike, but she was sticking to her post, taking care of *Lowestoft Lass*.

"Do you want to go across there now?"

"Of course I do. But you haven't come for me. You've come

for your clothes and your dinghy. You need to catch the tide and sail back down the river to your home."

"Yes – but I also came to look at those drawings you made."

Heike didn't seem to understand.

"You sketched the Thing that the Russians are searching for. Whatever it was that Donny and Liam dragged into Lowestoft."

Heike's face cleared. "Yes of course. When you spoke of drawings I was thinking so much of my grandfather, my *Vanaisa*. The whole of his story is in my books. But the sketches of the object are there also. Perhaps you like to copy them?"

"I'll do that. You got involved because you helped to take it off *Strong Winds* and then you carried it to the man called George. Was it heavy? Could you estimate the weight?"

"It wasn't heavy – maybe five, six kilos – otherwise there would have been more interference with the sailing of the junk. I have included measurements with my drawings."

"Okay. You go and spend some time on your grandfather's yacht and I'll stand guard here. How long before the tide turns?"

They both looked over the fishing boat's side to where the dinghies floated in suspended animation. The tide had reached its highest point.

"Not so long but you don't need to use the centreboard where it's shallow and I have both your oars together again." Heike saw that Anna didn't understand. "When I hit your friend, the big Russian agent grabbed the oar and he threw it in the river. But he threw it so hard that it stuck. The stupid man. So I went and fetched it. The tide leaves fast but your dinghy won't need too much water to get away. I think you have at least one hour."

"You'll be back then? There's a walkway built out to the yacht from the path that goes through the wood. It doesn't look very health-and-safety."

Heike was down to the cabin and up again quickly, bringing her backpack filled with sketchbooks.

"The drawings you want, they are here," she said opening the newest-looking book. "I draw a lot while I am studying. The others they are stories of my grandfather through his life. Your friend Donny didn't like them much."

"I don't need to look at them," said Anna, though she knew she would.

"I am not ashamed," said Heike, angrily. "I don't care for your opinion. I know my *Vanaisa* and my country and you don't."

"Fine," said Anna, "but you're wasting time."

She didn't bother trying to copy Heike's drawings of the Thing. Just snapped them with the camera on her phone. It was a box with openings: a flap, a filter, a photo lens, maybe. Giving no clues as to their functions. Data collection?

The box was fixed to an ordinary looking length of wire with cylindrical shapes at either end. Heike had labelled them '*ujukid?* / floats?' They both had significant cuts and gashes and one had torn through. She'd said Donny had been using Gold Dragon's knife to get the entanglement off the propeller. Maybe he'd made these marks. He was lucky he hadn't taken off his own wrists.

Heike had drawn the arrangement vertically. Float – wire + box – float. There were some fixings whose use was unclear. Some of them looked damaged. Heike had also made some guesses. At the base of her drawings she'd drawn an arrow downwards '*kaaluvit?* / weight?' and at the top, where there were the remnants of rope, '*markeri poi?*/marker buoy?' The end of the rope was drawn frayed. Presumably where little Liam had ploughed *Strong Winds* straight over it.

Poor Liam. Poor little vision-impaired Liam. Anna felt a terrible anguish. But surely these experts at Moorfields could make it all right again?

She needed to keep on distracting herself. If she'd had internet she'd have begun an image search using Heike's drawings.

But she didn't. And Heike wasn't back and the tide was going. Anna had changed back into her washed and dried clothes. Everything in *Theodora* was ready for a quick departure. There was nothing she could do except keep glancing anxiously along the path. Or over the fishing boat's side at the mud which was rising steadily towards her as *Lowestoft Lass* sank down.

Anna felt irritated. Then she got rational. There wasn't any law saying she had to sail down the river tonight. She could always walk back into town and catch a bus. Or ring her mother. Or even stay here.

She made herself comfortable and opened the oldest-looking of the sketchbooks. The drawings weren't so mature, pencil not so sharp, rubbings-out that had smeared, but Anna was soon gripped by the story they told. It began with a little boy growing up beside the water in a wooden house on stilts. A mother and some sisters and a father, who already looked old and who was pictured repairing and painting and towing boats: '*jahtklubi*'. There were no translations written here but Anna was getting what words she could by saying them aloud: 'yacht club'? One yacht was drawn larger and with more care than all the rest: *Racundra*. Two strong masts; hull broad as a soup plate but pretty too with curving sides and a pointed stern and a cheerful, snub-nosed bow.

Anna checked herself. Whatever Donny and the Allies thought, boats weren't people. It wasn't logical to call them words like 'cheerful' or give them human attributes like 'snub-nosed', yachts didn't have noses, there was sure to be a techie term.

Whatever. This yacht was neat and new and strongly-built and even Anna could see that she was the same boat that was lying just a few hundred metres away, ready to be flattened. It seemed as if Heike had come back to her drawings when she'd been a bit older and added careful dates. This one was labelled 'Riga 1922'. Ninety years ago.

In these early pages the yacht had two large people who came and went and the old man beside the lake who loved her. There was a sequence of departure and return. Voyages, with dates. The children and their mother waving from the shore. Proudly or dutifully? Other people in the yacht club, arms folded, looking sour. The two large people shaking hands in farewell. Two new, younger people took command. '*Inglis*'. The next pages showed the old man sad. The mother and the children, older now, packing their belonging into a cart, taking everything to a harbour where they were loaded into a bigger boat – still a sailing boat, but one designed for work.

Peteris, the boy in the story – presumably Heike's *Vanaisa* – had loved the voyage and his first sight of their destination, Tallinn. Once they got there he went a bit wild, bunking off school to hang around the harbour. His mother and sisters were busy, finding jobs, homemaking and settling in; the old father sat in the corner and moped.

☙ PEBBLE ❧

It was the sea scouts who changed Peteris's life. Anna had no idea they'd been about so long ago and in countries like Estonia but there they were, though she wouldn't have guessed the word – *'mere skaudid'*. Peteris was taller, wearing a uniform with his hair cropped close to his head, getting a badge, and his old father, cheerful now, helping transform an abandoned boat into something that the boys could use to get out to sea. Easy to see how Heike had inherited her shipwright passion.

Anna got up and went to check on *Theodora*. There was still a little water, but not much.

She began skipping through the sketchbook pages more quickly, as if Heike wouldn't come back until she'd finished. Peteris older still and crewing in a new yacht, the *See Adler*, smart and eager, cruising the Baltic with a doctor and his friends, all German names. But then it was the war and the story in the drawing became more and more horrific.

Anna could see why Donny hadn't liked them. His family had been in the British Navy: Peteris, orphaned and angry, had joined the German *Kriegsmarine*. He was sent to train in submarines. Learned to fire torpedoes. Heike had drawn him, making that salute. Heil Hitler!

With her head Anna understood this: 'My enemy's enemy is my friend'. If Peteris wanted to fight the Russians, joining the Germans was the logical thing to do. With her heart she found it hard as she followed the new submariner up into Arctic waters; the small boy from beside the lake was a Nazi now. Were all fighters Nazis? Surely they had to be? But the ships that he and the other U-boats in his wolf pack were attacking weren't Russian ships, they were British ships, carrying supplies to

Russia. 'My enemy's friend is also my enemy.'

Single U-boats, like lone wolves, silently tracking their prey. A date, a kill, a British ship, a U-boat number...

Anna put the sketchbook down, breathed deeply. She recognised that U-boat number.

"Surprised?" said Donny, coming close up behind her and putting his hands over her eyes.

"Don't!" said Anna, snapping the sketchbook shut and swinging round to face him. "Don't ever do that again!"

Donny laughed. Even when she was spitting mad, Anna would never be other than his dearest friend. Infuriating her was something he'd never have thought he would dare to do. But now he knew he could.

"Thought you had my exam timetable in your head. Didn't work out that it was Geology multi-choice this morning? Only lasted ¾ hour – and the amount I know, I could have been done in half the time. Nope. Don't say a word. I stayed the distance. Gave it best consideration. Ticks in all the boxes – whether I had a clue or not. And then I ran. Mum had *Strong Winds* humming and we made the trip in record time."

"But how did you...?"

"Know what had happened? Rev Wendy told us. She's praying for Liam. We're supposed to be praying too – but praying doesn't feel enough."

"It isn't."

"And I don't know enough either. What happened? Wendy says we may have to Forgive our Enemies but I need more information. Like who's the enemy. Was it that brat...?"

PEBBLE

"My friend, possibly-ex-friend, probably-still-my-friend, Zander? No, not him exactly. And even if it was, *your* new friend Heike has already got him back. She's broken his jaw. He's doubled up with guilt (as well as his stomach being bruised where Liam head-butted him) so he's called his mother's private ambulance and taken them all to London. Hello Skye, I'm very glad to see you."

Anna was talking with her fingers now. She was a lot better in BSL than she was in Russian.

She was about to start asking practical questions – like how they'd got *Strong Winds* up this astoundingly wriggly creek, where even she and Zander in a dinghy had stuck a few times – and Donny was about to tell her how it had all been okay because he'd had his mum with him and her eyesight was so good she could almost spot underwater seaweed.

But then he'd have fallen silent – whether he was talking with his tongue or his fingers – and he'd have felt sick with himself for being irritated when they'd run aground on a bend below Iken because Li couldn't see the withies. He'd have begun to wonder whether it would have made a difference if he'd taken him to get specs in Aldeburgh that afternoon instead of lying on the beach eating chips and stacking pebbles.

Except that Heike came running down the path, waving an old and clouded plastic pocket which held a single sheet of wilted paper.

"It's the crew list," she said, looking wildly at them all. She'd never met Skye before but there was no room in her head for greetings. "The list my father wrote for my grandfather to tell him that he would never voyage alone. It had slipped into the lining of *Ra*'."

She spread the paper on the wheelhouse table where they

could all of them see it. Skye wasn't looking at the paper. She couldn't read words. She was looking from this girl to her son. Reading their faces.

"Look," said Heike, "We are all there. Maroosia (that's my mother) He has written her as the cook; Vaclev (father) is *pootsman* – I can't think of your English word; my brother Arvo and me are crew. All of us were sailing with *Vanaisa* in our hearts. We are here still in the lining of his ship. It is proof."

"These others on the list," asked Donny, his voice had gone a little weird and he was signing too. "Hermann and Vanya? They don't have jobs."

"Her-mann," said his mother – who was usually mute. The colour had drained from her bright copper skin, her dark eyes were wide. She stepped towards Heike, reaching out unsteadily. She looked as if she might fall.

Skye was majestic. Donny and Anna were quick. They held her on either side, linked their arms intohers and helped her to sit down onto the wheelhouse bench as she continued to gaze at Heike.

"Her-mann," she said again. Her soul was in her eyes.

U-boot 711

17-2-1945 Barents See

CHAPTER SIXTEEN

A forgotten crew list

Bill hadn't understood that this hospital didn't have places to stay. They were expected and were seen quickly, efficiently and kindly in the children's emergency department. The female consultant asked Liam about his experiences over the past months, ever since he'd started losing his confidence at football. Listening to his son's answers made Bill feel terrible. He'd known nothing of this.

Then the doctor started asking him questions, not so much about himself, as about Eva, Liam and Luke's mum, who was dead and about Eva's family who Bill hadn't known so well. Her mum had some sort of MS and was in a home when they'd first met, and her dad hadn't exactly stuck around. Eva was angry with her father so she didn't have much to do with him. Bill wasn't even sure she'd told him they were married. Her mother hadn't lived long enough to know she had grandchildren.

Eva was convinced that she and Bill were going to be different. They were going to love each other and stick together and raise their children in a happy family of their own. In sickness and in health as long as they both did live. Then cancer had taken her – when she hardly knew her own younger child – and Bill hadn't any idea where any of her family might be now, although, as the doctor's questions went on and on, he did seem to recall that Eva had had an uncle who'd lost his sight.

"We didn't think nothing of it. Don't remember that I ever met the man. We didn't have much of a wedding, didn't reckon we needed anyone except ourselves. We was so young, so in love."

Liam'd never heard his dad talk like this.

"Have you any other children?"

"We got an older boy. Luke. He's the spit of my Eva. I often looks at him and think she ain't never really gone."

"You and your wife were never offered genetic testing?"

"I weren't a cripple then." Bill was angry.

"No, Mr Whiting. That wasn't what I meant. One of the possible reasons for a sudden – or relatively sudden – loss of vision such as Liam has experienced in his right eye is an inherited genetic condition. That's why I'm asking all these questions. We'll arrange testing for Liam immediately. And also for your other son. You don't have any daughters?"

"There's my Vicky – and I'm that fond of her sister, Anna…"

"But are they the daughters of your wife, Eva?"

"No, their mum's Lottie, We haven't never married."

"The condition I'm investigating, Mr Whiting, is mitochondrial. That means it's passed only via the biological mother. If Eva had any other children we'd need to test them as well. Obviously we'll know more when we can assess Liam's other eye, and when he's fully recovered from his concussion, but for now I'm going to ask Liam for a blood sample and send that for genetic analysis. It'll take a few weeks. We'll set you up with a series of appointments. If you're eligible you may be able to claim travel costs."

"We ain't staying here then?"

"There's no need. Your son is in what we call an acute phase. He'll do better in his own home. He's taken a bad knock. He needs to build up his resilience."

Liam had been listening as if they were in a different room and he had his ear crammed against the door trying to make out what they were saying but only catching fragments. He thought maybe there was a rim of blurred light around the central darkness of his open eye. The closed one was still a hot redness under the protective pad with flashes and crackles of sudden pain. He wanted to ask when he would get better but it was like one of those dreams where you open your mouth but you can't make any words.

"This acute phase," his dad was finding it hard, Lottie would have done this better but it weren't nothing to do with her. "How long do it last? And how are you treating him now so he can get on with getting better?"

The doctor's answer was a long one and full of waiting for this and checking for that and adaptive technology and packages.

Basically it was a no. Liam wasn't going to get better. Bill must have heard much the same when they told him he wouldn't be walking any more.

"But I could see that morning when we set out for school," Liam wanted to cry out. "Okay, it was blurry, but I could see. I was doing ok."

He was grabbing his amber in his pocket but it couldn't help him. He sort of squawked and stuck.

"What has happened is that the blow to your face, which has caused your left eye to swell and to close, has revealed that you no longer have any central vision in your right eye." She was talking properly to him, even though he hadn't managed to say nothing. "Your one eye's been doing the work of two, probably for several weeks, or even months. That's why your co-ordination hasn't been so good. You've been coping very well but recently you've been experiencing an increased blurriness – which suggests that the left eye is starting to fail. It's the classic pattern – if this is the condition I suspect."

"You need ter get on and do something then! Don't keep hanging about waiting fer tests. You need ter get on fixin' it!"

The doctor kept on explaining.

"Liam suffered a severe blow to the head when he fell onto the concrete. Vision loss is quite common after concussion and that's what your local hospital was checking for and we have confirmed those findings. Unfortunately for Liam, it may not stop there. There is damage from the fall – and I'm hopeful that with the body's natural healing processes there will be improvement – but it may not last. There's nothing more I can prescribe except rest – pain relief, anti-inflammatory medication, antibiotics – you have all of them. As the underlying problem is from a genetic cause, it's likely that only gene therapy will help – and that, I'm afraid, is in the earliest stages of research."

Bill and Liam said nothing. There wasn't anything they could say.

"I'll see you both again next week," said the doctor, trying to keep the Friday feeling out of her voice. "But what Liam must have now is rest."

"I don't want this anymore. There's no such thing as lucky stones." He was pulling the amber out of his pocket and shoving it in the direction of the doctor's voice. Being angry and hating her might mean he wouldn't start crying again. This was what his mum had left him. It was like a curse.

♀ PEBBLE ♀

He felt the doctor's hand close over his. She was refusing the stone, pushing it back towards him.

"You should keep your amber. Keep it for its own sake. Remember the day you found it. Remember where you were and who you were with. I'm so sorry this has happened to you, Liam," she added, really sounding as if she meant it.

Then she started talking to his dad again. "How are you travelling, Mr Whiting? Do you have anyone supporting you?"

Bill was saying they'd be okay and Liam was trying his best to hang on to his dad's arm and the doctor was insisting that she needed to take them to Patient Liaison when suddenly he was being pressed to a bosom he didn't know, smelling a scent he didn't recognise and feeling the unexpected touch of furs.

"My dear boy," said a warm and worried foreign voice, "I am so very sorry about all of this. Zander has explained as far as he is able. We have come to offer everything we can. Please let us help."

It was too much: those tears came pouring out again, pushing between the closed lids and getting stuck behind the dressings and the horrible bulging shield.

"He must have rest," the doctor said. "He must have sleep. That's all anyone can give him."

"The list had fallen between the lining and the outer skin," Heike was explaining. Donny was sitting close to his mother but had his hands free so he could sign as soon as she was able to understand. They'd thought she might faint but it was more like she'd gone into some sort of trance. Anna had fetched a glass of water and had checked there were no tight pieces of clothing.

With Skye's eccentric style of dressing this was totally unlikely, but she checked anyway.

Heike knew about first aid, of course she did, from her work in care homes, but she wasn't any help because she couldn't stop talking. "On the side where my grandfather slept. I was investigating for damage to the timbers. I had forgotten completely that my father did this. He had read that there must be a crew list. It gave him the idea that if he wrote our names, then the old man would not be so sad when he was leaving us, we would be coming too."

Anna, who was so rational, felt her throat constrict and the tears prickle behind her eyes. "I think that's a beautiful idea."

Heike smiled at her but Donny's face was tense. "Who are these people?" he asked again. He was pointing at the final two names, separated a little from the others on the list: Hermann and Vanya.

"I don't get this word." He pointed at it: *kummitused*.

"It means...I think...ghosts, maybe? Something that's in your head and it won't let go? You think it's real but it's not."

"Obsession?"

"Maybe. Hermann was my mother's brother – who is gone many years – and Vanya is his son who we have never seen. My grandfather would never stop thinking of him. He believed that the boy was born in England and his name was John. But he always called him Vanya. It was from some stories but it's the same name."

"John's my name."

Heike looked at him. "You said you are Donny."

"No, I'm John. When I was little I couldn't say it. And also it was the same name as my great-uncle who was in the navy. My granny brought me up – at least I thought she was my granny then. She had to fight for me and Skye. She was so strong. Except she couldn't really cope with me having her brother's name. It was to do with the way he died in the war. It totally messed her up."

Anna moved quietly to shut Heike's sketchbook. Donny didn't see what she was doing.

"Mum told me that my father's name was Hermann. She can't say many words but there was one day when I was upset and angry at not having a father and that was what she told me. 'Hermann' she said. Just like she did now!"

There were goosebumps running up and down his spine.

"Then, when we were talking properly again – signing – she told me that she met my father in the Northlands. That was her word. Later on I found letters and newspapers where my granny Edith was advertising for information around the Baltic States. She and Mum had been there on a holiday. I've no idea why. That was after they'd come back to England and Skye had discovered she was pregnant. I suppose I could have a DNA test or something."

Heike was looking down at her crew list and up at Donny and over towards Skye. Anna was cold with the other connection she had guessed. Skye was still staring at the Estonian girl.

"Hello, Mum," Donny took her hands in his. She had had a massive shock, even if it was a good one. He began signing into her palm. "You told me that I looked like my father, like…Hermann. Do I look like Heike? Do I, Heike, do I look like my dad?"

"I never met him."

"You do look alike," said Anna. Her voice was croaky. "I've been noticing it all along. I just didn't make any sense out of it. You're first cousins." If she needed her actress skills it was now. "I'm really happy for you. We should get out those papers old

Nokomis left. Where've you moored *Strong Winds*, Donny? You keep those papers in the locker with the ashes don't you? I'll fetch them. You need to stay with Skye."

Donny looked grateful. "We're moored directly astern. There's a jetty. I couldn't get why no one was using it already. It's on the final bend of the channel and it's got more water than anywhere. Must be private. I didn't check that carefully. We were running out of river."

"Cool. I'm on it. I'll bring Skye's beads as well. You okay for milk, Heike? We could all use some tea...Donny, your mum looks like she's shivering."

That did it. Donny went below for a blanket and Heike was lighting the gas. Never mind that it was still a beautiful summer evening. Anna stole Heike's sketchbook and slipped out while both of them were busy. She located the junk, agreed silently with Donny that it was an amazingly good mooring spot, found Gold Dragon's knife and amputated the page. She didn't leave it for anyone to find. She tore it up, burned it, then brushed every one of the smouldering fragments over the side into the creek.

A few moments later she was back on *Lowestoft Lass* with the file of letters and cuttings that Donny had found in the camper van what seemed like so many years ago.

It was a life-changing moment: Donny, who had never had any knowledge of his father as a person, was now sitting with his cousin – who he even looked like – and staring at a piece of paper which had his aunt and uncle, another cousin and his father's names on it. Heike was looking at the copies of all the unanswered letters confirming the existence of the cousin she'd thought of as a myth but who was opposite her now, drinking tea.

"What's our grandfather's name?" he asked. "I've only heard you calling him *Vanaisa*."

"His name is Peteris, Peteris Sehmel."

"Is that an Estonian name?"

"No. He was born in Latvia."

"I hardly know where that is."

"You can come and we will explore. My mother and my father won't believe this, that you are Vanya and you have been found! And *Ra'* is here! I don't know what my father will say. I have seen him angry with *Vanaisa* when he is talking of his longing for you when it is Arvo and I who are in the room. But he put you and your father on the list."

Donny took Skye's hand again and signed into it. "This is my cousin, Mum. Her name is Heike and she's from…the Northlands. Her uncle is Hermann, your…" He stopped. What word to use…? Her seducer? Rapist? Liar? Cheat?

Skye was signing back. "I loved him and he was your father. Please ask her where he is now."

"Mum wants to know where Hermann is now."

"We don't know. We don't think he's still living. All that my grandfather knew about you and your mother was from the letters that the Englishwoman kept writing. Not to him, you understand, but to officials, to politicians, newspapers…"

"These," said Donny, "all these letters that Nokomis sent and no one ever answered."

"These were arriving in our country from England. My grandfather was afraid they would cause trouble."

"What trouble?"

"It was a strange time. We had pushed out the Russians, but

had they truly gone? Would there be fighting, return to the old days, retaliations?"

Skye was signing. Donny translated for Heike.

"My mother says that you bring Hermann here with us. Back from the land of spirits."

So Skye didn't believe his father was still alive either.

Heike wasn't used to Skye. She smiled but looked a bit startled.

"Don't worry," said Donny. "When Mum's brother – that's her real mum's other child who she didn't know existed – turned up in our lives, he dropped straight down onto *Strong Winds*' deck from a helicopter! My dad's turned up in a plastic wrapper from the lining of a wreck – but all you did, when we first met, was give me the code for the facilities when I was nearly wetting myself!"

Anna could hear how profoundly happy he was, how something had shifted in the tectonic depths of her best friend's identity, her best friend, always. She was glad she'd done what she had.

"You must know something more about Hermann," she asked Heike, "Even if you didn't ever meet. What was his job, for instance?"

"My uncle was with the navy."

"Oh wow!" Donny almost shouted, "I always wanted that – to know that my sailing comes from somewhere."

"Maybe, but I think he was under the sea or an engineer. My family didn't talk about him much. It's possibly because it was the wrong navy. It is *Vanaisa* – who is also your grandfather as much as mine – who is the true sailor in your blood. You must come with me to look at his yacht. You must help me to save *Ra'*."

Talk about single-minded, Anna thought. Aloud she said, "There must be someone acting for Miss Grace who'll know what happened here after the night of the fire. We've got other problems though. And I don't just mean my sweet little brother. I mean the actual current threat."

"Russians." Heike only spoke it. She didn't spit.

"Her-mann."

Anna had been signing all the time she spoke. Just automatically trying to keep Skye included. Now Skye, with great effort, had produced those two syllables for the third time. Heike didn't know how much it took for Skye to speak at all. She treated it as part of the conversation and tried to answer.

"My mother said she couldn't understand why he was still working for them. Okay, he'd done his service when they were our rulers. He was sent to the Arctic and she didn't see him for four years. But why did he stay in? Even when they were leaving…"

"He was to make safe the rods of power. He did not expect he would have a long life," Skye was signing to Donny.

"He talked to you, Mum? But how could he?"

Skye looked at him with a profundity of love. "There are ways to speak that are not with words. You were his seed that I would carry safe."

This was getting way too personal. Heike most likely wouldn't understand but Anna would. It was embarrassing.

"It's okay, Donny," Anna was laughing. "We've all of us been conceived somehow! Meanwhile," she carried on, "I don't want to be a grinch, but we do have other issues and only this weekend to deal with them before it's exams again on Monday."

"I must speak to my college too," said Heike. "And I have to make sure that *Ra'* is safe. With this boat also to be protected and kept floating until Bill is back."

"And I'd just as soon *Strong Winds* didn't get trashed by any Russian spooks looking for something we haven't got," added Donny.

"So," said Anna, "I'm going to leave you three here enjoying your family reunion and I'm going to take the final dribble of water out of this creek and down the river to Bawdsey. That's three of you to protect three boats – Heike and Skye are tough enough, even if Donny's a bit of a wuss."

She smiled at him. He was her best friend and this news had made her at least 50 percent as happy as him but it was complicated and she needed to keep thinking for them all. "I'm going to have an in-depth conversation with my lawyer, Edward, as soon as I get a signal. He'll start by saying that there's nothing he can do to Act Professionally in his Capacity as my Trustee," Anna had got quite good at mimicking Edward's hrmph-hrmph seriousness, "but then he'll remember how he and my great-uncle were friends and how he knew some of Donny's lot as well and he'll talk himself round to working out something he can do to help. Like injunctions, which are ways to get protection. Those creekies are good but they can't guard *Ra'* for ever. And we must surely be able to fit a generator or something to keep *LL*'s pumps reliable."

"If there were facilities to lift her out," said Heike, "then I would be making sure that she didn't have these leaks."

This girl was going to be part of their lives now. She wasn't only someone with a skill; she was Donny's cousin.

"Did my father and your grandfather – *our* grandfather, I

mean – not get on?" Donny asked Heike, picking up something she'd said earlier.

"It was connected with the Russians, everything is connected with the Russians. Maybe I can explain another day? For now I am glad to meet my new aunt." She smiled rather shyly at Skye and held out her hand.

Anna hefted her school bag over the side and climbed down into *Theodora*, "Don't forget to keep lookout," she said. "I've got my phone and you've got Bill's Nokia brick and I'm suggesting we set up an on-the-hour-every-hour reporting system where one of you goes up to the top to get a signal and we check in for updates. This mud is gross. I'm going to have to punt and paddle till I reach the main river. Obviously, I could stay here and ring Edward from up the top but I also need to check out my own tribe and hear how my little brother's doing. You'll be okay."

She wasn't hanging about for them to agree. She was gone. Not looking back.

CHAPTER SEVENTEEN
A shelduck family

Anna wasn't a natural waterbabe and getting out of Fynn Creek was hard. The ebb tide had been running almost three hours already and the mud banks had risen high either side of the narrow stream. Every time she misjudged a bend she found herself aground. She couldn't work out where the wind was coming from, so the first stage of her journey was a mix of flapping sail and oars. It didn't look or feel pretty. To make it worse, there was a family of shelduck caught in the channel ahead of her. A mother and about ten tiny chicks all paddling as hard as they could go and obviously seeing her as some terrifying juggernaut.

The male duck was swimming behind them. He looked surprisingly large in his white, black and amber plumage and kept turning his head to glare at her. His beak was bright red with a fleshy crimson knob at the top which made him look as if he was suffering from high blood pressure. As she got closer he got angrier: he reared up in the water and lunged towards her.

Anna wanted to tell him that she didn't have a choice, that she couldn't do anything other than what she was doing, which was coming down the middle of this shallow, crazily-winding channel unable to even spread her oars out properly. She couldn't think how Donny and Skye had got *Strong Winds* up here.

The ducklings bobbed under water but when they bobbed up again she was still there. The male beat his strong wings and flew upwards from the creek. Not quitting but attempting to decoy her away from his family. She wished she could take the hint and follow him.

Then, when she reached the main river and the shelduck had finally scuttered away, she found she had seriously underestimated the wind. It wasn't a gale or anything but it was a fresh late evening breeze. The water was dark and cross-hatched with squalls. Donny or Xanthe, even Maggi, would have welcomed its power: Anna did not, particularly as it was blowing straight up the river from the direction she wanted to go. Maybe she should have stayed with the competent cousins – as she was now going to call them.

Anna felt unhappy about what she had done to Heike's sketchbook. She knew why she'd done it but there was no denying that it was wrong.

Just as there was no denying that the strong ebb tide – maybe wanting to be her friend and rush her down the river to Bawdsey – was engaged in direct wet warfare with the wind, which thought she'd be better turning tail and running up river to the town. She could have found somewhere to leave *Theodora* then caught a bus – or phoned her mother to come and collect her.

But there'd be mud there, too, and what sort of dinghy owner would she be if she phoned for a taxi as soon as the going got tough? It had been much worse last night, she reminded herself, as the quarrelling waves slapped the dinghy sides and splashed cold water over her. Last night, in the thunderstorm, she and Zander had been drenched by the rain, whirled by gusts from astern and frankly terrified by the flashes of lightening.

But it had been so…sort of elemental…and she'd been so

angry with Zander and sorry for him and urgent to get him away from Iakov that she hadn't exactly minded. She'd been frightened, of course, but it wasn't the same as this irritating tossing and soaking as little *Theo* struggled to sail with the tide but was constantly forced back by the sharp-peaked waves against her.

The journey took almost three hours. Twice she had to find places that would give her enough lee to pull the mainsail down and persuade the dinghy to lie quietly so she could phone Fynn Creek. It was Donny she spoke to both times. He'd nothing to report except to say again and again how amazing it felt to have this proof that his father had been real. How Heike felt like a cousin already. How she and Skye were beginning to get on.

Anna forced her cold face into smiles so he could hear that she was glad for him. He'd guessed she would be having a bumpy ride but she kept telling him she was fine and kept each call as short as she could. *Theodora*'s jiggling made her feel queasy. It was better when they were splashing into the wind and battling the waves.

The wind died finally and the last stretch of river calmed to a silver sheet.

Her head felt as if it had been wiped clean too.

Although it was still technically light, there was no colour left in the day. The Bawdsey landing looked uninviting. She wished she could just pull her dinghy up the beach and leave her there. But she couldn't. There were rules against that. Also there was sometimes vandalism or theft and *Theodora* had become precious – even though Anna didn't expect she'd be rushing to go sailing again any time soon.

The current sucked and eddied as the water forced its way

out through the narrow river mouth. Make a mistake here and you could be caught and carried helpless out to sea between those bare shingle banks. There wasn't any swimming here, it wasn't safe. She couldn't imagine that her vision of Vicky merrily bobbing about learning to row was going to happen in this place.

Anna dropped her sail, hauled up her centreboard, lifted the rudder inside the boat, then stepped onto the end of the launching slip. More mud and bladderwrack and slippery green weed. Eeurgh! There was nowhere to make *Theo* secure so she pulled her as far as she could. That wasn't very far. The dinghy, on land, was surprisingly heavy and Anna's whole body ached.

It would have to do. The light was fading and she needed to find the trolley that she and Zander had shoved deep under a clump of tamarisk in the early hours of the morning.

That same morning of this same day.

Since then she'd sailed up river through a thunderstorm; got Zander away to London; taken two AS level exams; walked to Fynn Creek; acted as boat guard, confidante and cheerleader; committed an act of vandalism, terrorised a family of shelduck and beat back down the length of the river against an unfriendly breeze. It was an understatement to say that she'd had enough.

But she still had to manoeuvre her dinghy onto the trolley. That involved shoving the trolley far enough into the river till it was submerged – which wasn't all that easy because the tide was so low she had to push the trolley off the end of the slip over various random lumps and obstructions which caught at its wheels while the mud squelched between her toes and she tried not to think about crabs. Then, with her other hand, she needed to push *Theodora* out into the river again, hanging on to her painter until she was floating free but NOT able to escape, then pull her in again quickly, guiding her onto the submerged trolley.

Anna wasn't big and she wasn't especially strong. Even when she'd finally persuaded the dinghy onto the trailer, and managed with a few lucky heaves to shift it sufficiently far forward that *Theodora* settled onto the two support bars, she couldn't pull the trolley back onto the slip. There was a ledge, too many broken stones. The wheels jammed against them.

Then she tried pushing the trolley a little further out (tying the dinghy firmly on with the painter), swivelling to avoid the launching slip and pulling it up the beach. But it wasn't really a beach, not that far down: it was just more mud and the wheels sunk in and stuck.

So her choices were to wait there another couple of hours for the tide to rise far enough to help her get the wheels of trolley onto the slip. Or give up.

Anna went with option two. She undid the painter, pushed *Theodora* off, still holding tight, then somehow managed to pull the trolley above the waterline and leave it there while she walked the dinghy across to the ferry pier and tied her to a post, illegally.

She was cold, tired, depressed and wet as she passed the lighted gatehouse – would they have helped her if she'd asked? – and set out along the drive to the Manor. The pinnacles were catching the last gleams of light and there were a few randomly-illuminated windows. Suddenly she remembered all that had been happening and what more could have happened while she'd been away. Anna summoned the last of her strength and hurtled towards her family.

Two super-luxurious coaches were parked outside the language school, pupils and teachers filing onto them, each with hand luggage and a single suitcase. Search wands were being run over each student as they boarded the coach. The suitcases were being screened as well. She didn't pause to wonder what was going on. She was running on empty now, stumbling upstairs to the top floor flat.

Luke and Lottie were in the sitting room with Vicky, who was refusing to go to bed. They were sitting on two sofas round a small table where they'd been trying to amuse themselves with snacks and games. Lottie leapt to her feet and hugged Anna passionately. Vicky wasn't far behind and a moment later Luke was in there too.

"Big Hug!" he said, trying to sound ironic, like he was on *Teletubbies*.

"Why didn't you phone?" asked Lottie. She looked haggard. "We knew you were sailing but it was getting so late. We were trying not to worry."

Why hadn't she phoned? She'd phoned Fynn Creek twice. But she hadn't even thought of phoning her family because… because until she'd begun walking up the drive she hadn't really thought of them. They were simply her destination, her taken-for-granted place.

If she had thought of them she could have asked them to come and help her with the dinghy. She'd have yelled at Liam or Luke if they'd failed to keep in touch with her when she was meant to be looking after them.

"I'm sorry," she said to her mother.

"You're here now, that's all that matters."

"Have you heard what the doctor said about Liam?" Luke asked her. She realised he'd been crying.

"Not properly. Not since when I came out of my second exam" (Had she really been taking AS levels today?) "How long will he have to stay in? What are they going to do? How soon can they get him seeing okay again?"

"They can't."

"*Can't?*"

"Can't get his sight back. Not in the eye that's gone. And the other one will likely go too. Might have gone already. Liam's blind, Anna!"

"But they're experts. It's the top place." Anna's faith, if she had one, was in experts.

"Turns out it's genetic. There's nothing they can do. Except hope it gets a bit better when he's got over the bang on the head. And all that 'better' might mean is a grey fog with a bit of light around the edges instead of complete black with flashes. It's inherited from our mum, Li's and mine."

Anna couldn't speak for a moment. A memory flashed in her head of her and Liam on the beach, talking about Zander's mother and her inherited illness, using statistical probabilities to get themselves over a quarrel and back on good terms. They hadn't begun to imagine the crashing human impact of being told that in your family it was normal to be ill – or blind – and there was nothing you could do about it because that was who you were.

"They must be doing research," was all that she could manage. "There's gene therapy these days. It's the fastest growing area." She was missing the point. She knew she was. This was truly awful news.

"But what about you, Luke? Your mum could see okay, couldn't she?"

Luke tried to answer normally but his eyes were welling up and he couldn't stop them. "It's about my only memory of her – her and me looking at the moon together. When she was sort of telling me she was pregnant with Liam. She couldn't have known." He swallowed back some tears and Anna noticed Lottie take his hand – and that Luke didn't pull away. Vicky was completely quiet, her thumb in her mouth. They must have spent ages talking and researching once they'd learned the bad news.

"Mum was a carrier. She probably never knew. One of her uncles had sight loss but Dad can't remember if there was anyone else. They never even thought about it. It's almost always males. And Li's so young. Younger than when people usually get it. Which means he was extra-susceptible and could mean I'm more likely, too. But they can test."

Anna's phone rang. It was on-the-hour check-in time.

"Sorry," she said to Donny. "I can't talk now. Are things okay with you? Really great. That's good. Yes – but it's not that easy right now. The Russians…?" (She'd forgotten all about the Russians.)

She needed to reassure Donny and get him off the phone. "I don't suppose you've heard anything from Zander?" she asked her mother.

"That's where Liam and Bill are staying. In their house."

"But Liam's in Moorfields! And Bill."

"Not now." Lottie was beginning to explain about the lack of beds and the kind offer from Raisa when Anna cut in.

"FFS! You've sent him and Bill to the spy house! Where's Iakov?"

"Who?"

"The agent, the fake bodyguard, the man who's been bullying and threatening and smashing things up!"

"You mean Mr Dzer... I can't remember his name."

"Yuck-off," said Luke.

"Yes, anyway, the new bodyguard...I'm sure he's left here. I saw the driver packing Zander's things. They'd have to leave, wouldn't they, if their job is to be with Zander?"

"Zander's been expelled," said Luke, "Because of you."

"Hi, Donny," said Anna. "I'm going to have to ring you back. I don't know if there's any threat right now but we definitely have to talk when I've got my head round what Luke and Lottie just told me."

Her little sister was looking so bewildered that she wasn't even sucking her thumb. "And Vicky sends her love."

That worked. Vicky brightened at once. "Tell Donny I've got a mermaid's purse for Auntie Skye."

"Yeah, thanks, Vicky," said Donny. "Yeah, thanks. I got that. Skye'll say thanks as well. Yeah. But, Anna, haven't you told them anything... about me being Vanya? About Hermann?"

"I've only just got here." She felt she was about to cry. "It's about Liam."

"It's bad news?"

"It's very bad. And it might get worse. I'm not not-caring about you and Skye. Or Heike. I need to process. Please, just let me call you back. Could you stay there? Or be back in 15?"

"My news can wait. It's waited all my life till now."

Anna ended the call with a mix of relief and dread.

"What was that?" Luke asked.

"It's a big thing for them. Needs telling properly – and I

will – but first, please tell me where Bill and Liam are?"

"Staying with your friends the Ivanovs. The hospital didn't want to keep Liam in. It turns out they don't have many overnight beds. He needs to be kept completely quiet. The rush hour journey back here after such a traumatic couple of days could have been too much."

"So he's in the KGB house!"

She didn't mean to say it like that. It was as if she was hurtling to the bottom of a bungee jump and couldn't tell whether the elastic was going to pull her up again or snap.

"What do you mean?" Lottie gasped.

Luke leapt up, fists clenched, "I told you Zander was a spy!"

Vicky turned bright red, scrunched up her eyes and began to bawl. When Vicky cried it was like a bomb going off.

Anna, who was still standing where she'd come in, sat down next to her sister and took her wet sailing jacket off so she could cuddle her. Luke sat down too, breathing a bit fast. Patted Vicky's hand, called her their Treasure. Lottie went into the kitchen and pinged a hot chocolate in the microwave for Anna. She placed food within reach for everyone.

"You have to tell us clearly what you mean," she said, sitting down opposite Anna and leaning forward intently. "I understood that the Ivanovs were your friends. You had been to their house. You didn't tell me there was anything wrong."

"You wouldn't have listened. You had all those meetings, remember?"

Lottie flinched. "Did you try to tell me?"

"No. Maybe I should have done."

"So, when Zander's mother telephoned and said that he'd

admitted hurting Liam, I believed that he was desperately sorry. I gather he's already had half a dozen new guitars delivered so Li can choose something to replace the one that was damaged. And it was you, Anna, who took Zander away from here last night and told him how he could get to Bill and Liam in the hospital – which appears to have been very useful…"

"He can't ever come back. He's been expelled." Luke said again.

"The principal was already angry before you did that late night flit. What *has* been going on?" Lottie asked her older daughter.

"That's what I've been trying to work out. It started in Lowestoft with *Strong Winds* and Donny and Liam and Donny's cousin Heike."

"Cousin?" said Luke. "The boatyard girl who slept in my bed?"

"Yes," said Anna. "That's Donny and Skye's big news – please don't let me forget to call him back. But the problem is that they picked up something under the boat – none of us know what – that Iakov wanted. That's the man who's been pretending to be the bodyguard. And – shut up for a moment, Luke! – the point is that Iakov's *not* KGB – I shouldn't have said that, it doesn't exist anymore. But there's a new one called SVR which is just as scary and that's what Iakov's in. Zander's father, Arkady, used to be in some other sort of Intelligence but now he's trying to be straight and he's totally paranoid. He's not in London at the moment. He's in Russia talking to the president."

"The KGB one who's just been re-elected?"

"*Not* KGB now…but yes. So the president's in charge of the SVR, which is what Iakov's in. Zander and his mother are really tense but they're not talking about it, even to each other, I don't think."

Then she got stuck. "But what I can't work out is how all this high level London and Moscow post-Cold War stuff connects up with that dodgy dive boat from Lowestoft."

She realised the others didn't know any of this.

"Donny made a mistake when he was trying to be helpful. He nearly told some people on a dive boat about the thing *Strong Winds* picked up and that made Iakov think they know where it is now. Except they don't because they left it with a man called George. And he's had a heart attack.

"Iakov and Zander and another man turned up at Fynn Creek and Heike took a swing at them but she only got Zander. She's Estonian and she's a bit indiscriminate. She just hates all Russians. It looks like Donny's half- Estonian as well. But his dad might have worked for the Russians."

"What I must do at once," said Lottie, "is ring Bill. Or I could drive to London. Would Bill recognise this Iakov?"

Anna thought for a moment.

"No. And we mustn't upset Liam."

"Liam can't see," said Vicky.

There was a silence.

"Bill says Liam holds onto his hand all the time. And I mean *all* the time."

"Even when Dad goes to the…?" asked Luke.

"Even then. But if I can't speak to Bill, I can at least text him. No I can't. He's got my phone. I'll ring Raisa Ivanov. Tell her I'm coming to fetch them now."

"Mum," said Anna. "Liam needs complete rest. You said so. He could even still get a brain bleed. We have to think this through. If Iakov's in London, it's probably bad. But it means he isn't here. So he can't be attacking *Strong Winds* or *Lowestoft Lass*.

And there's *Ra*'. I know you don't know all that. I told Heike I'd ring Edward tonight. Maybe it can wait till the morning…"

Lottie wasn't interested in anything except getting to Liam and Bill.

"You could text Zander," she said to Anna. "Send a message that way."

"He hasn't got a phone right now. Anyway he probably can't speak much. Heike broke his jaw," she added for Luke's benefit.

He was just opening his mouth to say how pleased he was and she was opening hers to take a long drink of the hot chocolate that had gone cold when there was a thump on the door.

"Open up! Suffolk Police!"

While they looked at one another, too shocked to move, three more bangs against the solid wood and a man's voice, telling others to stand aside.

Lottie moved quickly then. She ran across the room and turned the big brass handle.

"Can I help you?" she asked. "The door's not locked."

CHAPTER EIGHTEEN

A choice of guitars

There were three policemen, two men and a woman. The two men had guns and there was an extra person wearing some sort of decontamination suit. He – or she (they weren't introduced so you couldn't tell) – immediately began going over the flat with the same sort of wand that Anna'd noticed outside.

The woman officer glanced round checking the layout, then sent the two armed men to search the rooms to the seaward side and ensure the windows were locked.

"You have a warrant?" Lottie asked.

The officer showed her identification. "I apologise for the haste," she said, once she was certain that her orders were being carried out. "We have reason to believe that a wanted man may be heading this way. May I ask if you've seen or heard anything unusual over the last few hours?"

"No. Nothing."

"And you've all been in this single room? It seems late for the little one to be out of bed."

"I'd like to call my lawyer before this goes any further," said Lottie.

Anna was astounded. Her mother usually dealt with difficulties by charming people. It didn't mean she was a pushover, it was her tactic. But calling a lawyer sounded…quite aggressive.

The officer wasn't fazed. "Certainly. I'll need your formal

identifications first. You're Lottie Livesey and you and your family are the regular occupants of this flat. You're a singer and your record company is chief financial sponsor of the forthcoming Luminal Festival."

"Yes."

"And these young people…?"

"These are my daughters, Anna and Vicky, and my step-son Luke."

"And you've been together here this evening."

"I'll make the call now."

"I must ask you to remain in this room while you do so – for your own potential safety."

Lottie made the call from the landline but all Anna could work out was that she wasn't calling Edward. It was some duty lawyer connected with the PR company. Her mother lived in a strange world these days.

"I'm authorised to co-operate completely on matters relating to my family's personal security," she told the police officer, "But not to answer any questions that relate to my work or involvement with the forthcoming festival. They insist that you make no statements to the press without consultation. They can send someone if it becomes necessary."

The police officer nodded and carried on with her questions. She needed to know where they'd been that evening and what they might have heard or seen.

Anna didn't ask whether she could text Donny. She just did it.

"Can't talk. Police here. Check in 60?"

The search didn't take long. The scanning was much slower.

"Is that a Geiger counter?" Anna asked suddenly, listening to the changing pattern of clicks that the instrument was making.

"Yes. But please don't feel alarmed. There's radiation in every normal home."

"So you just turn up in any 'normal home' in the middle of the night to check it out. That's helpful. You've evacuated the language school." She understood what she'd seen now.

Lottie put her finger to her lips: Vicky, at last, had fallen asleep. Luke was on the sofa, thumbs busy on his Nintendo.

The two armed policemen had gone to search outside. The woman stayed. It looked as if she was writing up a report. In the silence they all heard a splutter of clicks as Liam's room was checked. The operative came to the door and signalled to the police officer. Anna and Lottie followed her.

"It's these, ma'am."

'These' were Liam's school shoes that Lottie had brought home from the hospital.

The shoes were immediately bagged up and also his socks and school trousers where the radiation traces were only slight.

Then the questioning began again. Whose were these clothes? Where was the child now? Where had he been?

The police officer began to sound more human as Lottie told the story of Liam's terrible day.

"I'm afraid," she said, "That this fits with our investigation to date. A dog, belonging to a young man who works as a gamekeeper on the former defence site, died recently from suspected radiation sickness, but we were not informed. Now the young man himself is unwell."

"Not the lad who found Liam? The one who called the ambulance?"

The word 'ambulance' sent the police officer into a spin. She made some hasty calls ordering the ambulance to be found and isolated and the paramedics identified and checked.

"There's something there that shouldn't be," said Luke, "Up on the old missile site." They didn't think that he'd been listening.

"We have placed the area out of bounds and will be carrying out a very thorough investigation with specially equipped personnel." The officer sounded as if she was already answering questions at a press conference.

"Don't worry," said Luke. "I'm not planning to go anywhere near the place, but you'd want to talk to that Russian. Except he left."

'Russian!' This was an even worse word for the police officer than 'ambulance' had been. Her fingers were already twitching towards her radio as she asked Luke to explain.

It turned out that he didn't mean Iakov, but Dimitri. When he'd been helping Liam on his clifftop lookouts several weeks ago he'd noticed Dimitri inside the defence site but couldn't work out how he'd got in.

"It wasn't the wild apple tree but it must have been something like that because I'd noticed the gates were locked when I was coming back from school. He must have had something that would have got him over the fence. Or under. But we won't never know now they've cleared it all away."

Then Anna decided that the police officer needed to be told about Dimitri's replacement, Iakov, and the intimidation of Zander and why Liam had been running onto the missile site where he'd been found. She even tried to explain about the possible data-collection box that had caught round *Strong Winds*' propeller.

Then the officer was calling Special Branch and Public Health and the Counter Terrorism unit and asking for the address of the Ivanov house in London to give to the Metropolitan Police.

"Stop," said Lottie. "Stop right there!" And she pulled the radio set away from the woman's mouth. "My step-son's in that house. He's suffering from trauma, head injury and sight loss. You are NOT, repeat NOT, going to risk any further injury to him by letting your Special Branch goons bursting in mob-handed like you came in here. Anna, get my PR company back on the line. Ask for the duty press officer. I'll make this a national scandal if you damage that child by your bully-boy tactics."

Anna hadn't a clue what the PR company number was but she made out she was doing what her mother asked.

"That's enough. Please, Ms Livesey. You don't seem to realise this is a matter of National Security."

"It's also a matter of my step-son's survival. There are a lot of people in that house. They could turn violent."

"Arkady Ivanov's ex-KGB." Anna decided to support her mother by dropping that one in, whether or not it was scrupulously accurate. "But he was official – like the president – so he's probably still got diplomatic protection. And Mrs Ivanov's quite fragile and there's a charity clinic there."

"I'm driving to London now," said Lottie. "I need to get my child out. *And* his father. Then National Security can do as it likes."

My child? Luke and Anna exchanged glances.

"Can we come?" asked Luke.

"If you leave this house, I cannot guarantee you'll be able to return immediately. It might risk a cross-contamination situation. We may need to place this building out of bounds."

"You've just checked it," Lottie snapped. "It's clean – apart for Liam's shoes and clothes. You've checked me. I'm clean. So are these children. You can check my car as well, but Liam hasn't been in it and I haven't gone onto the defence site. So I'm going to London now. And if we can't come back here, we'll go to the Erewhon Parva vicarage and claim sanctuary."

This was all going way too fast. Lottie had picked up her car keys and the police officer was about to get on her radio again. Anna really didn't think her little sister needed to be woken up into all of this. She hadn't liked the talk of National Security and Special Branch; she wished she'd never mentioned Arkady Ivanov's possible past.

"Mum," said Anna. "I'm really tired. And Luke is, too." She gave him a look. "If you set off by yourself now you could be back here before breakfast. We'll just go to bed. Vicky's asleep anyway. It doesn't need to be such a big deal. We've got the gatehouse security. It's a great idea picking up Liam and Bill. Then the police can get on with their job."

"We could detail one of our welfare officers to collect your husband and the child. Save you the journey?"

"Bill doesn't trust police and Liam would be frightened. I simply can't understand why you came in here like that. Getting ready to break down the door and carrying guns into a house with children. Why did you?"

"I'm not going to discuss operational detail," the officer sounded huffy. "I'll only say that we were acting on information received."

"In which case I dread to think how you and your colleagues might approach a house where you know there are foreign nationals and armed security. I'm going to get my child and my partner out of there. You can take the shoes and clothes but Liam won't be answering any of your questions until the doctors confirm he's completely well."

The police officer blinked and nodded. Lottie was given strict instructions about her need to rendezvous with Metropolitan Police before going anywhere near the Ivanov house and the officer grudgingly agreed that her presence might be useful if the situation escalated.

"The only thing that interests me about the situation is bringing Liam where he can be quiet and safe. When he needs to go to Moorfields again I'll drive him. And Bill," she added. Then she kissed them all and left.

Anna was truly too tired to care and Luke said nothing. They brought bedding into the sitting room and settled down near Vicky. Anna sent a single text for Donny to read when he next tried to check in. She wished she could have texted Zander. She understood that they'd made things really bad for him and Raisa but didn't see what else they could have done. Couldn't seem to think clearly at all. Lay down beside Vicky and put her arms round her. Slept.

Luke stayed awake in the darkness practising what it would be like to be blind. He shut his eyes and moved his head around, listening. They said your other senses sharpened if you couldn't see. He only felt dizzy and lost, though he knew exactly where he was, lying on the spare mattress he'd pulled in from his room.

His head hurt when he thought about Liam. This wasn't something that *might* happen to his younger brother. It *had* happened. Liam wouldn't be playing football or doing lookout from the cliff or searching the beach for lucky stones any more. Liam wouldn't be able to see the faces of the people around him or what they were doing or where he was. It was horrible.

Luke dreaded the genetic tests that he was going to have – they might show that the same fate waiting for him.

He reached for his Nintendo. He'd play while he still could, focus on capturing those Pokémon, blot out his problems.

Then he thought about Liam again. How he might be feeling right now. Decided one more time to practise using his other senses. Shut his eyes. Didn't move his head so randomly. Thought really carefully about touch, taste, smell, hearing.

The windows had all been closed and locked. There was no stirring in the air, no whisper from the sea. He checked his mouth for the sense of taste but as he'd been snacking all evening and hadn't cleaned his teeth, it was a bit like the inside of a rubbish bin. His sense of smell wasn't much better.

Luke listened. His sisters were asleep. He could hear their quiet breathing but he wasn't close enough to touch them.

Suddenly he was sharp and alert, gripped by a sense that wasn't on his list. It was a sense of danger. It felt like it came from inside his body; from his stomach, maybe. Every bit of him had gone hyper, even though he couldn't touch, taste, smell, hear or see anything that wasn't normal for the situation they were in. He felt frightened of the empty building, of the locked windows, of the dark night and the silence.

"Anna," he whispered urgently, "Why did they come here?

The police. They said they'd been given information about a wanted man. Who gave it to them? And what if they were right?"

But Anna didn't answer.

"We oughter leave, Anna. We oughter take Vicky and get out of here. Somebody might be knowing something that we don't."

Raisa Ivanov was sitting with the boy and his father as they slept. They were good people and the little boy had suffered a terrible blow.

She wished it had not been her son, Zander, who had precipitated the crisis though she understood it would have happened anyway. Zander had already gone to his room. A new phone had been delivered for him and he'd indicated that he needed to set it up. Then make a call.

His mother hoped that would be a message to his friend Anna, to thank her for her help and reassure her that they were caring for her young step-brother. After which she hoped he would be sleeping. As soon as he'd reached London she'd taken him to a top reconstructive surgeon who had fixed his broken jaw and prescribed strong painkillers and an early night.

She knew Zander was unhappy and under strain. So was she. The strain of separation. The strain of ignorance. They had heard nothing from Arkady since the message a week ago saying that he and the president were 'in discussions' and she was not to worry.

If her husband had told her that he and the president were going on a week-long vodka and caviar bender on a Lake Ladoga pleasure steamer with all the junior dancers of the Mariinski Theatre, she'd have taken it in her stride. But 'in discussions' was a phrase she didn't like at all.

Instead she distracted herself by focusing on the little boy and his father who she hoped she could help. She remembered the day of her own diagnosis, when she properly understood that her condition was inherited and inescapable, that it brought additional risks that could lead her to a premature death and long before that it would rob her of the ability to do the thing she loved most in the world, make music with her cello.

If anything the diagnosis had spurred her on to waste no time, try harder, practise longer, accept every opportunity to learn or perform. So she had tasted some of the delights of a successful career. She had that to remember now.

But this poor child was so young. He had had no warning, no knowledge – and no mother to comfort him. He was hurting. And his father was hurting too.

Once she was certain that Liam and Bill had everything material they could need, Raisa had settled in a corner of the large comfortable room, wrapped in her big cashmere shawl and she sang quietly, as if she was singing to herself. She sensed they were glad to have her there.

Earlier, the boy's father had caught some of her melodies and offered a few of his own. Songs from the rolling sea. Shanties he said they were called. They weren't songs she had ever heard before but she recognised some of the feeling behind them. Liam had remained completely silent but Raisa hoped it wouldn't be too long before one of the selection of guitars that were now stacked along the edge of the room would be nestling under his arm again.

Her house lay quiet around her. She had done all that was in her power to make it a place of healing. She was fearful that it might not be enough.

Zander had used his new phone to ring the principal of the language school. He thanked her for expelling him and explained that the man she had thought was his bodyguard was a dangerous SVR agent. He tried to explain that there wasn't any threat to the school but that she should tell the police about the agent. Especially if he ever tried to approach the family in the top floor flat.

It wasn't easy as he could only talk out of one side of his mouth and his head was packed with sedative and anaesthetic but he hoped he'd got the message across.

The principal had rung the police immediately.

CHAPTER NINETEEN
A travelling thumb

When Anna didn't answer, Luke lay still on his mattress for a few more moments trying to talk himself out of his panic. His stomach felt as if he was about to get diarrhoea, his skin was prickling as if it was being crawled over by an army of earwigs, the palms of his hands were cold and sweaty.

That time when he was on his own in *Lowestoft Lass* he'd forced himself to believe the woman next door on *Dree Vrouwen* was a harmless eccentric – which she wasn't. His instincts had told him she wasn't and he should have listened to his instincts. Now every nerve in his body was shrieking at him to get out of Bawdsey Manor and get his sisters out too.

He got up, looked at them, fast asleep together. Couldn't remember when he'd last seen Anna like that. Her arms were round Vicky, her black hair covering her pale face and she was completely gone.

The flat was so stuffy. Maybe he just needed some fresh air? Luke walked quietly back to his bedroom – you didn't have to tiptoe in the flat, it was so solidly built. His window slid open silently as he undid the fastening and pushed it up.

There was the sound of the sea. There was always the sound of the sea, pushing and dragging against the shoreline. The Manor was on top of a cliff and he was looking out from the top of the Manor. He could see the loom of Orfordness lighthouse to the north; the tiny pinprick lights of the navigation buoys; the moving clusters of light from ships – Liam wouldn't be using that identifier app of his anymore.

Nor would he, if he got this genetic sight loss too.

Luke turned away from the window and began to pack three small bags. What were his sisters wearing? He was in his jeans and sweatshirt, but Vicky was in her bed-time onesie and Anna had some odd combo of fleecy top and the shorts she'd sailed home in. Bare legs wouldn't do. Too pale in the dark. He rummaged quickly for more suitable garments. Then he had the job of waking them both and persuading them that they needed to get dressed and come with him out into the night.

They were good sisters, they trusted him. Even when he said they weren't going down by the main stairs or the lift. They were going to go out of his window and onto the roof. Then they were going to crawl round keeping underneath the parapet until they came to the short, straight, metal ladder that led down to the next floor and on to the twisting staircase that was the main fire escape and would take them safely down to ground level.

They didn't go on at him asking why, why, why. Anna asked a few questions about what he'd put into the bags and insisted on adding a phone charger, 12v adapter plug, a hair brush and her physics books.

"Even if there's World War Three scheduled for this weekend, I'll still need to turn up for exams on Monday. Maybe WW3's not such a far-fetched idea when you think how Liam's shoes set that machine gibbering. And I still haven't worked out what – or who – sent the police here in the first place. I need internet."

"We don't have time," said Luke. "I've packed water, food,

torches and warm top layers. And my Nintendo and Vicky's squashy parrot."

"Then we'd better all go to the toilet and put on socks and soft-soled shoes. Whatever's comfortable and has a good grip. Shoes we could run in if we had to."

Vicky hadn't said a word. She was big-eyed and bewildered, looking from one to the other. That last sentence sent her thumb back into her mouth.

"Chewy sweets would be good," said Liam. "In case we really have to stay quiet. And I've got the folding knife and marlinspike that the Ribieros gave me last Christmas."

"It'll be next Christmas if we don't go soon."

The landline rang then. A startling familiar noise that didn't sound right at all.

"Maybe it's Lottie or Donny – or Rev Wendy even…" Luke whispered eagerly.

"Or the police."

But it wasn't any of them: it was some newspaper wanting a statement from Lottie about Luminal.

Anna said her mother couldn't be disturbed and cut off the call.

"But it's midnight," she said to Luke. "That's weird."

"Maybe it was someone checking that we're here."

"Well, they're wrong, because we're not. Come, Vicky, you've been wanting to be allowed to do this for ages. And now you can, as long, as you're totally quiet and do everything we say. Luke's going first."

They were so careful that it really wasn't dangerous at all. The only awkward moment came when Anna realised she'd left the bottom section of the window open behind them and made herself climb back up to close it.

The building towered over them when they reached the ground. There were no lights or sounds, except for the sea. Or was that a motorbike in the distance?

"We can't go out down the drive," whispered Luke.

"Don't worry," Anna whispered back. "I've got the key to the beach gate. We'll go out that way, lock it behind us then wiggle through the tamarisk. That's what I did with Zander."

"Where are we going?" Luke's only instinct had been to get out.

"To the river, of course," said Anna, surprising herself. Earlier that evening she was never going near it again. "I need to shift *Theodora* anyway. I left her in the wrong place, though it could be the right place now. We could cross to the Ferry and sit under one of those huts till it's light. Then we can keep watching the entrance for Mum's car. You'd be okay with that, wouldn't you, Treasure?"

Vicky nodded but she didn't speak.

"If it gets to morning and she's still not home we'll take a bus into Felixstowe and go down onto the front." She knew the beach and its summer amusements were Vicky's idea of forbidden fun and Luke's too. Even if they didn't go there, the thought of it would help keep both of them cheerful through the hours ahead. "And if she's back before that, with Bill and Liam safe, we won't mind not going because we'll be so glad to be together again."

This wasn't so well-judged. It made Luke think about Liam and how there wouldn't be any more crazy golf and arcade games for him anymore. If he could keep his own sight he'd dedicate himself to quality brother time. Angel would understand. Mentally, he took Liam by the hand and guided him with them along the narrow path through the feathery bushes.

Then they were at the quay and Anna was motioning them to keep low along the side of the jetty and out of any possible sightline from anyone who might be on duty at the entrance of the Manor.

It was just after one in the morning. The tide was high and *Theodora* had floated out into the stream and was tugging at the end of her painter, apparently eager to return the way they'd recently come.

"No," said Anna to her dinghy, "I am so not going back up that river again. We are not a waterbus." Then she stripped all her clothes off and muttered to Luke to hold onto them and look the other way while she paddled cautiously down the wooden slope until she reached the end where she'd made the rope fast. Then she had to duck down underwater holding her breath until she could reach the knot and it took several attempts to untie it.

"Rookie error," commented Luke, sounding much more cheerful as she took her clothes back and gave him the dinghy to hold while she rubbed herself dry with a shirt. "You should have fastened the painter up much higher to allow for rise and fall and if you'd done a bowline with a big loop you wouldn't have had to go upending yourself like that."

It was unfortunate for him that Anna just that moment felt a long stringy clump of green seaweed drifting past her feet. She scooped it up and chucked it at him.

"I was only trying to be helpful," he complained.

"Was this boat our granny's?" Vicky asked Anna.

"Not exactly but it's got her name and I think we're meant to think of her when we use it. Ok, you two, all aboard."

"Remind me, Luke," she said later, when they were across on the Felixstowe Ferry side, and sitting in front of a hut on pillars ready to hide themselves among the jumble of old warps, redundant anchors and crab pots that had been stowed underneath. "Why are we not snoozing in the comfort of the Manor, waiting for Lottie where she's expecting us to be?"

They'd been watching the road on the other side of the river. You could see quite a long way back towards the village as well as into the Manor entrance. Nothing at all had arrived or moved. That motorbike they might have heard was probably one of the gate staff changing shift. The moored boats lay to the tide, there were sea bird calls from the marshes and the rustle of wind over water.

"Because I hate it." Luke shocked himself by telling her the truth. "It's not only because of looking like we're rich when we're not – except you are and probably Lottie soon – it's that I don't never feel at home. Like it's full of other people about to tell me I got no right to be there. There's your great-uncle and all them boffins and Wing Commanders and that – and there's the bloke who built it and kept adding more minarets every time he made another million. I keep expecting to meet his Lady Wife and she'll send me off to the servants' quarters."

Anna hugged Vicky to give herself comfort. People always forgot it was Vicky's house too.

"And I don't never feel safe. Can't look at them shingle banks without remembering the night we got stuck there with the witch women, can't look at them cliffs without wondering when they're falling down and can't look out to sea without wondering what new batch of trouble's coming across. That sea, it never stops. Except when you put headphones on to shut it out."

"I'm sorry," she said. It wasn't much.

"It ain't your fault; you didn't ask for all this to come landing in your lap."

"No." It had been such a humungous day. She was cold where she'd scrambled into the river to untie the dinghy. Drying with a T-shirt whilst staying modest in front of your step-brother wasn't completely effective. Vicky was warm, though. And Vicky would sleep if she and Luke stopped talking.

But she couldn't not listen to him. There'd been too much not listening.

"So, is that how Bill feels… and Liam?"

"Dunno about Dad. He's got LL to think about. And maybe adult stuff between him and Lottie. But probably yes for Li. It's why he's always on lookout. Thinks he's protecting us. Oh Anna, what we going to do if Liam's blind?"

"Shit, Luke, I don't know."

It was like looking into whirlpool and knowing that you'd soon be going down it, head first. There was nothing to be said after that, so they said nothing.

"That's Donny coming!" said Vicky, waking with delight.

"Signal him, Luke. Get him over this side of the river."

They all knew the sound of *Strong Winds*' engine, though it was amazing that Vicky'd been the first to hear it. And from her sleep! Luke didn't have a phone but he'd packed a torch. He couldn't think of anything to flash except short-short-short, long-long-long, short-short-short; dot-dot-dot, dash-dash-dash, dot-dot-dot; S.O.S.

Strong Winds had been heading to the visitor's mooring on the Bawdsey side. They saw her alter course towards Felixstowe Ferry. Anna had a torch on her phone so she pointed the beam at a vacant mooring buoy metres away from the steep beach where they were hiding. Donny picked it up like a pro.

Which he was.

And a star.

That, too!

They were out from under the hut, down into *Theodora* and pushing off from the shore before he could have put a hitch round his Samson post.

"Why're you here?"

"Is everything okay at Fynn Creek?"

"Is Auntie Skye here?"

"What's happening, Donny?"

All talking at once in urgent whispers as they were coming alongside and climbing aboard, tying *Theodora* to *Strong Winds* and urging each other to go down into the cabin where they could talk more easily.

"I came because of your text, Anna. I talked about it with Mum and Heike. You hardly said anything."

"I was tired."

"Whatever. But then I had to wait until there was enough water to get out of the creek. It's lucky there's some moon tonight. Why are you over this side of the river?"

"'Cos Lukey got spooked. So we had to get dressed in the dark and then we climbed down a ladder. All the way to the ground. And then we went out of the beach gate but we didn't go onto the pebbles, we came creeping through the bushes and then Anna had to take all her clothes off to go into the water because she'd tied the dinghy up wrong. And then she chucked seaweed at Luke and we came over here and hid under a hut. And I didn't say a single word all the way and if Mummy and Daddy don't get back with Liam in the morning, we're going to the beach at Felixstowe."

Donny sometimes felt like she was his little sister, too. "You're an Incredible, Vicky. *You* didn't do anything as babyish as chucking seaweed. Beach-visiting might be out, though. Have a read of this," and he shoved the Ipswich evening paper at them.

Anna read it aloud.

DEADLY RADIOACTIVE MATERIAL ON SUFFOLK BEACHES. PUBLIC ASKED TO STAY AWAY. FESTIVAL UNDER THREAT.

Significant traces of deadly radioactive material Strontium-90 have been found on Suffolk's most popular beaches. Holiday-makers and local residents have been asked to stay away from a stretch of coast several miles either side of Sizewell nuclear power station which is currently suspected to be the source of the contamination. Water samples are being taken as a matter of urgency while fishermen, sailors and all water sports enthusiasts are being warned off.

Experts stress however that there is no immediate danger to public health and these measures are merely precautionary while the investigations continue.

Questions are already being asked about the possible cancellation of the forthcoming Luminal festival,

controversially sited at Sizewell. Local singing star Lottie
Livesey, due to release her new album at the Festival,
was unavailable for comment but her partner, Bill Whiting,
speaking from London, said he thought it was a bit early to
make decisions until the scientists had taken a proper look.
'They've got a job to do, so giv'em proper time to do it,'
Mr Whiting said.

"That sounds like Dad," said Luke. "But what's he doing speaking for Lottie?"

"He's got her phone. The reporter must have found her number somewhere. Taken him by surprise."

Anna read on.

Mr Whiting also revealed that the singing star was
anxious about the health of one of their children and asked
that the family be given a bit of privacy at this time. He
declined to comment further.

Ms Livesey's family live in the spectacular Bawdsey
Manor, former research establishment and RAF defence
station, twenty miles south of Sizewell.

Ipswich Hospital has refused to comment on an
unconfirmed rumour of radiation sickness in the area.
Local public health officials confirmed that teams would
be checking all Suffolk beaches as a matter of routine but
stressed that there was no need for panic.

Strontium-90 is a 'bone-seeker'. After entering the
organism, most often by ingestion with contaminated
food or water, about 70–80 percent of the dose gets

excreted. Virtually all remaining strontium-90 is deposited in bones and bone marrow, with the remaining 1 percent remaining in blood and soft tissues. Its presence in bones can cause bone cancer, cancer of nearby tissues, and leukaemia.

Together with Caesium-137, Strontium-90 was among the most important isotopes regarding health impacts after the Chernobyl disaster. Previous nuclear accidents, nuclear weapons testing, and the by-products of nuclear fission mean there is always some presence of these isotopes in the environment. Detailed analysis of the beach results could take weeks. However public health experts insist the current ban is merely to ensure that there is no danger of cross-contamination while samples are taken.

Suffolk police are erecting temporary road blocks on all coast roads in the affected area while the test samples are taken. The environmental protection agency will be setting up an information line.

Best advice this weekend? Take your picnic to the park.

"That explains a lot," she said, handing it back and telling him quickly what had been happening with them, including the phone ringing just before they left. "I just wish we hadn't mentioned the Ivanov house."

Lottie had made a decision on her drive to London. She was going to play it straight. She was going to tell Bill or Raisa that she was coming, as she would normally. She wasn't going to rendezvous first with the Metropolitan Police and lurk around treating the Ivanovs as guilty till proved innocent. She and Raisa were fellow-musicians as well as fellow-parents.

She'd forgotten, however, that she'd only got Luke's phone so the Ivanovs' number wasn't in it. They were ex-directory, of course. She tried Bill but his phone was switched off. Lottie texted him anyway, set the sat nav and chose a download of sea shanties. That was the music that had brought her and Bill together in the first place and they were going to need every source of strength to help Liam now. They had to be better parents.

"But the police could be right," said Luke. "The contamination's got to be connected with the thing Yuck-off's been chasing. That was picked off Sizewell. And you said yourself that he's a Russian agent. If he's involved, so are they."

Anna didn't know what to think – and that wasn't normal for her.

Vicky had been sucking her thumb while they talked. She'd also been watching the Manor entrance hoping that her parents and Liam would come home. She touched Anna's arm and pointed. "Look!" she said.

There were blue flashing lights across the river. Three police cars and a minibus were parking on the quay. Already there were figures, hard to see in the dark, coming out of the vehicles and heading in different directions. It looked as if they could be unrolling tape, putting up barricades. Then one car started up again, turned into the drive and vanished, while another shifted position so it blocked the entrance.

"What do you want to do?" Donny asked Anna.

"I want to see what they're doing. But I definitely don't want to get involved."

He looked at his watch. "It's only just after high water. We could go out to sea, almost as far as the Woodbridge Haven buoy. Then come back inshore and anchor on the other side of the shingle. We won't get that close because it'll be ebbing but near enough to see what's happening. I wouldn't do it if there were any sort of wind and it'll shut *Strong Winds* out of the river till late morning, but we've got two dinghies…"

"Will Skye be okay – and Heike?"

"In practical terms the creekies are being brilliant and it's the weekend, so the demolition contractors won't work anyway. Socially – emotionally – they're doing their best to make an aunt-niece relationship. It's a bit like when Gold Dragon got to understand what Skye was like. But the other way round."

Luke was looking at Donny like he was talking in some foreign tongue.

"What do you mean an aunt-niece relationship?"

"Didn't Anna tell you? Heike came to England to learn to be a shipwright but she also came looking for her grandfather. And her grandfather might have been trying to come to England to look for her cousin called Vanya. This week – like, I dunno, two days ago or something – she spotted her grandfather's yacht: that's the old wreck in the lagoon at the top of Fynn Creek. Then yesterday – or whenever – she found a crew list and it seems like the old man's son, who Heike hasn't ever met, was called Hermann and he was…my dad. And that makes me…Vanya!"

Luke hadn't ever met Heike and he'd been struggling to follow Donny's excited explanation. The V-word did it. He jumped up.

"I used to know that old man! I spent most of my time in Fynn Creek trying to tell him that's who I wasn't! He's okay. Got the longest hair and beard you've ever seen and howls like a wolf. Used to help Miss Grace with the cows."

"So someone's going to help us to find him, if he's still alive." (You had to keep saying this with grandparents.) "Meantime, my dad's Hermann and I'm Vanya!"

"No you're not," said Luke, sitting down again. "That's some Russian name. You're Donny and you need to get on with taking us all out to sea."

CHAPTER TWENTY

A place to anchor

The night was quiet as *Strong Winds* left the river. There was a light breeze coming off the land so Donny set Anna and Luke to look out for the channel buoys and sailed out to sea. The junk's broad sails gleamed like the wings of a giant moth but he figured it was unlikely anyone would be looking their way and he didn't want to risk drawing attention by using the engine. He kept the depth sounder running and took them well beyond the hidden knolls before he gybed round, hardened his sheets and headed back towards the Bawdsey beach.

"How does it actually work?" asked Luke. He and Anna had come back into the cockpit, waiting to hear what they needed to do next. Vicky was tucked in the corner, wrapped in one of Great-Aunt Ellen's fleecy blankets. The whir of the depth sounder and the slap of the waves on the shingle were the only sounds.

"Sends a pulse down into the water and times how long it takes before the echo comes back." He could feel the tide beginning to push them northwards, which was helpful now they were beyond the knolls, but the seabed was uneven and he needed to anchor as close in as he could yet be sure of floating if they were still there at low water.

"There's about a three metre fall and we need two metres to stay comfortably afloat. So five's what we want now. I'm going to have to put the engine on for a moment. This year's survey showed a deep area close inside the shingle which would be perfect if we could find it."

The chug of the engine seemed shockingly loud in the quiet night.

"Have to hope we sound like a fisherman," said Donny, furling the sails as he spoke.

"Don't exactly look like one!"

"Then we have to hope no one's looking."

Donny wished he hadn't had this idea. Even if they found the deeper water the anchor was unlikely to hold well. It was okay in these conditions and with all of them on watch but if the wind got up or changed direction… He hadn't checked the weather forecast.

Here. This was the place. He turned the junk sharply to port and pulled the gear lever into neutral. Then he ran forward as she started drifting backwards. He dropped the anchor, checking the chain carefully as it paid out. At about eight metres he paused, listened with his hand on the anchor chain for the grinding slipping noise that would tell him the anchor had failed to bite into the ground. It was quiet. *Strong Winds* had stopped. The chain was taut. He relaxed and paid out another seven metres before he checked again. Then he went back to the cockpit and turned off the engine and the depth sounder as well.

"I could have done that," said Luke. He sounded hurt.

"Sorry. I'm used to being only me. Except for when there's Mum."

"Ssssh," said Anna. "There's stuff starting to happen at the house."

Lights at the windows. Lights moving on the beach below.

Strong searchlights put in position to illuminate the cliff paths. Possibly something where the road from the back of the village came down to East Lane.

"The police weren't being straight with us. They must have known much more than they said when they came bursting in."

"Why aren't they up at the missile site?" said Luke.

"Maybe they can't get that far along the beach yet. There was a rock-fall, remember. They need the tide to go down more before they can get to the cliff."

"But he'll have got away by then. They should have it surrounded from the road."

"Maybe they have."

Anna's brain was working better now. "The radioactive beach contamination and the accident at the site – I don't mean Liam, I mean the person who tried to help him, who called the ambulance, who's ill now. They have to be connected. Maybe it's too dangerous to search there in the dark."

"His dog died," said Luke.

Donny wasn't getting any of this so they explained quickly, still in low voices, how the police search had found radioactivity on Liam's shoes. And how the officer had let on that there'd been a tragedy with the gamekeeper's dog.

"And the keeper's ill too."

"He mustn't die. He rescued Li."

"She told us that they'd placed the whole site out of bounds and they were going to be investigating with specially equipped personnel."

"So, we have to make sure there's nothing left for them to find," said a deep and unexpected voice.

Arkady Ivanov had come alongside. He was on his own in a RIB and was wearing a uniform. It was black with gold epaulettes.

"There's no need to be alarmed," he said. "I have no weapons and my yacht needs deeper water than she can find here. I followed you in my tender. Its motor is virtually silent if you're not listening for it."

He gestured out to sea where, dim against the eastern sky, they could see the outline of something that looked like a small ship.

"My yacht," he said again. "She is for exploration. Today I am using her for my private business, though I chose to wear the uniform of an Admiral in the Russian navy. I was once before a Captain, first rank, but after such a long time has passed I felt that I could reasonably expect promotion."

"But I thought…that you were a businessman and you owned newspapers," stammered Anna.

"And when you met me in my house in London that was true. But since then I have been in Russia. I have had some discussions with the president. They were not pleasant discussions but we have made an agreement and I have accepted to be reinstated to a role that I had resigned more than ten years ago, with the promotion that you see. Then I must leave England and bring my money – and my family – back to Russia. But first I have to clean up a mess which has been made. It is not a good mess, it makes me very angry."

He didn't sound angry. He spoke calmly and a little sadly, sitting in his RIB with a hand on *Strong Winds'* gunwale but making no effort to come aboard. They noticed there were gold rings and a gold star on his sleeve.

"You mean contaminating our beaches and killing people's

dogs and getting them sick in hospital." Luke had jumped up with his fists clenched.

"If that's what has happened, then yes, and I am sorry for it. We have also lost a good man – a father – and that is finally why I have capitulated. I am sorry about the dog and about whoever is in hospital. If financial help is needed it will be given. I can promise you, however, there will be no lasting damage to your beaches and if I am successful now – with your help – I will be gone from your country and when the papers have finished with their stories, the affair will be done."

"And if not?"

"Then there may be lasting trouble. Still no one will be harmed in the short term (except perhaps the agent I have come to remove) but, if the relationship between our countries continues to grow more angry, I am fearful for the future. I do not want to see another war. Hot or cold."

"You've come to help Iakov escape?" said Donny incredulously.

"No way!" said Luke. "We're not going to help with that."

"That's not what I am asking."

"Then why have you come over to us?" asked Anna.

"Because I saw you. Not you, Annushka – I did not expect to find you, my son's friend, here. I came because I saw this yacht. I have been informed about this yacht – and of this young man," he looked at Donny. "And I believe it may be fated that they are here at this time."

This sounded a bit more than being the person who'd accidentally got some sort of something tangled round his propeller.

"Is it because I'm Vanya?"

"If you have been given a Russian name, then yes. I knew

your father at Paldiski and that was also a clean-up operation. But tonight it's because you are English that I'm asking you to help me."

"I don't know what you're talking about," said Donny. "But if you knew my father I suppose I'll have to do it and hope you'll explain later."

Arkady smiled. "It's not so bad. The thing is bad but I am not asking you or your companions to put yourselves in danger. Merely to bear witness to my actions."

Vicky was asleep anyway.

"It won't take long. It mustn't take long. The sun will soon rise and pursuit is already fierce. Someone has spoken when they should not have done. But I want you to see me. That I am here, in my uniform, come to remove a man who is carrying a dangerous cargo. I want you to tell whoever needs to know that this is not an act of aggression but a withdrawal. If anyone has been hurt then reparation will be made. I am very rich. The president tells me I must bring my money back to Russia and I have promised that I will, but only after all debts have been settled here."

"You'd better come and write that in my log book," said Donny.

"And I'll identify that it's you," said Anna. "Except no one will take much notice because we're too young."

"I still think you're a criminal," said Luke, as Arkady climbed on board.

"Then I can't change your mind, but all I can say is that for most of my life I have been trying to reveal or to clear up the criminal acts of others. That's why I left my country ten years ago and that's why I'm returning now."

I, Arkady Nikolayevich Ivanov, testify that at 2300 hours on Friday June 8th I supervised the removal of a Strontium-90 battery that had been stolen from a former USSR lighthouse in the Arctic and placed adjacent to the outfall from the Sizewell nuclear power plant to cause maximum panic and disruption without directly endangering life. This was not an act of aggression against the British people but an act of coercion against myself.

I have returned the battery to Russia using a Quebec-class submarine requisitioned by myself for this purpose.

I then discovered that the stolen battery had been temporarily stored in a bunker on a former defence site close to the school where my son is a pupil.

"Was," said Anna. "Zander has been expelled."
"That will please him," said Arkady and made the correction.

...was a pupil. I ordered the agent responsible to return to the site and ensure all was safe and in particular that any fragments of the battery casing had been removed, as these also would be radioactive in the longer term. I provided appropriate equipment and have pledged myself to ensure that this material is removed from British waters.

I authorise the British government to take whatever is necessary from my personal fortune to make reparation to anyone injured by these actions and to finance whatever additional testing operations are deemed necessary to *restore public confidence in the safety of the beaches and waters of the Suffolk coastline.*

Signed by me, before witnesses, Saturday June 9th.

"It's a bit like a last Will," said Donny when he and Anna had also signed.

"Good," said Luke, glaring at Arkady. "Wills are for when people are dead."

"I'll take a photo on my phone as a backup," said Anna, glaring back at Luke.

"Now I must get on." Arkady was climbing up the companionway to return to his RIB.

"What is this?" Anna asked him, showing him her photo of Heike's drawing of the Thing.

"It's a piece of monitoring equipment used to sample water quality. It will show quite clearly that the contamination has not come from the Sizewell nuclear plant. There may be other data-collection instruments stored inside." He chuckled, "You can thank your mother for that, Annushka. She and her colleagues have been so determined that their festival site must be squeaky clean. They gave the agent one big headache."

"It's not funny," said Luke. "It's caused massive trouble. My brother…"

Then he found he didn't want to talk about what had happened to Liam.

"There's a man in Lowestoft who had a heart attack because of it," Donny picked up from him. "And my cousin's boat was trashed and she's lost her jobs and might not be able to finish her diploma".

"Reparations?"

"Yes!" said Anna, with a flash of inspiration, deciding not to mention Zander's broken jaw. "She's discovered this old yacht…"

"It was her grandfather's yacht, my grandfather too…"

"And she needs to save it from being made into a car park…"

"And rebuild it…"

"But that will cost thousands…"

"Thousands," said Arkady, "are my small change."

"Then can you ring the college now, before you go, and leave a message on their phone that you'll be her sponsor if they give her the diploma? My Trust sponsored her to rebuild the dinghy but I can't afford a whole yacht – and anyway they wouldn't let me."

He made the call and pledged his wife and son to honour the debt if he wasn't able. Added it to the log book and signed again. Then he was determinedly down into his RIB.

"Are you sure you haven't got a gun?" asked Luke.

Arkady looked up at him. He opened his double-breasted uniform jacket to show a uniform white shirt with nothing more than a wallet-shaped bulge in the top pocket.

"No. I am not carrying a gun. Who would then believe that I act in peace? But I am carrying a dosimeter because I am worried about this agent. I don't like him. I don't like his methods or what he has done or why he has been employed to do it, but I am worried about him. I also have pills that he should take."

The eastern sky was brightening. Not glowing peach and gold as it had been on the day Donny and Liam left Lowestoft but a lurid red with dark clouds blowing like a giant's cigar smoke. Donny, hypersensitive, felt the first slight shift in the wind.

"We'll do our best to watch for you but if the weather changes I'm going to have to move. It's too shallow to come in closer."

"My captain has said the same. He has no choice, however, but to wait for my return."

There was something in his tone that Donny didn't like. "No choice?"

"He must wait. The systems of an explorer yacht are very complex and there are certain codes that are needed. These codes are protected by a password and I have changed it."

"But what if it comes on to blow and his anchors drag and the wind changes and he's being pushed onto a lee shore? Then he has to save the ship."

"In that case – if he cannot reach me – my wife will give authorisation. Meanwhile, he is compelled to stay. I cannot compel you – except I am trusting to your love of your country and the honour of your father's memory. I hope that will be enough."

"No pressure, then!" Donny exploded, as Arkady motored away.

"Told you," said Luke, who'd been beginning to feel friendlier towards the Russian.

"Clever, though," said Anna. "I bet it was him who taught Zander how to play chess."

"Donny, can we go now? I don't like it here. My tummy's feeling wobbly." Vicky had woken and pushed the blanket off. She looked pale.

"Y'r right Vic, this isn't such a good place anymore. I don't like the weather. You keep looking at that horizon. Right over there where the sun's coming up. We'll be moving in a moment. Anna, there's some wrist bands that Skye made in the cabin. Probably some ginger biscuits too. You'll need to look around a bit."

"I'll go," said Luke. "Or we'll have Anna turning green as well."

The wind had shifted, the tide was running hard, the mounds

of shingle were rising up out of the sea like alien islands and he could hear the waves breaking white on the seaward side. Donny's one thought now was to get his ship away from the land. He'd heave-to once he was somewhere near the Russian yacht. He couldn't do more than that. Honouring his father's memory or stopping the Third World War were all very well; his first loyalty was to his ship.

It was as if Anna read his mind. She'd always been good at that.

"You need to move *Strong Winds* further out. I understand that. And you're going to need Luke to look after Vicky, I get that too. But you don't, at this moment, need me. And I've got my own boat these days. There's nothing to stop me going closer in. I don't know what I think about Arkady Ivanov, but his family in London are being raided by Special Branch because of what I told the police. So at least I'll get as near as I can to being the witness that he asked for here."

CHAPTER TWENTY ONE

A white arm from the sky

The London house was softly floodlit inside its metal railings. The pavements were empty, as if they'd been cleared of any late night passers-by. As Lottie opened the window of her car ready to use the gate entry system, a policeman in dark clothes appeared immediately beside her.

"Ms Livesey?"

"Yes."

"We've been instructed to facilitate you to collect your husband and your child."

"Yes," said Lottie. This wasn't the right moment to explain that she and Bill hadn't ever married, were mainly living apart and that, technically, Liam wasn't related to her. Except, when she and Bill had got together all that time ago in Lowestoft – and became parents of Vicky – Luke and Liam were part of the whole new family that was made then, with Anna. When anyone asked Lottie how many children she had, her answer was always four.

"We can give you half an hour."

"I'll do my best."

The officer retreated and Lottie pressed the intercom. It was answered immediately but then there was a long wait while someone went to find Raisa.

"Hello, Lottie? You are here?"

She wished she'd managed to phone ahead.

"Yes. May I come in? I can explain."

What could she explain? That she'd come to remove Liam and Bill so that the police could come bursting in to this other woman's house.

"But, of course. The gates will open. Please drive to the front door. I will be there to greet you."

Raisa had wrapped an outsize and very beautiful shawl over her velour tracksuit. She didn't look as if she'd been to bed.

"I have been sitting with your men. We have been singing together and now they are both sleeping. You did not have to worry about them, though of course they will be delighted you are here."

"Thank you," said Lottie. "But I'm afraid there's trouble coming," and she explained the police search of Bawdsey Manor. "Your house is much larger. There are many people here and…"

"And we are foreign. They will come in harder." Raisa's voice was flat. She sounded very tired. "I understand. So you should take your family and go. I will need to speak with the nurses – we have some sensitive equipment in the clinic – and also Zander. His state of mind is not happy right now and he has been given some strong medicine to help him rest."

"That's what I'd planned to do. I would have phoned ahead, but Bill has my mobile and he'd turned it off. I have only Luke's. I am so sorry that I couldn't reach you in advance. He could have put it on silent."

"Bill turned your phone off because of the reporters." She saw that Lottie didn't understand. She pulled her iPhone from her pocket to show her the article about the contaminated beaches.

"There'll be more in your morning editions. He was protecting you – and Liam."

Lottie felt cold. What had she walked into here? And the threat to Luminal – when she'd worked so hard…

"Your husband didn't tell them where he was staying, however. How is it the police are here so soon, please?"

"Because of the contamination of the field behind the Manor. We didn't know about the beaches. But Liam was found on the defence site and his shoes showed traces of radioactivity and the young man who found him – who worked up there – is ill now. So Luke told them about Zander's bodyguard."

"Iakov?"

"No. The one who left. Who stole your car. Luke told the police that he had seen him on the old missile site."

"Dimitri! Oh that's terrible!" Raisa closed her eyes and muttered a few words that sounded like prayer. "Dimitri was a kind man – my husband and I have known him for a long time – but he was being blackmailed. There were threats to his family. We discovered too late. He stole the car to drive home to Kaliningrad. But he crashed and died. It was that which was used to force Arkady to return to Russia. The investigation after the crash showed that Dimitri had a radiation sickness. I have been giving iodine to all our staff. I am trying not to worry. I do not always succeed."

"I'm so, *so* sorry," said Lottie and hugged her. Then, after a moment, she said, "You know what we have to do now. We have to go out to the police, open your doors and invite them in. Together. I'm not going to leave you to cope with this alone. We need them to test everyone and look everywhere. We give them full co-operation. That way we'll protect our families, too."

Raisa nodded. She looked ill. The two women hugged again and went outside.

Anna hadn't felt as brave as she'd been trying to sound. She'd never sailed a dinghy at sea before and *Theodora* felt wildly unstable after the solidity of *Strong Winds*. Donny carefully didn't say anything but stood as near as he could on the deck of the junk and steadied the top of the mast as Anna struggled to get everything organised. She wished Luke hadn't said that about her getting sick.

"If it roughs up any worse you're probably still better trying to get back to us instead of running the dinghy ashore. That shingle's hard."

"I'm only going as an observer. They'll probably be finished and away by the time I get there. Then I'll come straight back. You'll keep as close as you can?"

"Sure. I understood what he was saying about wanting an English witness. I'm just not going to risk *Strong Winds* in shallow water off a lee shore."

"I'm ready now. Be good, Treasure. Look after her, Luke. Back soon," and she was away, heading towards the rather distant point where the Manor grounds ended and the old defence site began.

Theodora was bouncy and quite splashy. Anna's hair was whipping in her face and she was needing to use so much concentration for the sailing she began to think it was unlikely that she'd manage to observe anything at all. She ought to have a beanie or a headband or something.

She kept going anyway and after a while she remembered she had a pair of sun specs in her jacket. She fumbled around trying to hold the sheet and tiller in the same hand to keep the dinghy sailing in the right direction while she got them out. Eventually, she had the good idea of holding the sheet in her teeth. Then, once she had the glasses, she turned into the wind and let the sail flap while she pushed her hair back and crammed them on her head.

It was so worth it.

Now, as she and *Theodora* went flying along – well, if a twelve-foot wooden dinghy with a single, simple sail could be said to fly along – Anna was able to look where they were going without constantly flicking her head to get damp strands of hair away from her eyes. She felt more confident, too.

The sun was rising in the eastern sky behind her and the stretch of sea between her and the beach was brightening all the time. She thought she could see Arkady's RIB. The angle made it hard but he must be almost there. He'd have cut his speed before he tried to land. He'd want to be sure that the man he'd come to rescue was already waiting for him.

Anna began to think that her mission wasn't totally stupid. She'd probably meet them both when they were coming away from the beach, heading for the yacht, mission accomplished. Zander's dad would see her and he could show her whatever cargo he was carrying. She could take a photo – as long as this wind didn't get any worse. *Theodora* lurched to every gust.

Anna allowed herself a glance eastwards, out to sea. The explorer yacht was there, silhouetted against the blood-red sky. Heavy clouds were massing above her but Anna was comforted by the unmistakeable outline of *Strong Winds*, still heading in towards the land. Donny would be testing the depth to see how close he could come before he needed to heave-to and wait. The Russian admiral would have his witnesses, though she was certain they wouldn't be believed. She could only hope that no one would ever ask.

Lurid crimson light was creeping inland from the shore. The RIB had landed. Arkady must be confident that his man was there. She was way too far out to hear anything. She would only be able to report what she could see.

The light had almost reached the clifftop and Arkady was at its base. Waves were breaking more violently against the beach. Anna needed to slow down; she definitely didn't want to hit those pebbles. *Theodora*'s golden planks felt precious and thin.

Arkady was climbing up the cliff and there was a dark figure at the top. Something was pushed over the edge. It glinted briefly and smashed into him, knocking him backwards as it passed. The object continued unchecked, bouncing heavily until it reached the shore and rolled towards the waterline.

Arkady's body crumpled and lay still.

Anna stopped worrying about her dinghy. She pulled the centreboard up as far as it would go, adjusted the rudder and steered straight for the beach. She wondered about dropping her sail but remembered the water was ebbing away. She needed to keep momentum or *Theodora* would be sent spinning round. It was all science really. Anna liked science.

She didn't like peril. Adrenaline made her feel shaky, not brave. But that was Zander's dad lying there. Someone who had been trying to do the right thing.

In a very bad situation.

She looked up at the clifftop, dreading what or who might be coming down. She was very close now. Too close to turn back.

Disbelief.

What she seemed to be seeing, as she peered upwards, was a giant black slug, writhing in some grotesque dance.

As she stared, still playing her sheet to keep the dinghy heading in, the twisting slug seemed to gather itself and lift.

Up it soared, using the cliff edge thermals, then twisted away. A man in black was dangling from its cords, gliding expertly from the scene. He'd be long gone before the police arrived. The person they would find, when they reached the cliff edge, would be a billionaire, unconscious or dead, dressed in the uniform of a Russian admiral. And something nasty in a canister.

Anna stood up in the dinghy and shook her fist at the paraglider.

Then *Theodora* hit the beach and swivelled, scraping loudly against the stones. Anna was thrown forwards. She was struggling not to cry as she picked herself up, hurting and dazed.

Arkady's RIB was further up the beach. Both of them had landed on one of the flatter bits that were interspersed with the shingle ridges. The dinghy sail was being blown round behind the mast and the sheet was whipping away. Anna pulled everything back inside the boat. Then she set off towards the body, her legs shaking, clammy with fear.

Donny decided once again that Anna was totally the bravest person he knew.

He had Luke looking through binoculars describing all the

action he could see and Vicky watching the depth sounder while giving a continuous chant as the indicator moved. Vicky's concentration was amazing. She wasn't getting upset and she wasn't being sick. She seemed years older than five or six, or whatever she was now. When Luke described the sudden appearance of the paraglider, she allowed herself one quick glance and then went back to her job.

"I don't like that bad black bird," was all she said.

"Yuck-off!" said Luke.

Donny could see that the paraglider was heading north. He guessed it must be the SVR agent and was tempted to head that way himself, trying to keep him in view for as long as possible, though he could see that the billowing black silk in the rising wind was a much quicker form of transport than his solid yacht.

"He must have brought it on his motorbike," said Luke.

"Motorbike?"

"We heard it earlier. You weren't there then."

Escaping to Lowestoft, maybe? That was surely a long way to fly. Maybe he'd land at some lonely spot in between. But could paragliders keep on going in a straight line, didn't they have to loop round to gain height? He'd have the tide with him if he followed the glider now…

"What's Anna doing?" he asked Luke.

"Walking up the beach. I think she's trying to run. She's heading for Arkady."

"Don't know who he is," said Vicky. "One dot nine, one dot eight, one dot seven."

"Zander's dad. He was here when you were asleep." Donny

had to turn *Strong Winds* away from the shore. Needed two metres' depth to be safe.

"He's not too bad – for a Russian," Luke added. "That's his massive yacht we passed earlier. Anna's got to him now. She's kneeling down."

"One dot nine, two, two dot one, two dot two, two dot three…"

Donny reached forward and turned the engine on. Shoved the throttle hard down, trimmed the sheets and had *Strong Winds* heading out to sea as fast as she could go.

"Where're we going, Donny?"

"To talk to the captain of that yacht. I can't believe he's sitting there doing nothing. He must have other tenders. Ships like that probably have about four or five. He ought to be sending his crew in to rescue Arkady. And if he needs to ring Zander's mum to get permission, then he should. You keep on watching the shore, Luke. Vicky, you can have a break from the depth sounder if you keep that bad black bird in sight."

Coming alongside the Russian yacht wasn't hard – even though the weather was deteriorating. An onshore wind, blowing at right angles across a strengthening ebb tide, meant that the sea state was becoming choppy and unpredictable. Donny was glad to find that the yacht had quite normal decks – normal for a small ship, anyway. She wasn't all moulded and predatory like the superyachts he'd seen in photos. She had gates and ladders where people could come aboard or climb down for a swim or into a smaller boat. Davits too. One of the gates was already open with two chunky fenders either side. Probably waiting for the admiral's return.

A WHITE ARM FROM THE SKY

Her name was MY *Raisa*, which seemed endearing.

"Perfect," said Donny, getting his warps and fenders ready. "But don't stop watching, you two. Being witnesses is our main job, remember. I can manage *Strong Winds* on my own and there's sure to be someone who'll come and take a line, if only to ask what the hell we think we're playing at. Or however they say that in Russian."

"Probably with an AK47," muttered Luke.

No-one came.

Donny shouted 'Ahoy'. Luke and Vicky joined in with 'Hi' and 'Hello'.

No one answered.

"Do you think they're asleep?"

"It is still silly o-clock in the morning."

"We're going on board anyway. Be careful. Pick your moment. You two better go up on top. The view will be great but you must stick together. And Vicky, hang on tight up those ladders."

She looked at him with almost adult contempt; then she and Luke were racing each other to reach the highest deck first.

Donny took a deep breath and stepped cautiously inside as the vessels tossed against each other.

"Hello?", he tried.

It was eerily quiet. They couldn't all be…dead, could they? With some horrible, undetectable poison? He stopped again, listened, sniffed – that was a stupid thing to do – but all he could smell was a possible whiff of tobacco. He climbed the two short flights of stairs which he reckoned would lead to the bridge.

"Hello" he tried each time. "Hello?"

Then, "GEORGE!"

Lashed securely into an extremely comfortable-looking leather chair with his pipe and baccy in easy reach was George from the Mutford Mariners' Club. And over to the side of the well-equipped space were the instrument box and the wire and the neoprene floats that Donny had last seen when he'd disentangled them from underneath *Strong Winds*.

"Heard you callin'. Don't have no breath to shout back. Figured I'd save me speech till you found me. Untie me now, if you'd be so kind."

Donny didn't move. "We thought you'd had a heart attack. Everyone did. Heike was really upset."

"Have 'em all the time. Carry me off one day they will. Reckoned it were a good moment to throw a sickie. Got me doctor's note an' all."

The fat man was obviously unhealthy but Donny'd just noticed the hard, calculating blue-grey eyes hidden deep in his face fuzz. George had used his illness to fool them all. Set him and Liam and Heike up as decoy ducks for Iakov.

"What's that Thing doing here now?" he asked, as soon as he could trust himself to speak.

George followed his gaze. "That? What you and the young'un so kindly brought in? That's our insurance policy, Skipper's and mine. In case they ain't willing to listen to his side of the story over here. Or honour the bargain back home. Belt and braces, that's always been my motto."

"How is that Thing your insurance?"

"First, because it shows there wasn't nothing wrong off the Sizewell outfall – not until that black villain Dzerzhinsky dropped his present from the North Pole. And second, because we can prove it was him what sabotaged it. I'd had one of my members pop a little extra gizmo in there, recording date and time. Took a photo too – him and his fancy jet ski."

"Sabotaged it? But that's the equipment we ran over on *Strong Winds*…"

"Properly unlucky that was. For him. You were morning after the night before when he was half-way through making his own arrangements. You don't think it would have pulled up that easy if someone hadn't already had a go? Didn't you wonder what had happened to the anchor weight or why the marker buoy'd already half sunk?"

"Why should I?"

"Because you ain't got a nasty, devious mind. But blackheart Iakov has."

"Was it him who tied you up?"

George started to laugh but then it turned into a cough which went on and on until the sweat was pouring off his bald head.

"No," he said when he could finally speak again. "That were Skipper."

"Mr Ivanov? The admiral?"

"Yup. Known him for years as well. An' he knows me. Comrades. He knew I'd foller if he didn't tie me in."

George and the billionaire were comrades? What sort of set-up had he and the kids walked into?

"Where's everyone else?"

"Ain't anyone else. Only him and me. Rest of 'em left on the sub. He reckoned this bit was likely to be delicate. Is he alright?"

"No. Don't think so. I came to ask you for help." Donny

began untying George. The situation was way too complex for him but they couldn't leave Arkady lying on the shore. "My friend Anna's with him. I can't get close. And there's some cargo, too."

"What about blackheart?"

"Gone. Heading north on a paraglider. One of us is watching him but I should think he'll be out of sight by now."

"An' if I never see that one again, it'll be too soon. Now we need to get Skipper off. There's a good steady twin-hull that'll take us ashore nicely. Help me down young...what's yer name?"

"Donny," ('I think,' he added privately). "But your orders are to stay on board." It wasn't a question. "I'll check if our Vicky trusts you enough to keep you company. She's not six yet and she's very shrewd. Then Luke and I can both go."

George sighed. "I know myself I wouldn't be no use. Heart. An' lungs. But if you get Skipper back safe I can take him and his cargo all the way to Kaliningrad. Or Murmansk, if he prefers. She's a sweet ship this one. Get along an' call 'em down."

But at that moment Vicky came running in. "The bad black bird," she gasped, her eyes wide and round as cockle shells, "He drove right into the lighthouse. I was watching, though I almost couldn't see, and a big white arm came out of the sky and chucked him into it. And Luke looked with the binoculars and he says to tell you that the paraglider's on the ground and the man hasn't moved. But you're not to worry, he hasn't stopped watching for Anna and he thinks she's talking to the Russian man. Except it doesn't seem like he can move either."

"If you ain't Bob Whiting's little girl!"

"Oh, hello, Uncle George," said Vicky, reaching up to give

him a kiss. Her world was full of aunts and uncles, even when they weren't. "What are you doing here? You're meant to live in Lowestoft."

"I could be asking you the same," wheezed George. "And enquiring after your lady mother – whose name at this moment I can't recall. But we want to be getting' these lads on their way an' then we'll have plenty of time for yarnin'."

There was a really powerful telescope, almost more like a periscope, that could give 360° vision from inside the bridge deck.

"That were the other reason Skipper tied me up," said George. "'E reckoned I'd have another 'art attack if I were to see what he were up to. So you stand here, young Bridget."

"I'm Vicky."

"Different toppings, same ice cream. You keep a-watchin' and a-singin' out while I point these young hopefuls in the right direction. Left the junk warped up tidy have you, Jim?"

Donny assured him *Strong Winds* was secure alongside; then he called Luke and hurried to follow George's directions to start a solidly powerful twin-hulled motor boat with a broad stern deck.

"Amphibious, she is. Get Skipper up on 'er stern then bring him back steady. Sea's roughing up. She's got wheels if you find the right bit of beach and there's rubber treading you can roll out if yer need to. But yer not to put his filthy Yeranium on her. That's why I made him take the rubber one first trip. That's expendable. This one's nice."

George hesitated a moment, then brought out a bottle from his deep pocket.

"Best let 'im glug on this if 'e's 'ad a tumble."

Luke read the label: Oromorph. "My dad took that," he said. "It had him seeing monsters on the walls."

"Had enough of monsters this trip. I use it when me breathin's bad. But if the skipper's broke something he might be glad of it while yer movin' him."

"Okay," said Donny. "Sounds good."

"Can you get me back to my ship, Annushka?"

The metal canister pushed from the clifftop had struck Arkady in the centre of his chest, and then sent him backwards down the short steep slope onto the pebbles. His breathing was harsh, his colour grey and it was obvious to Anna that he was in deep shock. One leg was badly twisted. There was no way she wanted to touch him, let alone load him onto a boat.

She looked up and down the beach. It was deserted – except for him, for her and the canister that had rolled on towards the water's edge. *Strong Winds* had disappeared.

"I think my friends have gone to get help from your crew."

He couldn't laugh. "I have no crew. Only George. I left him tied in his seat so he could not see or follow. The rest left with the submarine. George and I can manage the yacht – and we had expected to have Iakov with us."

"So all that talk of codes and passwords…"

"…was a lie. Though my wife, Raisa, keeps the secrets of my soul."

He went deep, away, somewhere.

And came back.

"I may not have much longer. But if the canister is found here, everything has been for nothing."

"Okay." She remembered what he'd written in the logbook. "I'll see what I can do. Is it…?"

"Safe to touch? Yes. But not to open. Don't allow anyone to do that. It's also traceable. You must get rid of it."

"Okay," she said again and walked down the beach deciding which of the boats she should use to transport it to the distant yacht. The RIB would be more obvious, except she'd no idea how to work its motor. Could she row or sail *Theodora* towing it behind her?

The canister was unbelievably weighty. There was no way she could lift it.

That shouldn't have been a surprise. Anna'd been revising the periodic table. Uranium was one of the top ten densest elements. Densest also meant heaviest. The canister could have been packed with gold bars – but if they'd been gold bars she could have unpacked them. This container had to stay sealed.

Would it float? Of course not. Could she roll it? Maybe, if she used a lever. Then, if she got it into the RIB, would it sink? Probably not. A Rigid Inflatable Boat could take half a dozen adults if it had to.

Anna's clever brain was happiest calculating relative forces and tipping points. She was soon searching the beach for anything like a plank that she could use as a lever if she pulled the RIB to the water's edge, heeled it and manoeuvred the canister into it. She ignored the fact that there was only one of her with the standard number of arms (two) and that the waves had started hitting the beach in a worryingly random pattern.

The shingle was a plank-free zone. There weren't even breakwaters on this stretch. She'd have torn them down if there had been.

"Crap," she muttered, "I can't do this." Soon there would be people. Even if the public obeyed the warnings that were keeping them away from the coast, samplers and investigators would come along the beach. Or police officers would look over the low clifftop from the old missile site.

Anna hated defeat. So, it seemed, did Arkady. For one thing, he hadn't died yet. And when she went back and tried to talk about getting help, calling an ambulance or phoning his wife, he was only interested in getting the canister away.

"Try Annushka, try."

Then she looked at her own dinghy. *Theodora* – gift from God! – had everything. The canvas mainsail to provide a firmer surface, the mast to pull the dinghy onto its side, the centreboard for a ramp, those sturdy oars to work as levers.

"Okay," she said to Arkady, "if you concentrate on staying alive, I'll see what I can manage."

She became so absorbed in her improvisations that she was almost disappointed when Donny and Luke arrived with their state-of-the-art engineering miracle with its wheels and rubber matting. They had to agree, however, that they couldn't have lifted Arkady off the beach and onto the magically-flat stern deck without the dinghy mainsail. And then they used the oars, lashed together, to get under the canister, roll it onto the matting, down to the water's edge and finally, with extreme difficulty, up and into the RIB.

Then they all set off, towing the other two boats through the restless sea, with Anna cradling Arkady's head and telling him he was going to be okay; that he was going to make it back; that nothing had been left on the beach to incriminate his country. Then Luke reported that Vicky had witnessed the bad black bird – otherwise known as Yuck-off – being thrown against the Orfordness lighthouse by a white arm from the sky. And whatever Vicky meant by that, Luke's view through his binoculars, had confirmed that the agent and his parachute were on the ground and hadn't moved.

CHAPTER TWENTY TWO

A lump of amber

Strong Winds was waiting for the tide to get back into the Deben. The sea was bumpy; Vicky was tired and sick, Anna was angry and Luke anxious. Donny had said they mustn't even try the entrance until the flood had been running for at least three hours. But Donny would be almost a hundred miles away by now. MY *Raisa* had left just after five o'clock, heading northeast at her maximum speed, which was eighteen knots, and it was now after eleven.

Donny had left with her.

"You can do it, can't you Luke – if Anna's too cross? You can get *Strong Winds* home for me? I know the sea's a bit unsettled but you don't get sick and you took the witch boat into Lowestoft by yourself. You've taken SW's helm plenty of times."

"But you've always been there – or Gold Dragon was. And on *Drie Vrouwen* there was Xanthe, and Mr Vandervelde – though he wasn't exactly much use."

"But it was you who did it all. Come on Luke, every time you wake up in your Bawdsey Manor bedroom and look out of your window, you see the Deben entrance. You must know its shape better than anyone. All you have to do is spot the buoys, leave them on the correct side and listen to Vicky on the depth sounder. If it's less than two metres after the first red buoy you turn back and wait a little longer. But any time from eleven, you'll be fine. Except you mustn't let the tide push you sideways. You need to keep looking backwards as well as ahead. Use the engine. She's got plenty of diesel. If you don't feel like taking her all the way to Fynn Creek, you can pick up one of the moorings at the Ferry and I'll talk to the harbourmaster when I get back. I won't be away for long. Probably not even a week."

"But you'll miss your last three AS exams," said Anna. She was almost crying, she was so furious with him.

"But. But. But. So?" Donny had said. "Anna you have to get it. I'm through with school. I'd decided anyway. I'm not a child any more. I'm bored with lessons, I hate exams and I need to earn some money. I'll get paid for this. And, also, could you try to be rational and tell me what alternative there is? *Raisa*'s a beautiful ship with totally high tech equipment – she could probably take herself back to Russia – but she can't manage her own warps and anchors. Arkady's got a smashed leg and a chest full of broken ribs; George has chronic heart and lung issues. We've a canister of depleted uranium that's been round a dangerously radioactive core and needs to be taken right out of circulation. And the whole point of everything that's been done tonight has been to avoid an international incident – which will kick off the moment the coastguard decides to ask why this yacht's anchored here. It's not exactly Billionaire's Row."

Before that, when they'd got back to *Raisa* from the beach, Donny had worked out how to use the davits and Arkady had told them where they'd find a stretcher-trolley. Then he'd demanded to be taken, by ship's lift, to the bridge deck. Vicky and George were there. They'd been focusing on Orfordness.

George confirmed that the agent, Iakov Dzerzhinsky really

did appear to have hit the lighthouse. He'd come down hard and was lying there, shrouded in the black silk of his parachute.

"And may the Devil take his own, because we ain't collecting," he wheezed and everyone had looked anxiously at Arkady. He closed his eyes for a moment, paused as if in deep thought, then opened them and asked for the satellite phone. And another swig of morphine.

He had no difficulty getting though – to whoever it was. The conversation was brief, intense and in Russian. All they could make out was that the person on the other end was called Vladimir Vladimirovich. Or at least that was the name that was most frequently mentioned. It was a one-sided conversation. More like Arkady was giving the other person an ultimatum.

"That's it then," he said at the finish. "The president's office will arrange disposal. Now we must leave. Can you help us to get home from here, Hermann Sehmel's son?"

Donny had said yes at once, and that was when he and Anna had had the row. Though the row had been completely pointless, because Donny was going anyway.

Afterwards, he'd come on board *Strong Winds* and reminded Luke and Anna of her most basic features: engine, sails, anchor. He'd shown Vicky the locker where Gold Dragon would be travelling with them, along with the salt-stained book that had been dipped in the cold waters of the Barents Sea and which people could take with them when they were doing something unusually difficult or dangerous.

"Don't you want it?"

"I'll be ok. I'm with a Living Legend and an admiral of the Northern Fleet. Your job is to get *Strong Winds* back into the

Deben and up to that jetty in Fynn Creek, if you can. It's just behind *Lassie*. Anna knows where."

He ignored the fact that Anna wasn't speaking to him; he collected some clothes and his passport and shoved them in the old rucksack that had always travelled with him since he first arrived in Suffolk.

"Hug my mum from me," he told Vicky, "And don't forget to let her have that mermaid's purse."

"Can we track you?" asked Luke, looking up at the array of high tech equipment that crowned MY *Raisa*.

"They'll switch off the AIS and go dark," said Anna, bitterly. "Spies always do."

"They're not spies," Luke contradicted. "They're men on a mission."

"Like you are. Thanks, Luke. Time you got your engine going. Tide'll push her bows off if you have your helm down gently. I know the waiting's going to be tough but I promise you'll be okay. *Strong Winds* will look after you."

"Which is more than you'd do," spat Anna.

But Donny hadn't taken any notice. He'd checked that *Theodora* was securely attached astern and reminded them one more time about the need to wait for the tide. Then he'd stepped back on board *Raisa* and cast them off.

They'd had to wait almost six hours beyond the Woodbridge Haven buoy. It had possibly been the worst six hours of Vicky's life. As soon as she didn't have anything to do she'd started being sick. She had carried on long after there was anything left in her stomach. Anna had done her best to help by offering her sips of water, sweets to suck and nibbles of ginger biscuit but nothing had given any comfort except being held safe on Anna's lap. Which had left Luke to concentrate on trying to find the best direction to point *Strong Winds* so that she rode the waves as easily as possible and didn't roll wildly from side to side. He'd not been totally successful.

The Felixstowe Ferry harbourmaster had called them up on the VHF radio at about breakfast time to check they were okay.

"Mis-timed it, did you? Well, you're doing the right thing by waiting. Give me a call later if you want to know what the depth's looking like. Though I suppose with your boat you'll know the entrance well enough."

"If she could talk to us we would," commented Luke, but not to the harbourmaster.

The rough weather, which had been foretold by the red sky, had shaken and soaked them. The sea would seem to settle for a while but then there'd be the ominous changes in the clouds and darkening of the water and another squall would come shrieking by.

"I can almost see what Vicky meant by her white arm," said Luke, who'd been using the binoculars to watch the spiky waves breaking against the shingle mounds. "Every so often a wave just shoots upwards. Where the lighthouse is on Orfordness is like a corner sticking into the sea. It might be stronger there, with the tides and that."

"But Iakov must have been well above the water surface?"

"Was from the sky," mumbled their little sister. "There was fingers pointing up but the arm reached down."

Anna and Luke looked at each other. A freak wave? A sudden, spectacular gust?

"I read a book when some really bad guys got killed by a waterspout," said Luke, "and it ended: 'No questions were ever asked about them, so none were ever answered.' But I don't think we get waterspouts in Suffolk."

"Whatever. That no questions approach suits me just fine," said Anna. "I think we could head into the river now. Sorry I wasn't being very helpful earlier."

"I'm sorry I said all that about your house."

"That's okay. You might even have a point. Let's see whether we can't make it all the way home to *Lowestoft Lass*."

Once Anna had caught up on her sleep, she begged Heike for some Red Bull and caught up on revision. She was revising for two now – not for Donny, she'd put him right out of her head – but for Liam. And possibly for Luke and for people like Raisa because she was going to get the starriest top grades in the exam firmament and then she was going to become a doctor as well as a scientist and then she was going to do gene research. And find cures.

She also remembered her promise to ring Edward and find out what questions Heike should ask to establish her right to her grandfather's yacht and begin to discover where the old man might be.

Liam and Bill and Lottie stayed in London with Raisa until after their next visit to the hospital. The police search had been intense but had revealed nothing. There were no radiation traces, except from the linear accelerators and X-ray machines in the clinic.

"Do you treat cancer here?" Lottie asked Raisa.

"It's become necessary quite recently," her hostess answered but she didn't say anymore. The dark circles under her eyes had deepened dramatically.

Lottie knew that Raisa'd had a message from her husband because she'd passed on the message that Donny was helping to take the superyacht to her home port in the Baltic. She'd also heard from her own children that they were safe in Fynn Creek, moored astern of *Lowestoft Lass* and being lovingly mothered by Skye. Which left her free to support Bill, try to comfort Liam and ride out the storms over Luminal.

Then they came back to Bawdsey. The swelling on Liam's face had subsided so he had some vision back in his left eye and two new guitars.

He wasn't playing them, though. When they finally returned to the Manor he let go of his father's arm, said goodbye and went to his bedroom. Where he stayed hidden under his duvet, face to the wall, not wanting, it seemed, to look at any of his family.

"You'll all be gone soon," was the only explanation he gave. They knew that what he meant was that he wouldn't see them again after his left eye vision had failed.

He'd kept his lump of amber. He was using it as the doctor had suggested, as a souvenir of his last happy day: when he'd been lazing on the beach with Donny, building his pebble tower, certain that he had only to summon the courage to visit the optician and his problems would be solved.

When Heike came to visit she shocked herself by breaking down. To see the friendly little boy who'd looked after her so sweetly when she'd stayed here, lying in bed, staring at a blank wall waiting for total blindness was more then she could bear.

"Nē… nē…" she sobbed, burying her face in her work-toughened hands.

There was silence in the room as she struggled to control herself. The window had been closed. Liam didn't want to hear the sea. There was only the faintest sound as he rolled over towards her.

"What language is that?" he asked.

"It's Estonian; it's my language."

"It's my old man's language, at the care home. Can you go and explain to him why I can't come any more? He's got forgetfulness so it probably doesn't matter but I'd like him to be told that I hadn't forgotten him."

"He sang with your music?"

Liam nodded without answering and then turned away again. Heike realised just in time that the memory was too painful.

"Do you know what dementia's like?" she asked instead. And when he didn't speak she carried on: "I don't know either. But I did get sent on some training and we had to wear goggles that took away almost all of our sight, and ear muffs so our hearing got distorted, and thick plastic gloves that stopped us feeling things properly. I couldn't believe how horrible it was. Obviously they hadn't done anything to our brains but I felt absolutely that I was getting lost from myself. It was like being in a thick fog but so much worse. I was so lonely – and if my thinking had gone as well… I don't know how it would be…"

"Please will you go and see my old man?" he asked after another silence. "Tell him that I will come but I need to start practising my songs again. Tell him in his own language even if he's forgotten it."

But Peteris had not completely forgotten his language. Neither had he completely forgotten his granddaughter: though she needed to keep reminding him her name, in almost every other sentence. And Heike had found her *Vanaisa* though it was shocking to discover him without his beard and with his hair so short.

All the background information came rushing in faster than anyone could process it once Anna's lawyer Edward had got the necessary permission to talk to the lawyers representing Miss Grace, the former owner of the moorings – and the person whose money was paying for the old man's care home fees.

When Peteris had arrived in England he had been delirious, starving and without any papers (except the crew list which had already slipped into the lining of his yacht). Miss Grace, who lived on her own with her cows and her dog, had accepted him as a shipwrecked mariner. *Ra'* had been moored at her private landing stage – before the night of the storm which had ripped her away and dumped her on the far side of the lagoon – and the old man had settled to help her with the animals and to continue hoping that one day he'd find his Vanya.

She'd also allowed him to build a hut in her woods and made a deed of gift which gave him that small patch of property and made sure that, whatever happened to her, there'd be some money for him to be looked after. She'd done the same for her old mother, too.

Miss Grace hadn't died after the fire but her lungs had

failed. She was living in a coma and couldn't make any new arrangements or any changes to the arrangements that she had already made.

Her mother, old Mrs Everson, hadn't died either. She was still living in her little cottage near Pin Mill where Rev Wendy and Ellen visited her regularly. All of which meant that the farm above Fynn Creek couldn't be sold because there was no one to give their consent, except Miss Grace's mother – and she refused.

So when Bill and Lottie started thinking about the way they were going to reorganise their lives, the best idea they had was to ask old Mrs Everson if they could rent the Fynn Creek farm. They wanted to move there quickly so Liam could start learning his way around while he still had a small amount of vision left.

They could have animals at the farm and the dog, Ben, could come back and live where he'd been happiest in his confusing life so far.

Could the old man come back? That was a lot more complicated. The hut in the woods wouldn't be a good place for someone who'd forgotten how to feed himself, or to walk, or wash or keep warm. Heike had skills to help but Heike also had two major boat projects to manage.

Russian money was providing a shed to be built over *Ra'* and funds for a complete restoration, which would take years. The lagoon was still going to be filled in but it would be a place for boats to stand on when they needed repair, not only for cars. There would be a slipway and a hoist and it would be free for any of the current mooring holders to use until the new marina and houses were complete, which would also take years. Meanwhile the electricity supply had been reconnected.

Lottie sang from the lighthouse at the summer solstice – and nobody wondered what had happened to the bad black bird, because no one, except Anna, Luke, Liam and Vicky, believed he had existed. After Luminal, Lottie and Bill asked Miss Grace's mother for permission to convert the farmyard into recording studios and workshops. Plus a specially designed apartment where a very old man with dementia could live out his last days with a professional carer and family visitors and shanty songs.

Old Mrs Everson agreed at once. It was exactly the sort of place she'd like to die in herself, she said, except she was still quite happy living in her little cottage with its view of the River Orwell.

When Fynn Creek filled at high water there was a wide, clear space for rowing or sailing. It was surprising, Liam had discovered, how much you could enjoy sailing even when you couldn't see. You could feel the wind on your face and listen to the sound of the water, or advice from a friend who might be sitting in the dinghy with you or rowing nearby. You could sense the dinghy answering when you shifted your weight, moved the tiller or adjusted the simple sheet.

It was a sunny day, much later in the summer, when Liam was sailing there in *Theodora*. Luke's friend, Angel, was kayaking beside him, amusing herself with rolls and swerves and complicated freestyle moves. She was also telling him if he was getting too close to the banks or the reed beds. As well as the breeze,

⚓ A LUMP OF AMBER ⚓

Liam was learning to understand the current. It didn't ever actually stop – it was always one way or the other, even in this sheltered creek. But there was sometimes a moment when the water seemed to hold its breath.

He caught that moment now and loosed the mainsheet so *Theodora* slowed and drifted. Angel's paddle strokes slowed too. She steered her kayak alongside and gripped the dinghy's gunwale to check he was okay.

"The lion's mane pebble that I lost reminded me of you," he told her. "But the lump of amber, which I'm wearing round my neck, that's always going to be for Donny. I know he'll come back again one day."

But are there waterspouts in Suffolk?

Fact checker

Luke has learned about waterspouts from reading Arthur Ransome's *Peter Duck*, the third novel in the Swallows and Amazons series. That's where I first learned about them as well, reading and rereading the story in my bunk on board *Peter Duck*, the yacht he used to own. In those days, aged 10 and up, I didn't care whether waterspouts really existed, I was simply glad Black Jake and his crew had been knocked into splinters. Very much more recently I reread Brian Hammett's scrupulously edited *Racundra's Third Cruise* and was startled to notice that Ransome had seen a waterspout off the Baltic island of Runö in July 1923. The Ancient (Carl Sehmel) with whom he was sailing, commented that he had never seen one outside the Indian Ocean. I am so sad that Brian has died before I could thank him once again for this invaluable book.

Sehmel, who lived on the Stint See in Latvia, was the inspiration for Ransome's fictional character 'Peter Duck', who has retired to live near Lowestoft with his three daughters. There's a glimpse of Sehmel's family in K. Adlard Coles's *Close Hauled*. He and his wife did have three daughters, but no little boy called Peteris. From the moment in August 1925 when the Sehmels wave off *Racundra* for the last time as she sets sail for England, their continuing story, which Heike has recorded in her sketchbooks, is fiction. The real Carl Sehmel died in Riga, aged 80, in 1942.

The grim events in the Baltic States, however, are all too true: invasions, deportations, forced annexations. The later torpedoing of a British corvette by U-711 in the Barents Sea 17th February 1945 is also true, though not the identities of the people on board. I read about this incident in Richard Woodman's awe-inspiring history, *Arctic Convoys* and, in fictional form, it opened the first volume in this series, *The Salt-Stained Book*.

But are there waterspouts in Suffolk? Like Luke I didn't think there were and was puzzled by Vicky's 'white arm from the sky' which knocked Iakov's paraglider off course. If, however, you google 'waterspouts in Suffolk' you will be able to see what she saw – a waterspout off Thorpeness in August 2016 and another off Sizewell in May 2018.

The action of *Pebble* is set rather vaguely in the early summer of 2012, after President Putin was returned to power in Russia and before the London Olympics. I began writing in January of this year (2018) and had written the scene where Arkady believes (wrongly) that he is being poisoned some weeks before the actual poisoning of Sergei and Yulia Skripal in Salisbury in March and the subsequent death of Dawn Sturgess in June. As this book goes to press, officers of the Russian military intelligence service, the GRU, are being identified as responsible. I'm content to leave my villain as an agent in the SVR (Russia's foreign intelligence service) as this is the linear descendent of the KGB, which in turn has its roots in the activities of the Cheka, founded by Arthur Ransome's unappealing acquaintance, Felix Dzerzhinsky. I benefited greatly from listening to Dr Andrew Monaghan talking about his book *Power in Modern Russia* at the Felixstowe Book Festival this summer – and if the background to my story is a little anachronistic for 2012, well, it's only a story.

Is it a story for young people? I've no idea. I can only say that

I thought about my grandchildren a good deal as I wrote it. I would like to thank Digby for being exactly the right age for Liam and for agreeing to be photographed playing his guitar; Kemmel for loving the information book *A Pebble in My Pocket*; Gwen and Hettie for being such intrepid sailors and introducing me to the 'Cadet family' at the 2018 World Championships in the Baltic; and Quintus…? Quintus is the youngest, though a year or two older than fictional Vicky. He is a master of serious plausibility and I'd immediately believe whatever tall story he told me. I am so lucky to know them.

As well as recording my debt to the late Brian Hammett, I'd also like to thank John Benford of the Nancy Blackett Trust for organising a visit to Bawdsey Manor and to Peter Willis for the photos that he took. (It isn't a school any longer and there never was a top floor flat like the one inherited by Anna.) Thanks too to Liz Brooking and her colleagues at the Bawdsey Radar Trust for a fascinating visit and some evocative photos.

A trip to Orfordness lighthouse organised by the Orfordness Lighthouse Trust was made additionally memorable by the sea-fog as well as by the rusty debris from bomb-testing days strewn casually about. A peep through the window of a National Trust hut to spot a decommissioned Cruise missile felt positively mundane. It was when I trespassed, innocently and unexpectedly, onto the abandoned former RAF Bawdsey site and found myself standing on one of the empty Bloodhound launch pads that I really remembered what it had been like to be a mid-twentieth century child growing up in Suffolk. Such places were utterly off-limits then – and the more sinister because of it.

Thank you to Claudia, Francis, Frank, Peter Dowden, Peter

Maritime Titles from Golden Duck

The Strong Winds Series by Julia Jones (with illustrations by Claudia Myatt):
1 *The Salt-Stained Book* (available as an audiobook)
2 *A Ravelled Flag*
3 *Ghosting Home*
4 *The Lion of Sole Bay*
5 *Black Waters*
6 *Pebble*
7 *Voyage North* (forthcoming 2022)

The Yachtsman Volunteers Collection:
- *The Cruise of Naromis: August in the Baltic 1939*
  GA Jones (with an introduction & afterword by Julia Jones)
- *Man the Ropes: the Autobiography of Augustine Courtauld—Explorer, Naval Officer, Yachtsman*
  Augustine Courtauld (with an introduction by Susie Hamilton)
- *From Pole to Pole: the Life of Quintin Riley*
  Jonathon Riley (with a foreword by Noël Riley)
- *Maid Matelot: Adventures of a Wren Stoker in World War Two*
  Rozelle Raynes (with a foreword by Hugh Matheson and an appreciation by Richard Woodman)
- *We Fought Them in Gunboats* (HMS *Beehive* edition) (forthcoming)
  Robert Hichens

You may also be interested in *Uncommon Courage: The Yachtsman Volunteers of World War II* by Julia Jones, published by Adlard Coles, additionally available as an audiobook.

Books by Claudia Myatt:
- *Anglo-Saxon Inspirations: Designs to Colour and Create*
- *Keeping a Sketchbook Diary* (new edition forthcoming 2023)
- *One Line at a Time: Why Drawing Is Good for You and How to Do It*
- *Sketchbook Sailor*

We hold most titles in Claudia Myatt's RYA *Go Sailing!* series.

The East Coast:
- *The Deben* (biannual magazine)
  River Deben Association
- *Waldringfield: A Suffolk Village beside the River Deben*
  Waldringfield History Group

We also sell Robert Simper's books on East Coast history, people, and boats.

For a full list of Golden Duck titles, including the Allingham family series, *Wild Wood* by Jan Needle and the *Please Tell Me* activity books for older people, see golden-duck.co.uk. Most are additionally available as ebooks.

Willis, Georgeanna and Ruth for reading and commenting on the first draft of this book and to Megan Trudell for proofreading, copy-editing and typesetting. I think Claudia's drawings for this volume are the best ever (I possibly think that every time!) and I'd like to thank her for 'being' Heike and always thinking with her pencil while I talk. Several times every week I have the pleasure of conversation with a true Estonian, speaking English – that's Kaidi, a nurse at The Moat House where my mother lives. She is just one of the members of staff there to whom I am for ever indebted and to whom I am dedicating this book.

Thank you, Carol Wheen, for describing how it felt when your son Alexander effectively lost his sight by the age of eight and then the setbacks he endured through his teenage years. Alex has become a specialist in blind tennis and now manages a charity called Vision 4 Growth (www.vision4growth.org.uk). His problems were triggered by an accident; fictional Liam has a genetic condition called Leber's Hereditay Optic Neuropathy (LHON). Both Claudia and I have cause to be grateful to hospital eye departments over the past couple of years. There was a moment when I was afraid that I'd lose reading sight in both eyes. Thank you to Moorfields for averting this. And thank you to Francis and my lovely family for supporting me through the necessary operations, both practically and emotionally.